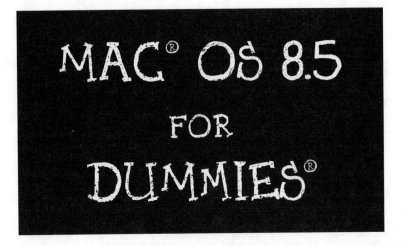

by Bob LeVitus

Foreword by Steven Bobker

IDG
BOOKS
WORLDWIDE

IDG Books Worldwide, Inc.
An International Data Group Company

Foster City, CA ♦ Chicago, IL ♦ Indianapolis, IN ♦ New York, NY

Mac® OS 8.5 For Dummies®

Published by
IDG Books Worldwide, Inc.
An International Data Group Company
919 E. Hillsdale Blvd.
Suite 400
Foster City, CA 94404
www.idgbooks.com (IDG Books Worldwide Web site)
www.dummies.com (Dummies Press Web site)

Library of Congress Catalog Card No.: 98-87908

ISBN: 0-7645-0397-9

Printed in the United States of America

10 9 8 7 6 5 4 3 2

1O/RV/RQ/ZY/IN

Distributed in the United States by IDG Books Worldwide, Inc.

Distributed by Macmillan Canada for Canada; by Transworld Publishers Limited in the United Kingdom; by IDG Norge Books for Norway; by IDG Sweden Books for Sweden; by Woodslane Pty. Ltd. for Australia; by Woodslane (NZ) Ltd. for New Zealand; by Addison Wesley Longman Singapore Pte Ltd. for Singapore, Malaysia, Thailand, Indonesia and Korea; by Norma Comunicaciones S.A. for Colombia; by Intersoft for South Africa; by International Thomson Publishing for Germany, Austria and Switzerland; by Toppan Company Ltd. for Japan; by Distribuidora Cuspide for Argentina; by Livraria Cultura for Brazil; by Ediciencia S.A. for Ecuador; by Ediciones ZETA S.C.R. Ltda. for Peru; by WS Computer Publishing Corporation, Inc., for the Philippines; by Unalis Corporation for Taiwan; by Contemporanea de Ediciones for Venezuela; by Computer Book & Magazine Store for Puerto Rico; by Express Computer Distributors for the Caribbean and West Indies. Authorized Sales Agent: Anthony Rudkin Associates for the Middle East and North Africa.

For general information on IDG Books Worldwide's books in the U.S., please call our Consumer Customer Service department at 800-762-2974. For reseller information, including discounts and premium sales, please call our Reseller Customer Service department at 800-434-3422.

For information on where to purchase IDG Books Worldwide's books outside the U.S., please contact our International Sales department at 650-655-3200 or fax 650-655-3297.

For information on foreign language translations, please contact our Foreign & Subsidiary Rights department at 650-655-3021 or fax 650-655-3281.

For sales inquiries and special prices for bulk quantities, please contact our Sales department at 650-655-3200 or write to the address above.

For information on using IDG Books Worldwide's books in the classroom or for ordering examination copies, please contact our Educational Sales department at 800-434-2086 or fax 317-596-5499.

For press review copies, author interviews, or other publicity information, please contact our Public Relations department at 650-655-3000 or fax 650-655-3299.

For authorization to photocopy items for corporate, personal, or educational use, please contact Copyright Clearance Center, 222 Rosewood Drive, Danvers, MA 01923, or fax 978-750-4470.

About the Author

Bob LeVitus (pronounced Love-eye-tis) was the editor-in-chief of the wildly popular *MACazine* until its untimely demise in 1988. Since 1989, he has been a contributing editor/columnist for *MacUser* magazine, writing the "Help Folder," "Beating the System," "Personal Best," and "Game Room" columns at various times in his illustrious career. In his spare time, LeVitus has written 29 popular computer books, including *Macworld Office 98 Bible* and *Mac OS 8 For Dummies*.

Always a popular speaker at Macintosh user groups and trade shows, LeVitus has spoken at more than 200 international seminars, has presented keynote addresses in several countries, and serves on the Macworld Expo Advisory Board. He was also the host of *Mac Today,* a half-hour television show syndicated in over 100 markets, which aired in late 1992.

LeVitus has forgotten more about the Macintosh than most people know. He won the Macworld Expo MacJeopardy World Championship an unbelievable four times before retiring his crown. But most of all, LeVitus is known for his clear, understandable writing, his humorous style, and his ability to translate "techie" jargon into usable and fun advice for the rest of us.

He lives in Austin, Texas, with his wife, two children, and a small pack of Welsh Springers and Vizslas.

ABOUT IDG BOOKS WORLDWIDE

Welcome to the world of IDG Books Worldwide.

IDG Books Worldwide, Inc., is a subsidiary of International Data Group, the world's largest publisher of computer-related information and the leading global provider of information services on information technology. IDG was founded more than 25 years ago and now employs more than 8,500 people worldwide. IDG publishes more than 275 computer publications in over 75 countries (see listing below). More than 90 million people read one or more IDG publications each month.

Launched in 1990, IDG Books Worldwide is today the #1 publisher of best-selling computer books in the United States. We are proud to have received eight awards from the Computer Press Association in recognition of editorial excellence and three from *Computer Currents'* First Annual Readers' Choice Awards. Our best-selling ...For Dummies® series has more than 50 million copies in print with translations in 38 languages. IDG Books Worldwide, through a joint venture with IDG's Hi-Tech Beijing, became the first U.S. publisher to publish a computer book in the People's Republic of China. In record time, IDG Books Worldwide has become the first choice for millions of readers around the world who want to learn how to better manage their businesses.

Our mission is simple: Every one of our books is designed to bring extra value and skill-building instructions to the reader. Our books are written by experts who understand and care about our readers. The knowledge base of our editorial staff comes from years of experience in publishing, education, and journalism — experience we use to produce books for the '90s. In short, we care about books, so we attract the best people. We devote special attention to details such as audience, interior design, use of icons, and illustrations. And because we use an efficient process of authoring, editing, and desktop publishing our books electronically, we can spend more time ensuring superior content and spend less time on the technicalities of making books.

You can count on our commitment to deliver high-quality books at competitive prices on topics you want to read about. At IDG Books Worldwide, we continue in the IDG tradition of delivering quality for more than 25 years. You'll find no better book on a subject than one from IDG Books Worldwide.

IDG
BOOKS
WORLDWIDE

John J. Kilcullen

John Kilcullen
CEO
IDG Books Worldwide, Inc.

Steven Berkowitz

Steven Berkowitz
President and Publisher
IDG Books Worldwide, Inc.

WINNER

*Eighth Annual
Computer Press
Awards ≥ 1992*

WINNER

*Ninth Annual
Computer Press
Awards ≥ 1993*

*Tenth Annual
Computer Press
Awards ≥ 1994*

WINNER

WINNER

*Eleventh Annual
Computer Press
Awards ≥ 1995*

IDG Books Worldwide, Inc., is a subsidiary of International Data Group, the world's largest publisher of computer-related information and the leading global provider of information services on information technology. International Data Group publishes over 275 computer publications in over 75 countries. More than 90 million people read one or more International Data Group publications each month. International Data Group's publications include: **ARGENTINA:** Buyer's Guide, Computerworld Argentina, PC World Argentina; **AUSTRALIA:** Australian Macworld, Australian PC World, Australian Reseller News, Computerworld, IT Casebook, Network World, Publish, Webmaster; **AUSTRIA:** Computerwelt Osterreich, Networks Austria, PC Tip Austria; **BANGLADESH:** PC World Bangladesh; **BELARUS:** PC World Belarus; **BELGIUM:** Data News; **BRAZIL:** Annuario de Informática, Computerworld, Connections, Macworld, PC Player, PC World, Publish, Reseller News, Supergamepower; **BULGARIA:** Computerworld Bulgaria, Network World Bulgaria, PC & Macworld Bulgaria; **CANADA:** CIO Canada, Client/Server World, ComputerWorld Canada, InfoWorld Canada, NetworkWorld Canada, WebWorld; **CHILE:** Computerworld Chile, PC World Chile; **COLOMBIA:** Computerworld Colombia, PC World Colombia; **COSTA RICA:** PC World Centro America; **THE CZECH AND SLOVAK REPUBLICS:** Computerworld Czechoslovakia, Macworld Czech Republic, PC World Czechoslovakia; **DENMARK:** Communications World Danmark, Computerworld Danmark, Macworld Danmark, PC World Danmark, Techworld Denmark; **DOMINICAN REPUBLIC:** PC World Republica Dominicana; **ECUADOR:** PC World Ecuador; **EGYPT:** Computerworld Middle East, PC World Middle East; **EL SALVADOR:** PC World Centro America; **FINLAND:** MikroPC, Tietoverkko, Tietoviikko; **FRANCE:** Distributique, Hebdo, Info PC, Le Monde Informatique, Macworld, Reseaux & Telecoms, WebMaster France; **GERMANY:** Computer Partner, Computerwoche, Computerwoche Extra, Computerwoche FOCUS, Global Online, Macwelt, PC Welt; **GREECE:** Amiga Computing, GamePro Greece, Multimedia World; **GUATEMALA:** PC World Centro America; **HONDURAS:** PC World Centro America; **HONG KONG:** Computerworld Hong Kong, PC World Hong Kong, Publish in Asia; **HUNGARY:** ABCD CD-ROM, Computerworld Szamitastechnika, Internetto online Magazine, PC World Hungary, PC-X Magazin Hungary; **ICELAND:** Tolvuheimur PC World Island; **INDIA:** Information Communications World, Information Systems Computerworld, PC World India, Publish in Asia; **INDONESIA:** InfoKomputer PC World, Komputek Computerworld, Publish in Asia; **IRELAND:** ComputerScope, PC Live!; **ISRAEL:** Macworld Israel, People & Computers/Computerworld; **ITALY:** Computerworld Italia, Macworld Italia, Networking Italia, PC World Italia; **JAPAN:** DTP World, Macworld Japan, Nikkei Personal Computing, OS/2 World Japan, SunWorld Japan, Windows NT World, Windows World Japan; **KENYA:** PC World East African; **KOREA:** Hi-Tech Information, Macworld Korea, PC World Korea; **MACEDONIA:** PC World Macedonia; **MALAYSIA:** Computerworld Malaysia, PC World Malaysia, Publish in Asia; **MALTA:** PC World Malta; **MEXICO:** Computerworld Mexico, PC World Mexico; **MYANMAR:** PC World Myanmar; **NETHERLANDS:** Computer! Totaal, LAN Internetworking Magazine, LAN World Buyers Guide, Macworld Netherlands, Net, WebWereld; **NEW ZEALAND:** Absolute Beginners Guide and Plain & Simple Series, Computer Buyer, Computer Industry Directory, Computerworld New Zealand, MTB, Network World, PC World New Zealand; **NICARAGUA:** PC World Centro America; **NORWAY:** Computerworld Norge, CW Rapport, Datamagasinet, Financial Rapport, Kursguide Norge, Macworld Norge, Multimediaworld Norge, PC World Ekspress Norge, PC World Nettverk, PC World Norge, PC World ProduktGuide Norge; **PAKISTAN:** Computerworld Pakistan; **PANAMA:** PC World Panama; **PEOPLE'S REPUBLIC OF CHINA:** China Computer Users, China Computerworld, China InfoWorld, China Telecom World Weekly, Computer & Communication, Electronic Design China, Electronics Today, Electronics Weekly, Game Software, PC World China, Popular Computer Week, Software Weekly, Software World, Telecom World; **PERU:** Computerworld Peru, PC World Profesional Peru, PC World SoHo Peru; **PHILIPPINES:** Click!, Computerworld Philippines, PC World Philippines, Publish in Asia; **POLAND:** Computerworld Poland, Computerworld Special Report Poland, Cyber, Macworld Poland, Networld Poland, PC World Komputer; **PORTUGAL:** Cerebro/PC World, Computerworld/Correio Informático, Dealer World Portugal, Mac*In/PC*In Portugal, Multimedia World; **PUERTO RICO:** PC World Puerto Rico; **ROMANIA:** Computerworld Romania, PC World Romania, Telecom Romania; **RUSSIA:** Computerworld Russia, Mir PK, Publish, Seti; **SINGAPORE:** Computerworld Singapore, PC World Singapore, Publish in Asia; **SLOVENIA:** Monitor; **SOUTH AFRICA:** Computing SA, Network World SA, Software World SA; **SPAIN:** Communicaciones World España, Computerworld España, Dealer World España, Macworld España, PC World España; **SRI LANKA:** Infolink PC World; **SWEDEN:** CAP&Design, Computer Sweden, Corporate Computing Sweden, Internetworld Sweden, it.branschen, MaxiData Sweden, MikroDatorn, Nätverk & Kommunikation, PC World Sweden, PCaktiv, Windows World Sweden; **SWITZERLAND:** Computerworld Schweiz, Macworld Schweiz, PCtip; **TAIWAN:** Computerworld Taiwan, Macworld Taiwan, NEW ViSiON/Publish, PC World Taiwan, Windows World Taiwan; **THAILAND:** Publish in Asia, Thai Computerworld; **TURKEY:** Computerworld Turkiye, Macworld Turkiye, Network World Turkiye, PC World Turkiye; **UKRAINE:** Computerworld Kiev, Multimedia World Ukraine, PC World Ukraine; **UNITED KINGDOM:** Acorn User UK, Amiga Action UK, Amiga Computing UK, Apple Talk UK, Computing, Macworld, Parents and Computers UK, PC Advisor, PC Home, PSX Pro, The WEB; **UNITED STATES:** Cable in the Classroom, CIO Magazine, Computerworld, DOS World, Federal Computer Week, GamePro Magazine, InfoWorld, I-Way, Macworld, Network World, PC Games, PC World, Publish, Video Event, THE WEB Magazine, and WebMaster; online webzines: JavaWorld, NetscapeWorld, and SunWorld Online; **URUGUAY:** InfoWorld Uruguay; **VENEZUELA:** Computerworld Venezuela, PC World Venezuela; and **VIETNAM:** PC World Vietnam.

5/7/98

Dedication

For Jodie, Andy, Robyn, Dad, Cousin Nancy, and all my other friends and relatives with new Macs. Now you can stop calling me at all hours.

And for my family — Lisa, Allison, and Jacob. Thanks for being there.

Author's Acknowledgments

Special thanks to my friends at Apple, who were there for me every step of the way: Tim "the shortstop" Holmes, Ken Bereskin, Keri Walker, and everyone on the Mac OS 8.5 development team; the Apple evangelists; and the Apple fellows. Thank you all. I couldn't have done it without your help.

Thanks also to superagent Carole "Damn-it-stop-calling-me-Swifty" McClendon of Waterside Productions, for dealmaking beyond the call of duty. You're a wonder!

Big-time thanks to the gang at IDG Books: Mike Kelly, Diane Steele, Mary Bednarek, and the big guy himself, John Kilcullen. Nobody does it better.

Extra special thanks to my editor, Tim "the Whipcracker" Gallan, who has been better than great.

Thanks to my family for putting up with my all-too-lengthy absences during this book's gestation.

And finally, thanks to you for buying it.

Publisher's Acknowledgments

We're proud of this book; please register your comments through our IDG Books Worldwide Online Registration Form located at http://my2cents.dummies.com.

Some of the people who helped bring this book to market include the following:

Acquisitions, Editorial, and Media Development

Senior Project Editor: Tim Gallan

Acquisitions Editor: Michael Kelly

Copy Editors: Stephanie Koutek, William A. Barton

Technical Editors: Debbie Gates, Steve Arany

Associate Permissions Editor: Carmen Krikorian

Editorial Manager: Leah P. Cameron

Media Development Manager: Heather Heath Dismore

Editorial Assistant: Donna Love

Indexer: Sharon Hilgenberg

Production

Associate Project Coordinator: Tom Missler

Layout and Graphics: Lou Boudreau, J. Tyler Connor, Maridee V. Ennis, Angela F. Hunckler, Todd Klemme, Anna Rohrer, Brent Savage, Janet Seib

Proofreaders: Kelli Botta, Nancy Price, Rebecca Senninger, Janet M. Withers

General and Administrative

IDG Books Worldwide, Inc.: John Kilcullen, CEO; Steven Berkowitz, President and Publisher

IDG Books Technology Publishing: Brenda McLaughlin, Senior Vice President and Group Publisher

Dummies Technology Press and Dummies Editorial: Diane Graves Steele, Vice President and Associate Publisher; Mary Bednarek, Director of Acquisitions and Product Development; Kristin A. Cocks, Editorial Director

Dummies Trade Press: Kathleen A. Welton, Vice President and Publisher; Kevin Thornton, Acquisitions Manager

IDG Books Production for Dummies Press: Michael R. Britton, Vice President of Production and Creative Services; Cindy L. Phipps, Manager of Project Coordination, Production Proofreading, and Indexing; Kathie S. Schutte, Supervisor of Page Layout; Shelley Lea, Supervisor of Graphics and Design; Debbie J. Gates, Production Systems Specialist; Robert Springer, Supervisor of Proofreading; Debbie Stailey, Special Projects Coordinator; Tony Augsburger, Supervisor of Reprints and Bluelines

Dummies Packaging and Book Design: Robin Seaman, Creative Director; Jocelyn Kelaita, Product Packaging Coordinator; Kavish + Kavish, Cover Design

♦

The publisher would like to give special thanks to Patrick J. McGovern, without whom this book would not have been possible.

♦

Contents at a Glance

Cartoons at a Glance

By Rich Tennant

page 219

page 135

page 337

page 371

page 7

Fax: 978-546-7747 • **E-mail:** the5wave@tiac.net

Table of Contents

· ·

Foreword

· ·

Some people say that Apple's Mac OS 8.5 is just a pretty face on old software. Some people say Bob LeVitus is just a pretty face. This book conclusively proves both sets of people wrong.

Mac OS 8.5 adds cosmetic improvements to the best interface in personal computing, but it's what it adds under the skin that really makes it worth your time and money. There's a whole bunch of new functionality and speed. A lot more of the code is optimized for Power Macs. And as usual, Apple only sketches out the new features and power in their documentation. Fortunately, there's no one better at analyzing and explaining the works of Apple than Bob LeVitus.

Bob's name is a working definition for Not Dull. No matter where you run into Bob — in conversation, around the poker table, or in his writings about the Mac — you are not going to be bored. You will pay attention, not that he'll give you much of a choice. And that's good. His opinions tend to be provocative and well thought out, his poker playing skilled enough to empty your wallet if you're not both good and lucky, and his knowledge of the Mac and ability to communicate it to readers unparalleled.

You need this book because Apple manuals are Apple manuals; you won't get a lot of explanation or help from them. To get at the new power, you could hire a consultant, but that's expensive and not at all necessary: Just read this book. It's a wonderful guide to all of Mac OS 8.5.

Like its System 7.x cousins, this book, *Mac OS 8.5 For Dummies,* might be better called *The Best Mac System Software Book Ever.* Bobby has gone past his usually really good writing level here, and taken a dry subject (who really gets excited about an operating system? A game, sure; and maybe even that exceptional productivity application, but the system software?) and created a book that makes you want to learn and use this important advance in Mac software.

He's also achieved the difficult trick of writing a book that works for first-time users as well as power users who have been using Macs since January 1984. That's no mean accomplishment. I've been writing for and editing Mac magazines since 1985 firsthand and understand (and stand in awe of) the magnitude of Bobby's achievement here.

This book is not free; Apple manuals come with the product. Why buy this book? Why not stick with the oh-so-pretty Apple manuals? Surely, they have everything you're going to find here? Well, no, that's not so. The Apple manuals are pretty. But readable? I don't think so. They're so dry that they should be declared a fire hazard. They're very full of themselves and at the same time so carefully worded that it seems certain their final editing was at the hands of Apple's legal staff.

They tell you the good parts, not the bad parts. And they'd choke before allowing that there are power tips that can really make you productive. Their "avoid all risks; take no shortcuts because it might not be perfectly 100% safe" approach means that the Apple manuals are incomplete.

You can't accuse *Mac OS 8.5 For Dummies* of being incomplete. It goes beyond the too-dry manuals and the too-brief magazine articles and tells you everything about Mac OS 8.5. After you digest it you have the choice of doing things the Apple manual way, or really using and enjoying your Mac.

Here's an example of manual dry versus Bob LeVitus: backing up. Apple tells you to do it. Period. Bobby tells you why you must back up frequently, the absolute best hardware and software tools, the tools to use if you can't afford the best tools, and the absolute need for multiple back up sets.

With a wonderful and refreshing attitude for a person who didn't grow up (or even ever live) in New York, Bobby gets vital information like his instructions on backing right in your face. He's never been shy, and if something is important, he makes sure you get it.

The greatest strength of *Mac OS 8.5 For Dummies* is the breadth and depth of its content. Mac OS 8.5 opens a lot of new ground for Mac users and this book covers it all. You're not going to find a better helper as you move into Mac OS 8.5.

The second greatest strength of *Mac OS 8.5 For Dummies* is its solid dose of in-your-face attitude. This is a readable helper that cares. All too many computer books today are either chores to read or in a couple of cases, simply unreadable because they seem to think dry seriousness is a "business-like" virtue. They're wrong. Readability counts big-time, and *Mac OS 8.5 For Dummies* can be as hard to put down as the latest potboiler. You not only learn from it, but you enjoy the process.

Mac OS 8.5 For Dummies jumps right to the top of the class in Mac system software books. Any book that surpasses it is going to have to be awfully good. And it wouldn't surprise me if Bob LeVitus is the author.

Steven Bobker

Introduction

● ●

*Y*ou made the right choice twice: Mac OS 8.5 and this book.

Take a deep breath and get ready to have some fun. That's right. This is a computer book and it's going to be fun. What a concept! Whether you're brand spanking new to the Mac or a grizzled old Mac-vet, I guarantee that discovering the ins and outs of Mac OS 8.5 will be easy and fun. They couldn't say it on the cover if it weren't true!

Why a Book for Dummies?

Because there wasn't a *...For Dummies* book about the Mac OS (though *DOS For Dummies, Windows For Dummies,* and *Windows 95 For Dummies,* all published by IDG Books Worldwide, Inc., are huge hits), and because the nice folks at IDG Books asked me if I wanted to write one. The result was the international bestseller *Macintosh System 7.5 For Dummies,* an award-winning book so good it was offered by now-deceased Mac cloner Power Computing instead of a system software manual.

And now I'm back with the all-new, totally revised, *Mac OS 8.5 For Dummies,* which combines all the old, familiar features of my earlier book with totally updated information about the latest, greatest offering from Apple.

So why a *...For Dummies* book about Mac OS 8.5? Mac OS 8.5 is a big, complicated personal computer operating system. *Mac OS 8.5 For Dummies* is a not-so-big (about 9 x 7 inches and not very thick), not-very-complicated book that shows you what Mac OS 8.5 is all about without boring you, confusing you, or otherwise making you uncomfortable.

In fact, you'll be so darned comfortable that I wanted to call this book *Mac OS 8.5 without the Discomfort* but they wouldn't let me. There are apparently some rules we *...For Dummies* authors have to follow, and using the word "Dummies" in the title is one of them.

And speaking of dummies, remember that it's just a word. I don't think you're dumb. Quite the opposite. I wanted to call this book *Mac OS 8.5 For People Smart Enough to Know They Need Help,* but you can just imagine what IDG Books thought of that. (If you're reading this in a bookstore, approach the cashier with your wallet in your hand, buy the book, and I'll think you're even smarter!)

This book is chock-full of information and advice, explaining everything you need to know about Mac OS 8.5 in language you'll understand.

It is supplemented with tips, tricks, techniques, and steps, served up in generous quantities. It all adds up to the only book in the world that makes learning Mac OS 8.5 both painless and fun. Can your beer do that?

How to Use This Book

We're gonna start off real slow. The first few chapters are where we get to know each other and discuss the basic everyday things you need to know to operate your Mac or Mac-compatible effectively.

The first part, in fact, is so basic it will probably bore you old-timers to tears. But hey, it's my sworn duty to show you all there is to know in the most painless manner possible. And I can't do that without a solid foundation. So long-time Mac users should feel free to skip through stuff they know to get to the better stuff faster.

A word of warning: If you skip over something important, like why you absolutely *must* back up your hard drive (see Appendix B), don't come crying to me when you lose all your valuable data in a horrendous disk crash. In other words, it's probably not a bad idea to read it all, even if you think you already know it all.

Another thing: We learn by doing. Perform the hands-on tutorials while sitting at your Mac. They're much less effective if you read them anywhere else.

Here are a couple of conventions I use in this book:

- ✔ When I refer to an item in a menu, I use something like File⇨Open, which means "Pull down the File menu and choose the Open command."
- ✔ For keyboard shortcuts, something like Command-A means hold down the Command key (the one with the little pretzel on it) and press the letter A on the keyboard. Command-Shift-A means hold down the Command and Shift keys while pressing the A key.

Finally, there are extensive cross-references throughout the book and a better-than-average index at the back. Use them freely.

How This Book Is Organized

Mac OS 8.5 For Dummies is divided into five logical parts, logically numbered parts one through five. It's better if you read them in order, but if you already know a lot or think you know a lot, feel free to skip around and read the parts that interest you.

Part I: Basic Training

The first part is very, very basic training. From the mouse to the desktop, from the menus to the tricky-for-beginners (but much improved in OS 8.5) Open and Save dialog boxes, it's all here. Everything you need to know to operate Mac OS 8.5 safely and sanely. Old-timers can skim through it; you newbies should read every word. Twice.

Part II: Making It Purr

Here, I discuss hands-on stuff, with chapters on organizing, printing, sharing (files, that is), and memory management. By the time you finish Part II, your system will be finely tuned and running like a champ.

Part III: U 2 Can B A Guru

Now we're cooking. This part is about how things work and how to make them work better.

Tips, tricks, techniques, control panels, scripts, and much more, plus the most useful chapter in the whole book, Chapter 14, which details each and every gosh darn file in your System Folder and why you need it or don't. If your Mac runs like a champ after Part II, wait'll you see it after Part III.

Part IV: The Infamous Part of Tens

Last but not least, it's the Part of Tens, which is mostly a Letterman rip-off, though it does include heaping helpings of tips, troubleshooting hints, and optional software and hardware ideas.

Part V: Appendixes

Appendix A lends a hand with installing Mac OS 8.5. Appendix B brow-beats you into routinely backing up the files on your hard drive.

Icons Used in This Book

Put on your propeller beanie hat and pocket protector. This is truly nerdy stuff. It's certainly not required reading, but it must be interesting or informative or I wouldn't have wasted the space.

Read these notes very, very, very carefully. Did I say "very?" Warning icons flag important information. The author and publisher will not be responsible if your Mac explodes or spews flaming parts because you ignored a Warning icon.

Just kidding. Macs don't explode or spew (with the exception of a few choice PowerBook 5300s). But it got your attention, didn't it? It's a good idea to read Warning notes carefully.

This is where you'll find the juciest morsels: shortcuts, tips, and undocumented secrets. Try them all; impress your friends.

This icon warns you that a hands-on tutorial with step-by-step instructions is coming. It's best to be at your Mac when you read these and perform the steps as you read them.

Me, ranting or raving about something. Imagine foam coming from my mouth. Rants are required to be irreverent, irrelevant, or both. I also try to keep them short, more for your sake than mine.

Mac OS 8.5 is chock full of new features. For those old-timers out there who remember Mac OS 7.*x,* 8.0, and 8.1, this icon alerts you to something you've not seen before.

One Last Thing

I'm thrilled at how this book came out — I think it's the best thing I've ever written. But I didn't write it for me. I wrote it for you and would love to hear how it worked for you. So please drop me a line or register your comments through the IDG Books Online Registration Form located at http:// my2cents.dummies.com.

Did it work for you? What did you like? What didn't you like? What questions were unanswered? Did you want to know more about something? Could you have stood to have learned less about something? Tell me! I've received more than 100 suggestions about previous editions, most of which are incorporated in here. So keep up the good work.

You can send snail mail care of IDG Books (they'll see that I receive it), or send e-mail to me directly at boblevitus@boblevitus.com.

I appreciate your feedback and try to respond to all e-mail within a few days.

Bob LeVitus
Autumn 1998

P.S. What are you waiting for? Go enjoy the book!

Part I
Basic Training

The 5th Wave   By Rich Tennant

"Well, the first day wasn't bad—I lost the 'Finder', copied a file into the 'Trash' and sat on my mouse."

In this part . . .

Mac OS 8.5 sports tons of new goodies and features. I'll get to the hot new goodies soon enough, but you have to learn to crawl before you walk.

In this part, you discover the most basic of basics, such as the de rigueur-for-books-with-*Dummies*-in-the-title section on how to turn your Mac on (it's very short). Next, I acquaint you with the Mac OS 8.5 desktop: icons, windows, menus, disks, and trash — the whole shmear.

So get comfortable, roll up your sleeves, fire up your Mac if you like, and settle down with Part I, a delightful little ditty I like to think of as "The Hassle-Free Way to Get Started with Mac OS 8.5."

Chapter 1

Mac OS 8.5 101 (Prerequisites: None)

Choosing Mac OS 8.5 was a good move. It's more than just a System software upgrade; Mac OS 8.5 includes dozens of new or improved features that make using your Macintosh easier, and dozens more that help you do more work in less time. In other words, it'll make you more productive, give you fewer headaches, reduce your cholesterol level, and make you fall in love with your Mac all over again.

I know you're chomping at the bit, but I'm going to start at the very beginning. This chapter mostly talks about Mac OS 8.5 in abstract terms. Don't bother to turn your Mac on yet, as there's no hands-on stuff here. What you'll find is a bunch of very important stuff that will save the beginner from a lot of headaches.

If you already know what System software is and does, how to avoid disasters, what a startup disk is, and how the startup process works, I suggest you read those sections anyway — to refresh your memory — and skim the rest.

Everyone else: Please read every word.

What Is System Software?

Along with the code in its read-only memory (ROM), the System software (often called the *operating system* or *Mac OS*) is what makes a Mac a Mac. Without it, your Mac is a pile of silicon and circuits, no smarter than a toaster. It's got a brain (ROM), it's got memory (RAM), and it's got ten fingers and toes (other stuff), but it doesn't know what to do with itself. Think of System software as an education, and Mac OS 8.5 as an Ivy League education. (A PC clone with Windows dropped outta high school in the 10th grade and flips burgers for a living.)

With Mac OS 8.5, your Mac becomes an elegant, powerful tool that's the envy of the rest of the computer industry. (Or so we Macintosh lovers like to think!)

Most of the world's personal computers use Windows. Poor schmucks. You're among the lucky few with a computer whose operating system is intuitive, easy to use, and, dare I say, fun. Windows — even Windows 98 — is a cheap imitation of the Macintosh System software. Try it sometime. Go ahead. You probably won't suffer any permanent damage. In fact, you'll really begin to appreciate how good you've got it. Feel free to hug your Mac or give it a peck on the floppy drive opening. Just try not to get your tongue caught.

What Does System Software Do?

Good question. It controls the basic (and most important) operations of your computer. In the case of Mac OS 8.5 and your Mac, the System software manages memory; controls how windows, icons, and menus work; keeps track of files; and does lots of other housekeeping chores. Other forms of software, such as a word processor, rely on the System software to create and maintain the environment in which the application software does its work.

When you create a memo, for example, the word processor provides the tools for you to type and format the information. The System software provides the mechanism for drawing and moving the window in which you write the memo; it keeps track of the file when you save it; it helps the word processor create drop-down menus and dialog boxes and communicate with other programs; and it does much, much more.

Now you have a little background in System software. Before you do anything else with your Mac, take a gander at the next section.

A Safety Net for the Absolute Beginner — or Any User

If you're a first-time Macintosh user, please, please read this section of the book very carefully. It could save your life. Well, now I'm just being overly dramatic. *It could save your Mac* is what I meant to say. I deal with the stuff that the manual that came with your Mac doesn't cover in nearly enough detail, if at all. If you're an experienced Mac user, read this section anyway. Chances are, you need a few reminders.

✔ **If you don't know how to turn your Mac on, get help.** Don't feel bad. Apple, in its infinite wisdom, has manufactured Macs with power-on switches on every conceivable surface: the front, side, back, and the keyboard. Some Macs (most PowerBooks) even hide the power-on button behind a little plastic door.

Like personal fouls in the NBA, authors are only allowed so many weasel-outs per book. I hate to use one so early, but in this case, I think it's worth it for both of us. I promise this is the first and only time I'll say "Look in the manual." Maybe.

✔ **Always use the Shut Down (Special menu) command.** Or press the Power key once and then click the Shut Down button to turn off your Mac. Turning the power off without shutting your Mac down properly is one of the worst things you can do to your poor Mac. It can screw up your hard disk real bad, or scramble the contents of your most important files, or both.

Of course, most of us have broken this rule several times without anything horrible happening. Don't be lulled into a false sense of security. Do it one time too many and your most important file will be toast.

The only time you should turn your Mac off without shutting down properly is if your screen is frozen or you crash and can't do anything else. This doesn't happen often, but when it does, turning your Mac off and then back on is the only solution.

Mac OS 8.5 actually scolds you if you don't shut down properly. If you break this rule, the next time your Mac is turned on, it will politely inform you that your Mac was shut down improperly and is trying to repair the damage, if any, as shown in Figure 1-1.

If you find the little "This Mac was shut down improperly" reminder annoying, you can turn it off in the General Controls control panel. I actually like it and leave the warning enabled. You should too.

✔ **Don't unplug your Mac when it's turned on.** See my blurb in the preceding bullet.

Figure 1-1:
Polite little
machines,
aren't they?

Your computer crashed or was not shut down properly
the last time it was used. Your startup disk is being
checked by Disk First Aid, and any problems will be
repaired.

If you are experiencing frequent crashes, please refer to
Mac OS Help for troubleshooting information. To turn off
your computer, press the Power key on the keyboard.

You can turn off this warning in the General Controls panel.

Verification and repairs completed successfully.

[Done]

✔ **Don't use your Mac when lightning is near.** Lightning strike = dead Mac. 'Nuff said. Oh, and don't place much faith in inexpensive surge protectors. A good jolt of lightning will fry the surge protector right along with your computer. There *are* surge protectors that can withstand most lightning strikes, but they're not the cheapies you buy at your local computer emporium. Unplugging your Mac from the wall during electrical storms is safer and less expensive. (Don't forget to unplug your modem as well — lightning can fry it, too.)

✔ **Don't jostle, bump, shake, kick, throw, dribble, or punt your Mac, especially while it's running.** Unless your Mac is ancient, it contains within it a hard disk drive that spins at 5,400+ rpm. A jolt to a hard disk while it's reading or writing a file can cause the head to crash into the disk, which can render many or all of the files on it totally and irreversibly unrecoverable.

✔ **Turn off your Mac before plugging or unplugging any cables.** This advice may be overkill, as even Apple seems to say that you can safely plug cables into the serial ports — the modem or printer ports — while your Mac is turned on. But other cables, specifically SCSI cables and ADB cables, should never under any circumstances be plugged or unplugged without first shutting down your Mac.

The one exception is if your Mac has USB ports, like the iMac, which you can plug and unplug safely while the Mac is powered up.

Okay, that about does it for bad stuff that can happen. If something bad has already happened to you, see Chapter 18.

What You Should See after Turning the Power On

After a small bit of whirring, buzzing, and flashing (the System software is loading), you should see a cheerful little happy Mac in the middle of your screen like the one in Figure 1-2.

Figure 1-2:
The Mac
startup
icon. Cute
as puke,
isn't it?

Soon thereafter comes a soothing blue Mac OS logo, with the message
"Welcome to Mac OS 8.5," followed by "Starting Up" and the infamous march
of the icons across the bottom of the screen. Makes you feel kind of warm and
fuzzy, doesn't it? These things indicate that Mac OS 8.5 is loading properly.

This might be a good time to take a moment to think good thoughts about
whoever convinced you that you wanted a Mac. They were right.

Anyway, in a few more seconds, the familiar Macintosh desktop will materi-
alize before your eyes. If you haven't customized, configured, or done any
other tinkering, your desktop should look something like Figure 1-3. Don't
worry if you don't see a desktop printer icon on your desktop (mine is
named HP LaserJet 4ML); I cover desktop printers in Chapter 7. And don't
worry if you don't see a little control strip hanging out near the bottom of
your screen; I cover the ingenious control strip in Chapter 12.

Figure 1-3:
The Mac
desktop.

A pop quiz on mousing

For those of you who need to hone your mousing skills, here's a little quiz.

1. How do you select an icon on the desktop?

   A. Stare at it intently for five seconds.

   B. Point to it with your finger, slap the side of your monitor, and say "That one, stupid!"

   C. Move the mouse pointer on top of the icon and click once.

2. When do you need to double-click?

   A. Whenever you find yourself saying, "There's no place like home."

   B. When you're using both hands to control the mouse.

   C. When you want to open a file or folder.

3. How do you select multiple items or blocks of text?

   A. Get several people to stare intently at the items you want to select.

   B. You need to attach multiple mice to your Mac.

   C. Slide the mouse on your desk, moving the on-screen pointer to the location where you want to begin selecting. Press and hold down the mouse button. Drag the pointer across the items or text that you want to select. Then let go of the mouse button.

4. How do you move a selected item?

   A. Call U-Haul.

   B. Pick up and tilt your monitor until the item slides to the proper location.

   C. Click the item and hold down the mouse button. With the mouse button still held down, drag the pointer to the new location and let go of the mouse button.

If you haven't figured it out by now, the correct answer to each of these questions is C. If any other answer sounded remotely plausible for you, sit down with your Mac and just play with it for a while. If you have kids at your disposal, watch them play with your Mac. They'll be showing you how to use it in no time.

In the unlikely event you didn't see the smiling Mac, soothing messages, and familiar desktop, read the next section — "What's Happening Here? (The Startup Process Revealed)" — very carefully. If this section doesn't set things right, skip to Chapter 18.

What's Happening Here? (The Startup Process Revealed)

When you turn on your Macintosh, you set in motion a sophisticated and complex series of events that culminates in the loading of Mac OS 8.5 and the appearance of the familiar Mac desktop. Fortunately, the mechanics of the process are unimportant. In brief, your Mac tests all your hardware — slots, ports, disks, memory (RAM), and so on. If everything passes, you hear a pleasing chord and see the happy Mac, the Mac OS logo, "Welcome to Mac OS 8.5," and "Loading" on your monitor as your Mac loads the System software it needs from disk to RAM.

You're not a failure

If any of your hardware fails when it is tested, you'll see a black screen with the dreaded sad Mac icon (see Figure 1-4) and hear a far less pleasing musical chord known by Mac aficionados as the Chimes of Doom. The fact that something went wrong is no reflection on your prowess as a Macintosh user. Something inside your Mac is broken, and it probably needs to go in for repairs (usually to an Apple dealer). If it's under warranty, dial 1-800-SOS-

Figure 1-4:
The Sad
Mac icon:
Look upon
this face, ye
mighty, and
despair!

APPL and they'll tell you what to do.

Before you do anything, though, skip ahead to Chapter 18. It's entirely possible that one of the suggestions there can get you back on track without your having to spend even a moment on hold.

Question Mark and the Mysterians

Although it's unlikely that you'll see a sad Mac, all users eventually encounter the flashing question mark (shown in Figure 1-5) in place of the usual happy Mac at some time in their lives. Don't worry. This one is a breeze. This icon means that your Mac can't find a *startup disk:* a floppy disk, hard disk, or CD-ROM containing valid System software.

When you turn on your Mac, the first thing it does (after the aforementioned hardware tests) is check the floppy disk drive for a startup disk (something with Mac OS 8.5 on it). If it doesn't find one there, it scans the SCSI bus. At this point, your Mac usually finds your hard disk, which contains a System Folder, and the startup process continues on its merry way with the happy Mac and all the rest.

Figure 1-5:
Your Mac is
having an
identity
crisis if you
see this
icon.

Think of the flashing question mark as your Mac's way of saying, "Please provide me with a disk that contains some System software."

If Apple can figure out a way to put a flashing question mark on the screen, why the heck can't the software engineers find a way to put the words "Please insert a startup disk" on the screen as well? The curtness of the flashing question mark is one of my pet peeves about the Macintosh.

I know, you're clever and smart (you're reading *Mac OS 8.5 For Dummies,* aren't you?), so you know that a flashing question mark means that you should insert a startup disk. But what about everyone else?

Get with the program, Apple.

The ultimate startup disks

Chances are, you have a copy of the ultimate startup floppy right there on your computer table. It's called Disk Tools, and it's one of the disks that you get with most versions of Mac OS. If you get a flashing question mark, pop Disk Tools into your floppy drive and your Mac will boot, just like magic.

Or, if your Mac (or System software upgrade) didn't include floppy disks, it instead included a bootable CD-ROM disk. To boot from a CD-ROM, you need to hold down the C key during startup on most Mac models. If that doesn't work, try holding down these four keys in the infamous four-finger salute: Delete-Option-Command-Shift.

A good way to remember this keyboard combination — which is generally used to start up from a disk other than your internal hard drive, including a bootable CD-ROM — is to think of the mnemonic device DOCS (Delete-Option-Command-Shift).

The legend of the boot

Boot this. Boot that. "I booted my Mac and . . ." "Did it boot?" It seems nearly impossible to talk about computers for long without hearing the word.

But why boot? Why not shoe or shirt or even shazam?

It all began in the very olden days, maybe the 1970s or a little earlier, when starting up a computer required you to toggle little manual switches on the front panel, which began an internal process that loaded the operating system. The process became known as *boot-strapping* because if you toggled the right switches, the computer would "pull itself up by its bootstraps." It didn't take long for the phrase to transmogrify into *booting* and *boot*.

Over the years, *booting* has come to mean turning on almost any computer or even a peripheral device like a printer. Some people also use it to refer to launching an application: "I booted Excel."

So the next time one of your gearhead friends says the b-word, ask if he or she knows where the term comes from. Then dazzle them with the depth and breadth of your knowledge.

Disk Tools or a bootable System software CD make the ultimate startup disks because, in addition to a System and Finder (the two files that must be present on a startup disk), they also have copies of Disk First Aid, Apple HD SC Setup, and Drive Setup, three programs that you may need if you see a flashing question mark. Disk First Aid can repair hidden damage to your hard disk; HD SC Setup or Drive Setup can install new hard disk drivers. Both Disk First Aid and Apple HD SC Setup/Drive Setup are described more completely in Chapter 18, and Apple HD SC Setup and Drive Setup are described in Appendix A.

Now what?

So you've gotten your Mac to boot from the Disk Tools disk or System Software CD-ROM but there's still this little problem. Like you'd prefer that your Mac boot from your (much faster) hard disk than that piddly little Disk Tools floppy or System software CD-ROM. Not to worry. All you need to do is reinstall Mac OS 8.5 (see Appendix A).

Those of you who are going to upgrade from an earlier version of Mac OS to Mac OS 8.5 may want to read Appendix A right about now. The rest of you, the ones whose Macs have already booted from a hard drive with Mac OS 8.5 installed, can breathe a sigh of relief and skip ahead to the next chapter.

How do you know which version of the Mac OS your computer has? Simple. Just pull down the Apple menu and choose About This Computer, the very first choice in the list. A window will pop up in the middle of your screen (see Figure 1-6). In the upper-right corner of this window you'll find the version number of your System software. As you can see, the About This Computer window not only tells you the version number of the Mac OS you're using, but it also details your RAM usage. (You can find out more about RAM usage and memory in Chapter 9.)

Figure 1-6:
I'm using
Mac OS
Version 8.5.
Look. It
says so
right there
on the
upper right!

One Last Thing Before We Move On . . .

If the stuff on your hard disk means anything to you, you must back it up. Not maybe. You must. Which is why I recommend that you read Appendix B right now instead of later. Unlike an earlier section in this chapter, Appendix B is a safety net for everyone. Before you do any significant work on your Mac (or even if your most important file is your last saved game of Marathon Infinity), you need to realize how important it is to back up.

Dr. Macintosh sez, "There are only two kinds of Mac users — those who have never lost data and those who will." Which kind will you be?

I beg you: Please read Appendix B now before something horrible happens to your valuable data.

Chapter 2

Meet the Desktop

. . . .

. . . .

This is where I get down to the nitty-gritty; this is the chapter about the Macintosh desktop. Your desktop is the center of your Macintosh universe. Just about everything you do on your Mac begins and ends with the desktop. The desktop is where you manage files, store documents, launch programs, adjust the way your Mac works, and do much more. If you ever expect to master your Mac, the first step is to master the desktop.

Once again, those of you who have been using Mac OS for a while may find some of the information presented in this chapter repetitive; many of the features discussed in this chapter are unchanged from earlier versions of the Mac OS. Still, you'd be foolish to skip it completely. If you do, I assure you you'll miss sarcasm, clever wordplay, shortcuts, awesome techniques, a bad pun or two, and lots of good advice on making the desktop an easier place to be. If that's not enough to convince you, I also provide a bunch of stuff Apple didn't bother to tell you. (Like you read the manual anyway. . . .)

Tantalized? Let's rock.

I Think ICON, I Think ICON

Icons, those funny little pictures on your desktop and in your windows, represent containers, and these containers hold things that you work with on your Mac, like programs, documents, System software items, discarded files (the Trash icon), and more. All icons appear on your screen as little pictures with their names attached.

The first icon you should become familiar with is the icon for your hard disk. It's in the upper-right corner and is named Macintosh HD, unless you've renamed it (see Figure 2-1). In upcoming screen shots you'll notice I've renamed mine Spawn.

If you want to give any icon a different picture, you can find out how in the very next chapter.

Figure 2-1:
A plain
vanilla hard
disk icon.

The look you want to know better

Icons come in all shapes and sizes. After you've been around the Macintosh for a while, you get a kind of sixth sense about what an icon contains just by looking at it. For example, application (that is, program) icons are often diamond shaped. Unless, of course, they're rectangular or square or oddly shaped (see Figure 2-2).

Figure 2-2:
Application
icons come
in many
different
shapes.

Okay, so application icons are all over the place. Document icons, on the other hand, are almost always reminiscent of a piece of paper (as shown in Figure 2-3).

Figure 2-3:
Typical
document
icons.

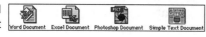

See? You're already acquiring that sixth sense. Application icons are all over the place; document icons look like paper. Kind of.

Now let's talk about the four kinds of icons: application, document, folder, and System software.

(There are actually five kinds of icons. Aliases are an icon type in their own right. But I'm trying to keep things simple; I discuss these most excellent icons soon enough. Like in the very next chapter.)

Applications are programs, the software that you use to accomplish tasks on your Mac. Your word processor is an application. So are America Online and Adobe Photoshop. Titanic: Adventure Out of Time and Marathon are applications. (They're also great games.)

Documents are files created by applications. Letter to Mom, which you created in ClarisWorks, is a document. So are Bob's Calendar and Expense Report.

Folders are the Mac's organizational containers. You put icons, usually application or document icons, into folders. You can also put folders inside other folders. Folders look like, well, folders. Some folder icons have pictures; most don't. (See Figure 2-4.)

Figure 2-4:
Typical folder icons.

untitled folder   System Folder   Control Panels   Fonts

System software is the stuff in your System Folder — the System, the Finder, control panels, extensions, and almost everything else. The files that make up your System software have many purposes, most of which will be second nature to you by the end of this book. For now, I'll just talk about the icons, though.

System software icons usually have a distinctive look as well. For example, the System and Finder have distinctive, Mac-flavored icons. (See Figure 2-5.)

Figure 2-5:
The System and Finder icons.

Finder   System

Control panel icons usually have a slider bar at the bottom or on one side (as illustrated in Figure 2-6).

Figure 2-6:
Control
panel icons
generally
have a
slider bar.

Extension icons usually look like jigsaw puzzle parts. (See Figure 2-7.)

Figure 2-7:
Extension
icons
usually
display a
puzzled
look.

But that's where the metaphor breaks down. The rest of your System software icons may look like just about anything. (See Figure 2-8.)

Figure 2-8:
Other
System
software
icons may
look like
almost
anything.

I have lots more to say about all of these kinds of icons, and I do so in upcoming chapters. But that's enough about what icons look like. I'm sure you're anxious to do something with icons already.

Open sesame

There are three ways to open any icon. (Okay, there are four ways, but, as I said, I'm saving aliases for later. You don't need to know just yet.) Anyway, here are the ways:

✔ Click the icon once to select it; then point to the File menu (it's the one that says File) and press the word File. Remember, a press is half a click. Don't release the mouse button yet. A menu drops down. Move the pointer downward until the word Open is highlighted (see Figure 2-9). Then release the mouse button.

(I probably could have saved a whole paragraph by simply saying "Choose File⇨Open." But you may have been pulling down a menu for the first time. I wanted to be safe.) The icon opens.

By the way, in case you hadn't noticed, I just showed you how to choose an item from a menu. Don't go hog-wild. There's lots more to know about menus, but I cover it in the next chapter. In fact, all of Chapter 3 is about menus.

✔ Double-click the icon by clicking it directly twice in rapid succession. If it doesn't open, you double-clicked too slowly.

✔ Select the icon and then use the keyboard shortcut Command-O. That means you press the Command key, the one with the pretzel and the apple on most keyboards, and then press the O key while continuing to hold down the Command key.

If you look at Figure 2-9, you can see that the keyboard shortcut appears on the menu after the word Open. Pretzel-O. Any menu item with one of these pretzel-letter combinations after its name can be executed with that keyboard shortcut. Just press the pretzel (Command) key and the letter shown in the menu — Command and N for New Folder, Command and F for Find, and so on — and the appropriate command is executed.

Figure 2-9: Selecting the Open command.

It's never too soon to learn good habits, so I'll mention here that experienced Macintosh users use the keyboard shortcuts as often as possible. Keyboard shortcuts let you get things done without opening the menu, which means that you don't have to reach for the mouse, which means that you get more done in less time. It's a good idea to memorize shortcuts for menu items you use frequently.

Although the letters next to the Command-key symbol (I'm done calling it a pretzel now) in the Finder's menus are capital letters, you don't have to press the Shift key to use the keyboard shortcut. Command-P means that you hold down the Command key and press P. Some programs have keyboard combinations that require the use of Command-Shift, but these programs let you know by calling the key combination something like Command-Shift-S or Command-Shift-O. Or they indicate the shift part with a little up-facing arrow. You don't have to worry about the capitalization of the letter.

The name game

Icon, icon, bo-bicon, banana fanna fo-ficon. Bet that you can change the name of any old icon. Here are two ways:

- ✔ Click the icon's name directly. Don't forget to release the mouse button.
- ✔ Click the icon and then press the Return or Enter key on your keyboard once.

Either of these ways selects the icon's *name* and puts a box around it, waiting for you to type. (See Figure 2-10.)

Figure 2-10:
You can change an icon's name by simply typing a new one; when the name is highlighted, as shown, just start typing.

In addition to selecting the name, the cursor changes from a pointer to a text-editing I-beam. An I-beam cursor is your Mac's way of telling you that it's okay to type now. At this point, if you click the I-beam cursor anywhere within the name box, you can edit the icon's original name. If you don't click and just begin typing, the icon's original name is completely replaced by what you type.

If you've never changed an icon's name, give it a try.

And don't forget: If you click the icon itself, the icon will be selected and you won't be able to change its name. (Selecting the icon itself enables you to move, copy, print, or open it, but I'm getting ahead of myself.) If you do this, press Return or Enter to edit the name of the icon.

Other various and sundry icons

Before I get off the subject of icons completely, and because this is the chapter where you meet your desktop, I'd be remiss if I didn't mention a couple of other icons that you'll probably find there. The most important of these is . . .

The Trash

The Trash is a special container where you put the icons you no longer want on your hard or floppy disk. Got four copies of SimpleText on your hard disk? Drag three of them to the Trash. Old letters that you don't want to keep? Drag them to the Trash as well. To put an icon in the Trash, drag it on top of the Trash icon. When the tip (cool people call it the *hot spot*) of the pointer is directly over the Trash icon, the icon inverts (as shown in Figure 2-11).

Figure 2-11:
Dragging a
file into the
Trash.

When the Trash inverts (that is, turns black), release the mouse button and, voilà, whatever you dragged to the Trash is trashed. But it's not gone forever until . . .

. . . you choose Special⇨Empty Trash. You know how the garbage in the can in your kitchen sits there until the sanitation engineers come by and pick it up each Thursday? The Mac OS Trash works the same. When you put something in the Trash, it sits there until you choose the Special⇨ Empty Trash command.

TIP

You can also use the Mac OS 8.5 contextual menu➪Empty Trash command by putting your cursor directly over the Trash icon and holding down the Control key on your keyboard as you click. You should see a menu like the one shown in Figure 2-12.

Figure 2-12:
Emptying the Trash the contextual menu way. (Hold down the Control key when you click the Trash icon.)

Think twice before you invoke Empty Trash. After the Trash has been emptied, the files it contained are gone forever. Figure 2-13 shows what a full and empty trash can look like. (Of course, you read Appendix B and you've backed up your hard disk several times, right? So even though the files are gone forever from your hard disk, you can get them back if you like, right?)

Figure 2-13:
Empty trash can on the left; full and bulging trash can on the right.

TECHNICAL STUFF

Utility programs that let you retrieve a trashed file after you empty the Trash are available. Norton Utilities and Tech Tool Pro are the two most popular. They don't have a 100-percent success rate, so you should still consider the Empty Trash command fatal to files.

TECHNICAL STUFF

What the heck's the Finder, anyway?

You may have noticed that I use the words *Finder* and *desktop* interchangeably. As you probably know, the Finder is one of the files in your System Folder. The Finder is the super-program. Among other things, it creates the desktop metaphor — the icons, windows, and menus that make up the Macintosh desktop. Unlike with ordinary programs, you can never quit the Finder. Like Katz's Deli, the Finder never closes. And unlike with ordinary programs, you don't have to open the Finder to use it. The Finder is always open; it opens automatically when you turn on your Mac.

Because the Finder is, among other things, responsible for creating the desktop and its menus, many people, myself included, use the words *Finder* and *desktop* interchangeably. You can, too.

The only time it gets confusing is when you are talking about the Finder icon in your System Folder. Just say "the Finder icon" instead of "the Finder" and you'll sound like a pro. It can also be confusing when you're talking about the background you see on your screen (mine is Mac OS wallpaper), which is also called the desktop.

As with all icons, you can open the Trash (you can find at least three ways to open an icon earlier in this chapter) to see what's in there. You can tell there's something in the Trash because the Trash icon bulges when it's full (as shown in Figure 2-13).

If you drag an icon that's *locked* to the Trash, you'll see a message telling you to hold down the Option key when you choose Special⇨Empty Trash to delete locked items. (To unlock locked icons, select the icon and then choose File⇨Get Info or its keyboard shortcut, Command-I, and then click the little box marked "locked.")

Close encounters of the icon kind

If you've used System 7.5, Mac OS 7.6, or Mac OS 8 for very long, you've probably encountered a couple of other icons. You probably have an icon for a desktop printer on your desktop, which you can see in Figure 2-14.

Figure 2-14:
Mac OS
8.5's four
default
desktop
icons with
my desktop
printer icon
above them.

Each Desktop Printer icon represents one printer available to your Mac or one set of printer-specific settings (scale, tile, crop, and so on). You may have more than one Desktop Printer icon. If you don't have even one, don't fret. You can make one in Chapter 7.

If you performed a full install of Mac OS 8.5, you will see three or four other icons on your desktop: Browse the Internet, Mail, Register with Apple, and Get QuickTime Pro. (Refer to Figure 2-14.)

This is probably a good time to mention that if you need help with any part of Mac OS 8.5, you can choose Help Center from the Help menu and get assistance instantly. (See Figure 2-15.)

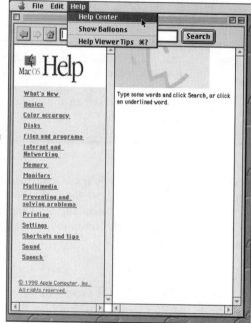

Figure 2-15:
You can learn a lot about Mac OS 8.5 by exploring the Help Center. So what are you waiting for?

I cover Mac OS 8.5's amazing Internet capabilities as well as more about the Browse the Internet and Mail icons in Chapter 15.

If you have any other icons on your desktop, ignore them for now. They probably won't hurt anything.

Windows (Definitely Not the Microsoft Kind)

Windows are such a fundamental part of the Macintosh experience that Microsoft blatantly ripped off the name for their operating system add-on.

If you're relatively new to the Mac, you might want to read this section while sitting at your computer, trying the techniques as you read them. I've always found it easier to remember something that I read if I actually do it. If you've been abusing your Mac for a while, you've probably figured out how windows work by now, but you may not have tried some stuff in here. Your mileage may vary.

Doin' windows

Windows are a ubiquitous part of Macintosh computing. Windows on the desktop show you the contents of disk and folder icons; windows in applications usually show you the contents of your documents.

I've already showed you three different ways to open an icon, so you know how to open a window. When you open a window, its icon turns fuzzy gray (see Figure 2-16), which is your Mac's way of letting you know that the icon's window is open. Clever, eh?

Figure 2-16:
A fuzzy gray (that is, open) icon.

Zooming right along . . .

Notice how the Spawn window in Figure 2-17 says "9 Items" near the top, but only one item seems to be showing. That's easily remedied. To make a window larger, click the *zoom box,* one of the two boxes in the upper-right corner of most windows (circled in Figure 2-18). This action causes the window to grow, and it should reveal the rest of its contents.

Figure 2-17:
This window says that it contains nine items, but you only see one. What gives?

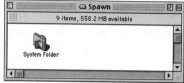

Figure 2-18:
When you click the zoom box in the upper-right corner of the window (circled at left), the window expands to show all the items it contains (right).

I say "should" because if a window contains more icons than the window can display, it grows as large as it can and still leaves room for your disk and Trash icons on the right side of the screen when you click the zoom box.

Click the zoom box again to return the window to its original size.

That shady window feeling . . .

If you want to collapse the window so just its title bar shows (see Figure 2-19), either double-click in the title bar or click the windowshade box (circled in Figure 2-19).

Figure 2-19:
Clicking the
windowshade
box shrinks
the window
so just its
title bar
shows.

Click the windowshade box again to return the window to its original size.

Windowshade's double-click feature can be turned on and off in the
Appearance control panel, which is covered in Chapter 12.

Cutting windows down to size

Another way to see more of what's in a window is by using the *sizer* in the
lower-right corner. It's shown in Figure 2-20 on the left. Click the sizer and
drag downward and to the right to make the window larger, as shown on
the right in Figure 2-20. You use the sizer to make a window whatever size
you like.

Figure 2-20:
Click and
drag the
sizer and
then drag
down and
to the right
to make a
window
larger.

Notice the faint white lines when you drag; they're there to show you the
size the window will be when you release the mouse button. Go ahead and
give it a try; it's fun, it's easy, and it's free.

A scroll new world

Yet another way to see more of what is in a window is to *scroll*. You scroll using *scroll bars*, which appear on the bottom and right sides of any window that contains more icons than those that you can see in the window. (See Figure 2-21.)

Figure 2-21:
Scroll bars.

There are four ways to scroll:

Way #1: Click a *scroll box* and drag, as shown in Figure 2-22.

Figure 2-22:
You can scroll by clicking and dragging a scroll box.

Way #2: Click a *scroll arrow,* as shown in Figure 2-23.

Figure 2-23:
You can also scroll by clicking a scroll arrow.

Way #3: Click in the gray *scroll bar* area, as shown in Figure 2-24.

Figure 2-24:
You can
also scroll
by clicking
in the gray
scroll bar
area.

If the scroll bar is white, then there are no items to scroll to — everything that the window contains is visible.

Clicking the gray scroll *bar* scrolls the window a lot; clicking a scroll *arrow* scrolls the window a little; and pressing and dragging the scroll *box* scrolls the window an amount that corresponds to how far you drag it.

Way #4: Use the keyboard. Select an icon in the window first and then use the arrow keys to move up, down, left, or right. Using an arrow key selects the next icon in that direction and automatically scrolls the window, if necessary.

You can also press the Tab key on the keyboard to select the next icon alphabetically. So if I clicked SimpleText and then pressed the Tab key, the System Folder (the icon that comes next alphabetically) would be selected. If the System Folder wasn't showing when I selected SimpleText, the Spawn window would scroll automatically to reveal the System Folder after I pressed the Tab key.

For what it's worth, the Page Up and Page Down keys on extended key-boards function the same as clicking the gray scroll bar area (the vertical scroll bar only) in the Finder and many applications. But these keys don't work at all in some programs, so don't get too dependent on them.

Transportable windows

To move a window, click anywhere in the *title bar* (shown in Figure 2-25) and drag the window to its new location. Figure 2-26 shows an example of moving a window by dragging its title bar. The title bar is the striped bar at the top of the active window. It contains the window's name, as well as the close box, the windowshade box, and the zoom box.

Figure 2-25:
A title bar.

[□   ⌐ Spawn   🗖🗗]

Figure 2-26: Click and drag the title bar to move a window to a new location.

The window moves to its new position as soon as you release the mouse button.

You can also move a window by clicking any side of it. Figure 2-27 shows all the places you can click and drag to move a window.

Figure 2-27: Click and drag any edge of a window, or its title bar, to move it to a new location.

Just below the title bar is the window's *status line,* which tells you the number of items the window contains (9) and the amount of space available on this hard disk (65.3MB).

Ladies and gentlemen, activate your windows

In order to work with a window, the window must be active. Only one window at a time may be the *active window*. To make a window active, click it anywhere — in the middle, on the title bar, or on a scroll bar. It doesn't matter where.

The active window is always the frontmost window, and inactive windows always appear behind the active window. The active window's title bar has black lines; its size, zoom, and close boxes are defined, as are its scroll bars. Inactive windows show the window's name but none of those other distinctive window features. See Figure 2-28 for an illustration of active and inactive windows.

Figure 2-28:
An active window in front of an inactive window; notice how the active window's features — scroll bars and boxes, close box, title bar, and so on — are clearly defined.

Shutting yo' windows

Now that you know just about all there is to know about windows, I suppose I ought to tell you how to close them. Here we go again with the ways. There are four ways to close an active window:

Way #1: Click the *close box* in the upper-left corner of the title bar. (See Figure 2-29.)

Figure 2-29:
You can click the close box to close a window.

Way #2: Choose File⇨Close Window. (See Figure 2-30.)

Figure 2-30: You can use the Close Window command in the File menu to close an active window.

Way #3: Use the keyboard shortcut Command-W. Note that in Figure 2-30, the Close Window command in the File menu has this keyboard shortcut listed next to it.

If you're like me, by the end of the day, you have windows open all over your desktop, sometimes a dozen or more. Wouldn't it be nice if there were a way to close them all at once with a single "close all windows" command? But you don't see a Close All command in the menus, do you?

Well, there is one, but Apple, in its infinite wisdom, has hidden it from mere mortals. To make this useful command come out and play, merely hold down the Option key as you close the active window using Way #1, Way #2, or Way #3. In other words, hold down the Option key when you click the active window's close box, hold down the Option key when you choose File⇨Close Window, or hold down the Option key and the Command key while you press the W key (Command-Option-W).

Apple didn't hide the Close All command very well. As Figure 2-31 illustrates, if you press the Option key before pulling down the File menu, Close Window is magically transformed into Close All.

Way #4: Use the contextual menu shortcut, as shown in Figure 2-32. Just hold down the Control key on your keyboard when you click any window to get the contextual menu.

Figure 2-31:
Hold down
the Option
key while
pulling
down the
File menu
and you'll
see the
Close All
command
instead of
the Close
Window
command.

Figure 2-32:
Hold down
the Control
key when
clicking a
window to
pop up the
contextual
menu.

Congrats: You now do windows

That retires the side. You now possess a massive, all-encompassing, thoroughly pervasive knowledge of windows and how they work. You can do windows with the best of them.

And I have good news for you: Windows in 99 percent of all applications (programs) that you will ever encounter work the same as windows in the Finder. Just about every application has active and inactive windows with title bars, close boxes, zoom boxes, scroll bars, scroll arrows, and scroll boxes.

Windows are windows, for the most part. As you use different programs, you'll probably notice that some of them (Microsoft Word, for example) take liberties with windows by adding features such as page counters and style indicators to the scroll bar area. Don't worry. You know how to do windows. That stuff is just window dressing (pun intended).

Disk Could Be the Start of a Beautiful Friendship

Groan. I apologize, but I assure you that you don't want to hear the alternatives. Though I don't think there's such a thing as a good pun, in retrospect, this one *is* particularly odious. Sorry.

For all the lowdown on what floppy disks are and where they came from, you ought to see David Pogue's *Macs For Dummies* (published by IDG Books Worldwide, Inc.). I limit my discussion to stuff you do with disks when they're on the desktop.

You should think of the disk icons that appear on your desktop as if they were folders. When you double-click them, their windows open. You can drag stuff in and out of a disk's window, and you can manipulate the disk's window in all the usual ways.

Initialization and erasure

Brand new disks usually need to be *initialized* — prepared to receive Macintosh files — before they can be used. I say "usually" because you can buy new disks that are *preformatted* and are already initialized. It only takes a couple of minutes to initialize a disk, so don't pay a whole lot more for preformatted disks unless you really believe that time is money.

When you pop an uninitialized disk into your Mac, it will walk you through all the steps necessary to initialize it.

Surprise! PC disks work as well!

One of Mac OS 8.5's most excellent features (if you have friends unfortunate enough not to own Macs and you want to share files with them) is the fact that it reads both Mac and DOS floppy disks without any user intervention. DOS disks are formatted for use with personal computers running DOS or Windows. If a friend has a Windows computer, you can read his or her disks by just sticking them in your floppy drive. Your unfortunate friend, on the other hand, can't do diddly squat with your Mac-formatted disks — yet another reason why Macs are better.

When you insert a disk formatted for DOS, you'll see a distinctive PC disk icon like the one in Figure 2-33.

Figure 2-33:
A PC-
formatted
disk on
your Mac
desktop.

There are two other disk formats that you might run into: ProDOS is the Apple II format, rarely used anymore, and Macintosh HFS Interchange Format is a weirdo format nobody I know uses for anything.

Getting disks out of your Mac

You know about everything there is to know about disks except one important thing: how to eject a disk. Piece of cake, actually.

And, of course, there are five ways.

Way #1: Click the disk's icon to select it. Then choose Special⇨Eject or use the keyboard shortcut Command-E.

Way #2: Drag the disk's icon to the Trash.

This drives me nuts. Anything else you drag into the Trash dies (or at least it does when you select Empty Trash). Why does dragging a disk to the Trash eject it?

Way #3: Select the disk and then choose File⇨Put Away (or use its Command-key shortcut, Command-Y).

Way #4: Click the disk while holding down the Control key; then use the contextual menu's Eject command.

Way #5: Use the keyboard shortcut Command-Shift-1. Notice how even though the disk has been ejected and is probably in your right hand, its icon still appears on the desktop, albeit with an unusual ghostly gray pattern. (See Figure 2-34.)

The ghostly gray indicates that the disk is not currently mounted (inserted). Note that a dismounted disk's icon is not the same as that of a disk with its window open. The icon of a mounted disk with its window open is shown in Figure 2-35.

Figure 2-34:
The icon
of a disk
ejected
with
Command-
Shift-1.

Figure 2-35:
The icon of
a mounted
disk with its
window
open.
See the
difference?

Why would you want the icon for an ejected disk on your desktop? So you can copy files from one floppy disk to another even though you have only one floppy disk drive. A whole section on copying files is coming up in a few pages.

If you use the Eject command, drag a disk's icon to the Trash, or use the Put Away command, the disk's ghost icon is *not* left on the desktop. If you use Way #1 or Way #2 to eject your disk, you can get rid of its ghost image by dragging the ghost icon to the Trash or selecting it and choosing File⇨ Put Away. Unless you plan to copy files from one floppy to another, you don't want floppy disk icons on your desktop after you eject the disks. Ways #3 and #4 are the most commonly used methods of ejecting a disk.

If you insist on leaving ghost icons of long-ago-ejected disks on your desktop, it's only a matter of time before your Mac presents you with the dreaded "Please insert the disk" dialog box, which is shown in Figure 2-36.

Notice that there is no OK or Cancel button in the dialog box in Figure 2-36. There's no way out but to insert the disk your Mac is asking for.

Okay, I lied. There is a way out. Press Command-period. This keyboard shortcut cancels the dialog box and lets you drag the ghost disk icon to the Trash. Command-period is a good shortcut to remember. In most dialog boxes, Command-period is the same as clicking the Cancel button.

Figure 2-36:
When you
leave
ghosted
disk icons
on the
desktop,
your Mac
may ask for
the disks
back.

The dreaded "Please insert the disk" dialog box usually appears if you try to open the icon for an unmounted disk or try to open any of the files in the unmounted disk's window.

Get in the habit of dragging disks to the Trash or using the Put Away or Eject commands to get disks off your desktop. These techniques eject the disk and get rid of its pesky ghost icon. Unless you plan to copy files from one floppy to another, which you don't do all that often, avoid the Command-Shift-1 method of ejecting disks.

Up the Organization: Copying and Moving Files and Folders

Now that you know icons and windows and disks, it's time to get serious and read about something useful, like how to work with folders and how to move and copy icons from folder to folder and from disk to disk.

Know when to hold 'er, know when to folder

If your hard disk is a filing cabinet, folders are its folders. Duh. You use folders to organize your icons.

Makin' folders

To create a new folder, first decide which window you want the new folder to appear in. Make that window active by clicking it. Now either choose File⇨New Folder or use the shortcut Command-N. A new, untitled folder appears in the active window with its name box already highlighted and ready for you to type a new name for it. (See Figure 2-37.)

Figure 2-37:
A brand-new untitled folder.

Name your folders with relevant names. Folders entitled sfdghb or Stuff — or worst of all, names like Untitled — won't make it any easier to find something six months from now.

Usin' 'em

Folders are icons; icons are containers. Folder icons (like disk icons) can contain just about any other icon.

You use folders to organize your stuff. There's no limit to how many folders you can have, so don't be afraid to create new ones and put stuff in them.

At the very least, you should have a System Folder. (If you don't, read Chapter 1.) Until you get a *lot* of stuff, may I suggest that you start out with Application and Document folders, at the very least? You can even have the Mac create these two folders automatically by using the General Controls control panel. (More about that in Chapter 12.)

Later, when you get more files, you can subdivide the Documents folder into meaningful subfolders like those shown in Figure 2-38.

As your subfolders get fuller, create subfolders within them. The idea is to have enough folders so that no one folder ever has hundreds of items in it, while simultaneously avoiding folders with only one or two items in them. Strive for balance. And try not to go deeper than four or five levels. If you find yourself creating subfolders that you have to open eight folders to get to, consider reorganizing the stuff in levels five through eight so that your folder hierarchy is no more than five levels deep. Trust me, you can save a lot of time if you don't stash stuff ten folders deep.

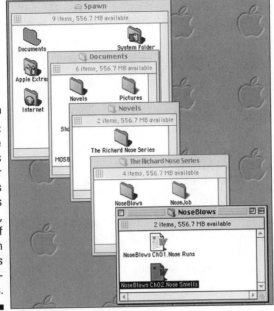

Figure 2-38:
The
Documents
folder
contains
numerous
subfolders,
each of
which
contains
sub-
subfolders.

Moving and copying folders

You can move icons around within windows to your heart's content. Just click and drag within the window.

Now I'll run through how you move an item into a folder. For example, take a look at how you move One Folder into Another Folder. As you might expect from me, the King of Ways, there are two ways to do it.

- ✔ As shown in Figure 2-39, drag the icon for One Folder onto the icon for Another Folder and release when Another Folder is highlighted. This technique works regardless of whether Another Folder's window is open. If its window is open, you can use the second way.

- ✔ Drag the icon for One Folder into the open window for Another Folder (or disk), as shown in Figure 2-40.

Figure 2-39:
Placing one
folder into
another.

Figure 2-40:
You can
also move a
folder by
dragging its
icon into
the open
window of
another
folder.

Notice the little gray border that appears around Another Folder's window in Figure 2-40. This is your Mac's way of telling you that if you release the mouse button right this second, the One Folder icon will be moved into Another Folder. If you move the pointer out of the Another Folder window, the gray border disappears.

You can use these two techniques to move any icon — folder, document, System software, or program icons — into folders or disks.

Before you read the next section, you should know that if you try to move an item from one disk to another disk, it will be copied, not moved. Always. Without exception. If you want to *move* a file or folder from one disk to another, you have to trash the original manually after the copying is complete.

But what if you don't want to move something from one place to another on your hard disk? What if instead you want to copy it, leaving the icon in its original location and an identical copy in the destination window?

You might be thinking, why would I want to do that? Trust me, someday you will. Say you've got a file called Long Letter to Mom in a folder called 1987 Correspondence. You figure Mom's forgotten it by now, so you want to send the letter again. But before you do, you want to change the date and delete the reference to Clarence, her pit bull, who passed away last year. So you want a copy of Long Letter to Mom in your 1998 Correspondence folder.

There are three ways to copy, but the first two are the same as you saw in the One Folder and Another Folder example, with one small difference — you must hold down the Option key during the dragging portion of the move. In the Finder, Option-dragging an icon to any folder icon or window copies it instead of moving it. So you Option-drag the Long Letter to Mom icon onto either a folder icon or an open window to deposit a copy.

When you copy something by dragging and dropping, the mouse pointer changes so that it includes a little plus sign (+) next to the arrow. Neat.

Now you have two copies of the file Long Letter to Mom, one in the 1987 Correspondence folder and another in the 1998 Correspondence folder. Open the one in the 1997 folder and make your changes. Don't forget to save. (There's more about saving in Chapter 5.)

If I were you, I'd change the name of the 1998 copy, as having more than one file on your hard disk with the same name is not a good idea, even if the files are in different folders. Trust me, having 10 files called Expense Report or 15 files named Randall's Invoice can be confusing, no matter how well organized your folder structure is. Add something distinguishing to file and folder names so that they're Expense Report 10/98 or Randall's Invoice 10/30/98. You'll be glad you did.

The third way to copy a file is to use the Duplicate command in either the File or the contextual menu, which I cover in depth in the very next chapter.

Moving and copying disks

Moving an icon from one disk to another works the same as moving folders in the previous example. Because you're moving the icons from one disk to another disk, the copy part is automatic; you don't need the Option key. As I mentioned before, when you move a file from one disk to another, you're automatically making a copy of it. The original is left untouched and unmoved. If you want to move a file from one disk to another, copy it. You can then delete the original by dragging it to the Trash.

Copying the entire contents of a floppy disk to your hard disk works a little differently. To do this task, select the floppy disk's icon and drag it onto your hard disk's icon, onto your hard disk's open window, or onto any other folder icon or open folder window.

When the copy is completed, a folder bearing the same name as the floppy disk appears on your hard disk. The folder on your hard disk now contains each and every file that was on the floppy disk of the same name.

Be careful copying disks containing System Folders to your hard disk. You never want to use the preceding technique to copy a floppy to your hard disk if the floppy has a System Folder. One hard and fast rule of the Mac is that you should never have more than one System Folder on your hard disk.

If a floppy disk contains a System Folder and you want to copy everything else to your hard disk, do the following: Create a new folder on your hard disk. Then select every icon in the floppy disk's window *except* the System Folder and drag all the selected icons onto the new folder's icon or window.

To select more than one icon, click once and drag. You see an outline of a box around the icons as you drag, and icons within or touching the box become highlighted. (See Figure 2-41.)

Another way to select multiple icons is to click one and then hold down the Shift key as you click others. As long as you hold down the Shift key, each new icon you click is added to the selection. To deselect an icon, click it a second time while still holding the Shift key down.

Figure 2-41:
To select
more than
one item,
click and
drag with
the mouse.

Be careful with multiple selections, especially when you drag icons to the Trash. It's easy to accidentally select more than one icon, so it's possible to put an icon in the Trash by accident if you're not paying close attention. So pay close attention.

Meet the desktop

Earlier in this chapter, I say that the terms *Finder* and *desktop* are used interchangeably, referring to the total Macintosh environment you see — icons, windows, menus, and all the other cool stuff. Well, just to make things confusing, the background you see on your screen, the gray or patterned backdrop behind your hard disk icon and open windows, is also called the *desktop*.

Any icon can reside on the desktop. Just move icons to the desktop from any window. It's not a window, but it acts like one. You can move any icon there if you like; the desktop is a great place for things you use a lot, like folders, applications, or documents that you use every day.

It's even better to use aliases of things you use often so that you can keep the originals tucked away in one of your perfectly organized folders. But I don't talk about aliases until Chapter 3, so for now, just tuck that little tidbit away in the back of your mind.

In Figure 2-42, you see two icons on my desktop that you haven't seen before: Disk First Aid (application icon) and Internet Explorer (alias icon).

Disk icons always appear on the desktop, as does the Trash icon. The desktop printer, Browse the Internet, Mail, Get QuickTime Pro, and Register With Apple icons are created when you install Mac OS 8.5.

My other icons were moved from inside Spawn to the desktop by me to make them easier to use.

Items on the desktop behave the same as they would in a window. You move them and copy them in the same way as you would an icon in a window — except that they're not in a window; they're on the desktop, which makes them more convenient to use.

Got it? It's convenient. It's fast. Put stuff there.

But not too much. If you keep putting stuff on the desktop, eventually it gets very cluttered. That's the time to put infrequently used icons back in the folder or disk window they came from. Fortunately, your Mac makes this task easy, even if you've forgotten which folder they were in. Select the icon or icons that you want to be moved back to where they came from and then choose File➪Put Away. Each icon is magically transported back into the folder or disk icon from which it came and no longer appears on the desktop. Neat, eh?

Figure 2-42:
My desktop
with some
stuff on it.

One Last Thing . . .

I'd be remiss (again?) if I didn't at least mention here that you can change the background pattern of your desktop. Though it's covered in full and loving detail in Chapter 12, if you're sick of the Mac OS desktop pattern seen in almost every screen shot so far, you can do either of the following things:

- ✔ Choose Apple menu⇨Control Panels⇨Appearance.
- ✔ Hold down the Control key, click anywhere on the desktop, and choose the Change Desktop Background menu item.

Either one will lead you to the Appearance control panel, where you can choose from dozens of desktop patterns and pictures.

I am particularly fond of the Desktop Pictures feature. I use the 3-D UFO picture Apple supplied as my everyday background. (See Figure 2-43.)

Figure 2-43:
My desktop with some stuff on it and a 3-D UFO picture as my desktop background.

Chapter 3

A Bevy of Delectable Menus

- -

- -

*L*ike icons and windows, menus are a quintessential part of the Macintosh experience. In this chapter, I take a brief look at each and every Finder menu item.

I'm trying to provide an appropriate level of detail based on the menu item's importance. Trust me here. In earlier editions of this book, I said that Mac OS 7.*x*'s Label menu was dumb; apparently Apple agrees because that menu is gone from Mac OS 8 and later. (The old Label menu's functions are available from either the File menu or contextual menus in Mac OS 8.5.)

Anyway, I start with a few menu basics and then move on to the menus in almost the order they appear on your screen: File, Edit, View, Special, Help, and Application. Last, but not least, I look at the context-sensitive contextual menus. Because the Apple menu is so long and so important, I'm going to give it its own chapter, the very next one after this one.

Menu Basics

Mac menus are often referred to as *pull-down menus*. That's because, to use them, you click their names to make the menus appear and then pull (drag) down to select an item. Piece of cake, eh?

Ever since Mac OS 8, the menus now stay down after you click their names. They stay down until you either select an item or click outside the menu's boundaries.

Command performance

As noted previously, many menu items have Command-key shortcuts after their names. These key combinations indicate that you can activate the menu items without using the mouse by pressing the Command key (notice I refrained from calling it a pretzel) and then pressing another key without releasing the Command key. And, as I've said before and will say again, memorizing the shortcuts you use often pays.

It's elliptical

Another feature of Mac menus is the ellipsis after a menu item's name. Ellipses, in case your English teacher forgot to mention them, are the three little dots (...) that appear after certain menu items' names. According to the Bible (actually, the *Chicago Manual of Style,* but for writers, it may as well be the Bible), "Any omission of a word or phrase, line, or paragraph . . . must be indicated by ellipsis points (dots). . . ."

Apple is true to this definition. Ellipsis points in a menu item mean that choosing the item will bring up a dialog box where you can make further choices. Choosing a menu item with an ellipsis never actually makes anything happen other than opening a dialog box, where you make further choices and then click a button to make things happen.

Dialog box featurettes

Dialog boxes may contain a number of standard Macintosh features such as *radio buttons, pop-up menus, text entry boxes,* and *check boxes.* You see these features again and again in dialog boxes, control panels, and elsewhere. So take a moment to look at each of these featurettes while I demonstrate how they're used.

Radio, radio (buttons)

Radio buttons are called radio buttons because, like the buttons on your car radio, only one can be pushed at a time. Radio buttons always appear in groups of two or more; when you push one, all the others are automatically unpushed. I think eggheads call this setup "mutually exclusive." Take a look at Figure 3-1 for an example of radio buttons.

In Figure 3-1, Normal is currently selected. If you click the radio button for Urgent, Print at, or Put Document on Hold, Normal is deactivated.

Figure 3-1:
A group of radio buttons. Only one radio button in each group may be selected at a time.

Menus redux pop-up style

Pop-up menus are called pop-up menus because that's what they do — they pop up after you press them. You can always tell a pop-up menu because it appears in a rounded rectangle and has a double-arrow on its right. Figure 3-2 shows a pop-up menu before you click it; Figure 3-3 shows the same menu after you click it and hold the mouse button down.

Figure 3-2:
Pop-up menus have a distinctive look, with a shadow and a two-headed arrow.

Okay, so now you've looked at two features, radio buttons and pop-up menus, and they both do the exact same thing: enable you to make a single selection from a group of options. Sometimes a radio button is associated with a text entry box, which happens to be the feature I cover next.

Championship boxing text entry style

Text entry boxes enable you to enter text (including numbers) from the keyboard. When a text entry box appears in conjunction with a radio button, the text entry box or boxes matter only if the associated radio button is pressed. Take a look at Figure 3-4. You can enter text in the two text entry boxes next to the From radio button, but if you click the All radio button, your text disappears. Conversely, if you click in one of the text entry boxes and type, the From radio button automatically becomes selected.

Had Apple chosen to use a pop-up menu instead of radio buttons in the Figure 3-4 example, the menu would have taken up more valuable screen real estate. So that's the reason for two featurettes that do the same thing.

And now you know how to use both.

Checkmate

The last featurette you see frequently is the check box. Check boxes are used to choose items that are not mutually exclusive. In a group of check boxes, you can turn each one on or off individually. Check boxes are on when they contain a check mark and off when they're empty. Figure 3-5 shows five check boxes, three of which are on.

Figure 3-5:
In this example, three out of five boxes are checked.

Image & Text:
☑ Substitute Fonts
☑ Smooth Text
☑ Smooth Graphics
☐ Precision Bitmap Alignment
☐ Unlimited Downloadable Fonts

Unlike radio buttons, which force you to choose one and only one item, check boxes are independent. Each one can either be on or off.

Here's a nifty and undocumented shortcut: Check boxes and radio buttons can usually be activated by clicking their names (instead of clicking the buttons or boxes). Didn't know that, did you?

File Management and More: Meet the File Menu

The File menu (shown in Figure 3-6) contains commands that enable you to manipulate your files and folders.

Menu items that can be used to act upon the item or items selected (the Documents folder in Figure 3-6) in the active window (or on the desktop) appear in black and are currently available; menu items not available at the current time are displayed in gray. You cannot select a gray menu item.

Figure 3-6:
The File menu.

In this example, only three items are disabled — Print, Put Away, and Show Original. That's because you can print only documents, not folders, and the selected item in the active window is a folder (Documents). The Put Away command is dimmed because you can put away only items that reside outside of windows on the desktop itself. The Show Original command is dimmed because it works only if the selected item is an alias. (I cover aliases a little later in this chapter.) The rest of the commands appear in black and are valid selections at this time.

New Folder (Command-N)

I talked about this command in the last chapter, but just for the record, New Folder creates a new, untitled folder in the active window. If no window is active, it creates a new folder on the desktop.

You probably do a lot of new-folder making, so it may be a good idea to memorize this command's keyboard shortcut, Command-N. It comes in handy later, as most software uses the shortcut Command-N to create a new document, another thing you do a lot of.

If your memory is bad, use this mnemonic device — N is for New.

Most menu items, or at least most common ones, have keyboard shortcuts that have a mnemonic relationship to their names. For example, New is Command-N, Open is Command-O, Get Info is Command-I, Make Alias is Command-M (which is good news because in earlier versions of the Mac OS, you had no keyboard shortcut for Make Alias), and so on.

Open (Command-O)

This command opens the selected item. Not much more to say, except to remind you that, in addition to the menu command and its shortcut Command-O, a double-click also opens this icon.

Print (Command-P)

This command, which prints the selected item, is active only if the selected icon is a document. Furthermore, it works only if you have the application that created the document on your hard disk. If you try to print (or open) a document when you don't have the application that created it, you see a dialog box like the one shown in Figure 3-7.

Figure 3-7:
Try to print
or open a
document
when you
don't have
the program
that created
it and
you may
see this
dialog box.

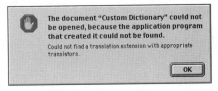

I talk about what translators are when I discuss Macintosh Easy Open in Chapter 12. For now, leave it at this: If you select a document icon and then use the Open or Print command, the command works only if you have the application that created the document or another application that is capable of opening that type of document.

That's where the translator part comes in (refer to Figure 3-7 again). Many programs can open files created by another program, but only if the right *translator* is available. I'll save the details for later.

Move to Trash (Command-Delete)

This command, new to Mac OS 8 and later and long needed, moves the selected icon to the Trash. Don't forget that the icon (that is, the item the icon represents) is not deleted from your hard disk until you choose the Empty Trash command from either the Special or contextual menu.

Close Window (Command-W)

This command closes the active window. Don't forget, if you hold down the Option key before you click the File menu, this command changes to Close All.

I talked about this command in Chapter 2, so I'll just move on.

Get Info (Command-I)

When you select any icon and choose the Get Info command (or use its keyboard shortcut Command-I), a Get Info window opens (see Figure 3-8).

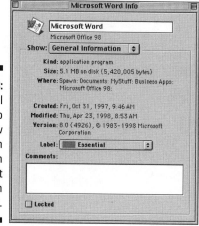

Figure 3-8:
A typical
Get Info
window
for an
application
(Microsoft
Word, in
this case).

The top portion of the Get Info window provides details about the icon, such as what it is (application, document, disk, folder, and so on), how big it is (5.1 megabytes, which equals 5,420,005 bytes), where it is on my disk (Spawn: Documents: MyStuff: Business Apps: Microsoft Office 98), when it was created (Halloween 1997), when it was last modified (Thursday, April 23, 1998, at 8:53 AM), and its version number (8.0).

The bottom part is called the Comments box because that's where you type your comments about the icon. In earlier versions of the Mac OS, these comments would disappear whenever you rebuilt your desktop or restored it from a backup; and, as I discuss in Appendix B, you should rebuild your desktop and back up your hard disk on a regular basis.

Since Mac OS 7.6, an icon's comments *do* survive rebuilding the desktop. They don't always survive restoration from backup, so use them at your own risk.

You see two additional parts in the Get Info box — Memory and Sharing. You choose them from the Show pop-up menu. Memory deals with the application's memory requirements. This stuff gets a little complicated, so I don't go into it here. (If you just can't wait, skip ahead to my dandy and easy-to-understand explanation in Chapter 9.) Sharing deals with file sharing, which you find out about in Chapter 8.

The last item in an application's Get Info box is the Locked check box. When an application is locked, its name can't be changed, and it can't be emptied from the Trash. (I mentioned locked files and the Trash briefly in Chapter 2, as you may remember.)

If you try to empty the Trash when a locked item's in it, you see a message telling you to hold down the Option key before you choose Special⇨Empty Trash. Holding down the Option key when you choose Empty Trash empties the Trash even if locked items are in it.

While I'm on the subject, do you hate the dialog box you see each time you try to empty the Trash? (You know — the one that reads: "The Trash contains X items. It uses X K of disk space. Are you sure you want to permanently remove it?") If you never want to see this pain-in-the-bottom dialog box again, select the Trash icon, invoke the Get Info command (Command-I), and uncheck the Warn Before Emptying check box.

Documents, folders, and disks each have slightly different Get Info boxes. Folders and disks can't be locked; documents and applications can.

Sharing

The Sharing command, which you find in the Get Info submenu, enables you to decide who can share your files. So much can be said about Macintosh File Sharing that I could write an entire chapter about it. And in fact, I have. If you're interested, take a look at Chapter 8.

Label

Maybe it's just me, but I've never really gone much for the Label feature. And I hardly know anyone who uses it diligently, which is the only way it's useful. Anyway, the Label submenu, which looks a lot neater in color than it does in Figure 3-9, enables you to organize your files yet another way — by label.

Figure 3-9:
Use the
Label
submenu to
assign
labels to
icons as
shown.

Artistic icons

The Get Info box serves another more frivolous but fundamentally fun function — it enables you to change any icon's picture to anything you like.

Don't like the Mac's folder icon? Give it a new one. Here's how: Find an icon you like — say it's a skull. Select it and select the Get Info command. Now select the folder that you want to give the skull icon to (call it untitled folder for convenience) and open its Get Info window. In the upper-left corner of the skull icon's Get Info box, you see the skull picture.

Click the skull. A box appears around the skull icon indicating that it's now selected. Choose Edit⇨Copy.

Now click the untitled folder icon in its Get Info window and choose Edit⇨Paste. The results of this last step are shown below.

There you go! This technique works on any icon — disk, folder, application, or document. And if you can't find an icon you like, you can create a picture in any graphics program, select it, choose Edit⇨Copy, and then paste it into the Get Info box of any icon. Furthermore, online services such as America Online, as well as Macintosh user groups and the Internet, offer humongous collections of icons for your pasting pleasure.

To apply a label to an icon, select it and then choose the appropriate label from the Label submenu, as shown in Figure 3-9. Again, labels are more useful on a color screen, as they tint the icon the appropriate color. You can also choose a label from a pop-up menu in the icon's Get Info box.

Because the Find command can search by label, you have reason to use labels. Still, unless you're very organized and remember to label every file (which, unfortunately, must be done in the Finder, not when you save from within an application, when it may actually be useful), labels aren't much use.

The Dilemma: On one hand, several users (well, actually just two) took the time to write me and say they found labels useful. On the other hand, thousands of people didn't.

On the *other* other hand, severely obsessive, compulsive, or anal-retentive Mac users can have hours of pleasure assigning those pretty labels to their icons.

So labels: Yea or Nay? It's your call.

You can change the names and colors of your labels by using the Finder's Preferences dialog box, which I discuss in just a few pages (as it lives in the Edit menu, which is coming up really soon now).

Duplicate (Command-D)

Duplicate duplicates the selected icon. More precisely, it makes an exact copy of the selected icon, adds the word *copy* to its name, and places the copy in the same window as the original icon. Figure 3-10 shows the results of using the Duplicate command.

Figure 3-10:
The Duplicate command in action.

The Duplicate command can be used on any icon except a disk icon.

Make Alias (Command-M)

Aliases are a wonderful, fabulous organizational tool introduced with System 7. An *alias* is a tiny file that automatically opens its *parent* file. To create an alias for any icon, select the icon (the parent) and then choose File⇨Make Alias or press Command-M.

(By the way, you can also make an alias by Command-Option-dragging an icon, or you can Control click an icon and choose the Make Alias command from the contextual menu that appears. Contextual menus, which are very cool, are covered at the end of this chapter.)

When you open an alias, the parent opens.

An alias is different from a duplicated file. For example, my word processor, Microsoft Word 98, uses 5.1 megabytes of disk space. If I duplicated it, I would have two files, each using 5+ megabytes of disk space. An alias of Microsoft Word, on the other hand, uses a mere 3K.

Due to a variety of complicated and unimportant reasons having to do with sector size and hard disk size, your mileage may vary depending on the size of your hard disk. In general, the smaller the disk, the smaller the aliases will be.

When you make an alias, it has the same icon as its parent, but its name appears in *italic* type and the suffix *alias* is tacked onto its name. A tiny arrow also appears on its icon. Figure 3-11 shows an alias and its parent icon.

Figure 3-11:
An alias icon looks identical to its parent 'cept for the italics and the little arrow.

You can put aliases in convenient places such as the desktop or the Apple Menu Items folder (so that they appear in your Apple menu). You can also use the Add to Favorites command to automatically create an alias and place it in the Favorites folder so that it appears in the Apple menu (see the following section).

At least a dozen ways exist in which aliases can help organize your Macintosh existence, and I talk about all of them in Chapter 6.

Add to Favorites

This command creates an alias of the selected item and puts it in the Favorites folder. Thereafter, it appears in the Apple menu's Favorites submenu.

Put Away (Command-Y)

Choose Put Away to move the selected icon from your desktop to the window it was in before you moved it to the desktop. This command works even if it's been years since the icon was moved to the desktop and you don't remember which folder it came out of.

The Put Away command is only active when an icon on the desktop is selected; it is dimmed whenever any icon in a window is selected. Put Away is also dimmed when the Trash icon is selected.

And, as mentioned previously, the Put Away command ejects a floppy disk and removes its ghost icon from the desktop. In other words, Put Away has the same effect on a floppy disk as dragging its icon to the Trash does.

Find (Command-F)

Use this command when you need to find an icon on your hard disk and you can't remember where you put it. This command is a Mac OS 8.5 feature that really kicks earlier versions' butts. It even has a new name: Sherlock.

You have three different ways to invoke the Sherlock (here I go again with the ways):

- ✔ Choose File⇨Find.
- ✔ Use the keyboard shortcut Command-F.
- ✔ Choose Apple⇨Find (using the Apple menu).

Whichever way you choose, the next thing you see is the Sherlock dialog box (as shown in Figure 3-12).

Figure 3-12:
The
Sherlock
dialog box.

Just type in the name of the file that you're looking for and then click the
Find button or press the Return key. In a flash, you see the Items Found
showing every file on the disk you searched that matches the word you
typed in the text entry box window (see Figure 3-13).

Figure 3-13:
The Items
Found
window.

In Figure 3-13, 14 items on my hard disk (Spawn) contain the word *Bob*.

After I found all these files, I selected the one I wanted — Letter to Bob
Leeds. At this point, I have three ways to open the file:

   ✔ Choose File➪Open Item.

   ✔ Use the keyboard shortcut Command-O.

   ✔ Double-click the file in the top or bottom part of the Find File Results
     window.

If you prefer to open the folder that contains the item, you have three ways to do that:

- Choose File➪Open Enclosing Folder.
- Use the keyboard shortcut Command-E.
- Double-click the folder in the bottom part of the Items Found window.

If searching by name alone finds too many files, you can narrow your search by clicking the More Choices button in the Sherlock dialog box and adding one or more additional criteria for the search. These criteria include the following: Size of file, Kind of file (application, alias, and so on), Label (see the Label menu section, later in this chapter), Creation Date (date the file was created), Modification Date (date the file was last saved), Version Number (is or is not), Lock Attribute (file is locked or is not), Folder Attribute (empty, shared, or mounted), File Type code, and Creator Type code.

Figure 3-14 shows what the Sherlock dialog box looks like after you click the More Choices button.

Figure 3-14: This search finds only files with names that include the word *Bob,* that are smaller than 128K, and that were created before 1/1/98.

Mac OS 8.5 introduces two new ways to find stuff, By Content and Search Internet. Just click the appropriate tab at the top of the Sherlock dialog box to use these Find methods.

Find By Content enables you to search for words within documents. So, for example, if you're looking for a letter that you wrote containing the phrase "You are a scumsucking dog," you can search for the word *scumsucking* in every document on your hard disk(s). You do need to *index* your disk(s) before using this feature, but doing so's an easy (albeit slow) process. To index your disk(s), simply click the Index Volumes button at the bottom of the window and then click the Create Index button in the new window that appears.

Because indexing takes a long time, you can schedule it to take place while you're not around. Click the Create Index button and then place a checkmark next to the volumes (that is, the disks) that you want to schedule for indexing. Now just click the Schedule button and choose a convenient time and day for the indexing to take place. Presto. As long as your Mac is on at that time, it creates the index automatically without any intervention from you.

If that process seems too complicated or you want to index your disk right this second, just click the Index Volumes button, click the volume (disk) that you want to index, and then click the Create Index button. Now go out for coffee.

The second new find feature is Search Internet. Again, to use this feature, click the appropriate tab at the top of the Sherlock dialog box. Assuming that you have an available Internet connection (see Chapter 15), the Sherlock dialog box connects to the Internet, searches all the engines that you check in the Sherlock dialog box, and returns the results, along with summaries, in a new window — all without launching a browser. It's fast, it's fun, and it's one of Mac OS 8.5's most useful new features.

I need to use another weasel-out here. I could write an entire chapter about using the new Sherlock features but another one of the rules that we *Dummies* authors must follow is that our books can't run 1,000 pages long. So I'm going to give you the next best thing: Open the Help Center (by choosing Help➪Help Center from the menu bar) and search for the word **Find**. Searching for that term provides you with the information that you need to get the most out of the new, improved Find command. It's almost as good as reading it here.

Show Original (Command-R)

Show Original works only on aliases. Select any alias icon and then choose this command to reveal the parent file of the selected alias.

Page Setup

Choosing Page Setup opens the Page Setup dialog box, which is where you specify the type of paper in your printer (letter, legal, envelope, and so on), page orientation (longways or wideways), and scaling (100 percent = full size).

In addition to the command here in the Finder, you also find a Page Setup command in almost every program that you use. A whole chapter on printing's coming up in a little while (Chapter 7, to be exact), so I'm leaving this topic alone for now. (That's also why I didn't waste space here on a screen shot.)

Print Desktop/Print Window

This command is a little tricky. If no windows are active, the command is called Print Desktop. If a window is active, the command's name changes to Print Window.

If you choose Print Desktop, your Mac prints a picture of your desktop, with its icons and Trash (but not the menu bar), exactly as you see them on-screen. This image generally requires two or more pieces of paper.

If you choose Print Window, your Mac prints a picture of the active window, showing all the icons it contains, even if you'd need to scroll to see the icons on-screen. If the window contains a lot of icons, printing this document may require more than one sheet of paper.

And if a document is selected when you choose the Print command, the application that created the document launches automatically, and you see a Print dialog box. (Printing is covered in full and loving detail in Chapter 7, which is why no screen shot of this one appears either.)

The Edit Menu (Which Shoulda Been Called the Clipboard Menu)

In contrast to the File menu, which has commands that mostly deal with file management and are exclusive to the Finder, the Edit menu's commands and functions are available in almost every Macintosh program ever made (see Figure 3-15).

Because almost every program has an Edit menu and because almost every program uses the same keyboard shortcuts on its Edit menu, it behooves you to know these keyboard shortcuts by heart, even if you remember no others.

The Edit menu should probably have been called the Clipboard menu because most of its commands deal with the Macintosh Clipboard.

Figure 3-15:
The Edit
menu.
Memorize
these five
keyboard
shortcuts
even if you
never
memorize
anything
else.

Edit	
Undo	⌘Z
Cut	⌘X
Copy	⌘C
Paste	⌘V
Clear	
Select All	⌘A
Show Clipboard	
Preferences...	

If you read the little sidebar about the Clipboard, you find out 75 percent of what you need to know about the Edit menu. Still, because IDG's paying me to be thorough, and because the Finder's Edit menu has a couple commands that aren't Clipboard-related, I go through the Edit menu's commands one by one.

Undo (Command-Z)

This is a great command! You're gonna love it. Undo undoes the last thing you did. Try it:

1. **Create a new folder in any window or on the desktop.**

   It's called untitled folder.

2. **Change the name untitled folder to Undo Me.**

3. **Without clicking anywhere else or doing anything else, choose Edit⇨Undo or use the keyboard shortcut Command-Z.**

The folder's name should magically undo itself and change back to untitled folder.

Neat, huh? Don't forget about this command 'cause it can be a lifesaver. Almost every program has it.

Now for the bad news: The Undo command is ephemeral, like the Clipboard. It undoes only your last action, and as soon as you do something else, you lose the ability to undo the original action. To see what I mean, repeat the exercise and change untitled folder to Undo Me. But this time, click another icon before you undo. What's that, you say? The Undo command is grayed out and not available any more? I told you. When you clicked the other icon, you forfeited your chance to use Undo.

Unfortunately, Undo doesn't work with things such as moving icons or copying files. In fact, as you find out more about using your Mac, you discover lots of actions that can't be undone. Still, Undo is a great command when it's available, and I urge you to get in the habit of trying it often.

Incidentally, the Undo command *toggles* (that is, switches back and forth) between the new and old states as long as you don't do anything else. So in the first example, if you chose Edit⇨Undo again without clicking anywhere else, the name would transform back to Undo Me. And if you chose Edit⇨ Undo again, it would change back to untitled folder. You can continue to undo and redo until you click somewhere else.

The Clipboard

Essential to your understanding of the Mac and essential to your understanding of the Edit menu is an understanding of the concept of the Macintosh Clipboard. In one sentence, the Clipboard is a holding area for the last thing that you cut or copied. A thing can be text, a picture, a portion of a picture, an object in a drawing program, a column of numbers in a spreadsheet, or just about anything that can be selected. In other words, the Clipboard is the Mac's temporary storage area.

As a storage area, the Clipboard is ephemeral, which means that its contents are temporary. Very temporary. When you cut or copy an item, that item remains on the Clipboard only until you cut or copy something else. Then the Clipboard's contents are replaced by the new item, which remains on the Clipboard until you cut or copy something else. And so it goes.

To place the item that's on the Clipboard somewhere else, click where you want the item to go and then paste. Pasting does not remove the item from the Clipboard; the item remains there until another item is cut or copied.

Almost all programs have an Edit menu and use the Macintosh Clipboard properly, which means that you can usually cut or copy something in a document in one program and paste it into a document from another program. Usually.

The Clipboard commands in the Edit menu are relatively intelligent. If the currently selected item *can* be cut or copied, then the Cut and Copy commands in the Edit menu will be enabled; if the item can't be cut or copied, the commands are unavailable and grayed out. And when nothing at all is selected, the Cut, Copy, Paste, and Clear commands are grayed out.

The contents of the Clipboard don't survive a restart, a shut down, or a system error or crash. The Clipboard is ephemeral in the sense that any of these events purges its contents, so when your Mac comes back to life, the Clipboard is empty.

Cut (Command-X)

The Cut command removes the selected item and places it on the Clipboard. Follow these steps to see this command in action:

1. **Create an untitled folder.**

2. **Select only the word _untitled_.**

   The word _untitled_ should be black or colored with white letters; _folder_ should be white with black letters.

3. **Choose Edit⇨Cut, or use the keyboard shortcut Command-X.**

The word _untitled_ disappears from the folder's name. Where did it go? You cut it! It's removed from the folder and is now waiting on the Clipboard.

(You can, of course, use the Undo command at this point to make _untitled_ reappear, as long as you haven't clicked anything else.)

Show Clipboard

I know I'm not covering the commands in the order that they appear on the Edit menu, but there's a method to my madness. If you don't believe that the word _untitled_, which you cut in the previous section, is on the Clipboard, choose Edit⇨Show Clipboard. A window will appear, telling you the type of item (text, picture, sound, and so on) on the Clipboard and displaying it if it can be displayed (see Figure 3-16).

Figure 3-16:
The Show Clipboard command displays the current contents of the Clipboard.

Here's another way to display the Clipboard's contents: Open the Clipboard icon in your System Folder. Because some programs don't have a Show Clipboard command, it's convenient to make an alias of the Clipboard file and put the alias in your Apple Menu Items folder so that it appears in your Apple menu. (Don't panic. I'm going to talk about the Apple menu in the very next chapter.) Then, even if you're in a program that doesn't have a Show Clipboard command, you can select the Clipboard alias from the Apple menu. This technique saves you two steps; without it you'd need to first go back to the Finder and then choose Edit⇨Show Clipboard. Choosing the Clipboard alias from the Apple menu does both steps automatically.

Copy (Command-C)

Copy makes a copy of the selected item and places it on the Clipboard. The original is not removed, as it is when you cut. Try it. Select your System Folder and choose Edit⇨Copy or use the keyboard shortcut Command-C. Now choose Edit⇨Show Clipboard. The Clipboard contains the text *System Folder*.

It's that simple.

Paste (Command-V)

You've been cutting and copying but not doing much with the stuff on the Clipboard except looking at it to make sure that it's really there. Now, to use what you cut or copied, do as follows:

1. **Create a new folder.**
2. **Change the folder's name to Elvis Costello.**
3. **Copy the word *Elvis* to the Clipboard.**

   (C'mon, you know how.)

4. **Create another new folder and select its name, which should be untitled folder if you've been following my instructions.**
5. **Choose Edit⇨Paste.**

The new folder is now called Elvis. Pasting doesn't purge the contents of the Clipboard. Don't believe me? Choose Edit⇨Show Clipboard to confirm that Elvis is still alive and well and on the Clipboard.

Which is where he stays until you cut, copy, crash (the three Cs of Macintosh computing), or restart or shut down.

Clear

Clear deletes the selected item without involving the Clipboard. It works the same as pressing the Delete key on your keyboard. Use it when you want to make something disappear forever.

Clear can usually be undone as long as you haven't done anything else like click, type, save, or use a menu.

Select All (Command-A)

Select All selects all. If a window is active, Select All selects every icon in the window, regardless of whether you can see them. If no window is active, Select All selects every icon on the desktop.

Go ahead and try it a couple of times. I can wait.

Select All has nothing whatsoever to do with the Clipboard. So why is it on the Edit menu? Who knows? It just is and always has been.

Preferences . . .

The Preferences item in the Edit menu combines a bunch of items (as shown in Figure 3-17) formerly found in the Views and Labels control panels, both of which were discontinued in Mac OS 8, plus a couple of nifty new features that you meet in a second.

Figure 3-17:
The General tab of the Finder's Preferences.

Here's a quick tutorial in the Finder Preferences window:

General tab

Click the General tab at the top of the Preferences window to access the following three features:

Simple Finder

The Simple Finder check box emasculates your Mac and makes it harder to use by removing a lot of useful commands from its menus (see Figure 3-18).

Figure 3-18: Regular Finder menus (top) and Simple Finder menus (bottom).

Simple Finder is recommended only for absolute rank novices. As you can see in Figure 3-18, Simple Finder hides many useful menu items — such as Move To Trash, Make Alias, and so on — and thereby (at least in my humble opinion) reduces the usefulness of your Mac. If you have young children or old parents, this setting may be useful, but if your gray matter functions normally, just say "No" to the Simple Finder choice. In other words, unless you're computerphobic, don't bother with the Simple Finder for yourself.

Spring-loaded folders

The option for spring-loaded folders is turned on or off with a check box. Spring-loaded folders are a nifty feature that pops folders open when you hold an icon over them. They are opened only until you release the mouse button. Then they close automatically.

This option's easier to demonstrate than write about, so follow along with this tutorial if you want to see a neat new Finder feature in action:

1. **Check the Spring-loaded folders check box on the General tab.**

2. **Set the Delay before opening slider to Short.**

3. **Close the Preferences window.**

4. **In the Finder, click any icon and drag it on top of any folder that contains at least two subfolders — but *don't* release the mouse button yet.**

   The folder you've dragged the icon onto should spring open.

5. **Move the icon over one of the subfolders inside the original folder — but don't release the mouse button yet.**

   That folder springs open. If you were to release the mouse button right now, the original icon you clicked would be deposited in this subfolder.

6. Move the icon so that it's not over any windows or folder icons.

Folders that have sprung open spring closed after you move the icon away from them.

In other words, spring-loaded folders let you move or copy an item deep into your folder hierarchy by automatically opening and closing folders for you with absolutely no double-clicking. Play around with this feature for a while and you'll wonder how you ever got along without it.

Grid Spacing

Grid Spacing deals with an invisible grid that the Finder maintains for your convenience. The invisible grid is available only in Icon views (which I cover in the very next section). Here in the Finder Preferences window you can only choose from Tight or Wide spacing.

The invisible grid can be turned on or off on a folder-by-folder basis using the View Options window (also explained in the upcoming section on the View menu). Furthermore, if you have the grid turned off in View Options, hold down the Command key when you drag any item to have it snap to the invisible grid; alternatively, if you have the grid turned on in View Options, hold down the Command key to temporarily disable the invisible grid and move the icon anywhere you like.

Views tab

Click the Views tab to set the Standard Views for your folders. These settings govern all folders unless you use View Options to customize the view of a specific folder. In other words, the settings that you make in this window become the default settings for all folders.

Because I'm going to explain these options in the very next section, I'll skip over them for now. Just remember that the settings you make here in the Preferences window apply to all folders except the ones that you use View Options to change.

Labels tab

The options on the Labels tab enable you to change the names and colors of the labels in the File menu's Label submenu.

To change the name associated with a label, double-click its name in the Finder Preferences window and type a new one. To change a label's color, click directly on the color itself and a Color Picker window appears (see Figure 3-19).

Figure 3-19:
A Color
Picker
window
appears
after you
click a color
in the
Labels tab
of the
Finder
Preferences
window.

I know that all the colors in the Color Picker look gray in the picture, but on a color monitor, they're in color — I promise. To select a new color, just click the color wheel or change the Hue Angle, Saturation, and/or Lightness settings.

Color Pickers are a little hard to explain, but basically, they're just different windows that enable you to pick a color. The left side of the Color Picker window enables you to choose from six different kinds of Color Pickers. I generally use the HSV (hue, saturation, value) Picker shown in Figure 3-19, mostly because I consider it the easiest to use. But Apple now provides many other ways for you to pick colors. So I recommend you play with all of them just a little. Just click a Color Picker — Crayon Picker, CMYK Picker, and so on — on the left side of the window and then play with the resulting controls on the right side of the window to pick a color.

Whee!

A View from a Window: The View Menu

The View menu governs the way icons look in a window or on your desktop. The View menu affects the icons in the active window or, if no window is active, it affects the icons on the desktop. The similar settings found in Finder Preferences govern all windows *except* ones you use the View menu to modify.

The first two parts of the View menu have to do with what the icons and windows look like; the third part of the View menu has to do with how icons and windows are arranged and/or sorted.

The first part: As icons, as buttons, or as list

Viewing by icon is the "Macintosh" view, the one most closely associated with the Macintosh experience. It's also, in my humble opinion, one of the two least useful views, as those big horsey icons take up far too much valuable screen real estate. And, as you'll see in a minute, list view offers a nifty navigational extra and saves space as well.

The window in Figure 3-20 uses the icon view.

Figure 3-20:
My hard disk window viewed as icons. Pretty and very Mac-like, but a total waste of perfectly good screen real estate.

In all fairness, I must say that there are many perfectly happy Macintosh users who love the icon view and refuse to even consider anything else. Fine. But as the number of files on your hard disk increases (as it does for every Mac user), screen real estate becomes more and more valuable.

By the way, if you like the icon view, they now make monitors as big as 21 inches.

The button view (shown in Figure 3-21) is no better and wastes just as much screen space as those blocky big icons. The biggest difference is that buttons require only a single-click to open them (as opposed to the double-click that opens normal icons).

The only thing the icon and button views have over the list view is the capability to arrange the icons anywhere you like within the window. Big deal.

Finally, the view I love and use most, the list view (shown in Figure 3-22).

Figure 3-21:
The same
window
viewed as
buttons.

Figure 3-22:
The same
window
viewed
as a list.

The triangles

In list view, folder icons have a little triangle to the left of their names. This is the outline metaphor, and it's available only in the list view. You click the triangle to reveal the folder's contents right there in the same window.

In my humble opinion, this is a much better way to get to an icon buried three or four folders deep than clicking through the folders themselves. Figure 3-23 shows the slow and tedious way of getting to the icon named NoseBlows Ch01.Nose Runs. Figure 3-24 shows the cool, savvy, and efficient way of getting to the same icon.

In Figure 3-23, I had to double-click four folders to get to NoseBlows Ch01.Nose Runs. When I got to it, I had four windows open on the desktop.

In Figure 3-24, I had to single-click four triangles to get to NoseBlows Ch01.Nose Runs. When I got to it, only one window was open, keeping my desktop neat and tidy.

Figure 3-23:
Getting
to the
document
NoseBlows
Ch01.Nose
Runs the
usual way,
by opening
windows.

Figure 3-24:
Getting
to the
document
NoseBlows
Ch01.Nose
Runs the
fast way,
using the
outline
triangles.

Easy copying and moving

There are other advantages to the triangles-outline metaphor. First and foremost, you can copy or move items from separate folders in one move, as Figure 3-25 illustrates.

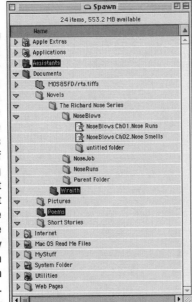

Figure 3-25: Moving or copying files from two or more separate folders is easy if you're using the list view (but impossible to do in one step by using icon or button views).

In the list view, you can copy or move items from different folders with a single motion, without opening multiple windows. In either of the icon views, on the other hand, moving files from two or more different folders requires opening several windows and two separate drags.

Another feature of the triangles appears when you hold down the Option key and click a triangle. This action reveals *all* subfolders to the deepest level (see Figures 3-26 and 3-27).

The bottom line is that I have almost all of my windows displayed in the list view by name. Finally, I almost always use the triangles to reveal the contents of folders and rarely have more than a couple of windows open at a time.

The View Options command, which I talk about in a moment, offers additional controls and enables you to choose stuff such as the size of the icons and which columns appear in list view. If you feel adventurous, go ahead and play with it a little now.

Figure 3-26:
A regular click on the Documents triangle reveals only the next level of folders.

Figure 3-27:
An Option-click on the Documents triangle expands all its subfolders.

You can also move among icons by using the keyboard. If a window is active, make sure that no icons are selected and then type the first letter of a file's name. Regardless of which view you chose, the first icon that starts with that letter will be selected. To move to the next icon alphabetically, press the Tab key. To move to the previous icon alphabetically, press the Shift and Tab keys at the same time.

If no window is active, typing a letter selects the first icon on the desktop that starts with that letter. The Tab and Shift-Tab commands work the same with desktop icons as they do with icons in a window.

If you have many icons that start with the same letter, you can type more than one letter (that is, type **sys** to select the System Folder, even if you've got folders called Stuff and Slime in the same window).

The second part: As window or as pop-up window

The second part of the View menu enables you to choose between regular old windows and nifty new pop-up windows, which enable you to arrange frequently used windows at the bottom of your screen for quick access (see Figure 3-28).

Figure 3-28:
I have three
pop-up
windows:
Hardy Boy
(open),
Documents,
and
My Stuff.

To open a pop-up window, click its name at the bottom of your screen; to shrink it back down, click its name again. When you open one pop-up window, any other open pop-up window closes automatically (but regular windows remain open).

You can drag any icon onto the name of a pop-up window at the bottom of your screen; the pop-up window will scroll down, revealing its contents.

Pop-up windows are a nifty new feature introduced in Mac OS 8. I recommend you play with them a little now and decide whether they suit your work style. (I still haven't decided; I fluctuate between using them and not.)

The third part: Clean Up, Arrange, Reset Column Positions, and View Options

These last few commands on the View menu help you keep your stuff in order.

Clean Up

The Clean Up command aligns icons to the invisible grid; it is used to keep your windows and desktop neat and tidy. (If you like this invisible grid, don't forget that you can turn it on or off for the desktop and/or individual windows by using View Options.)

Clean Up is only available in icon views or when no windows are active. If no windows are active, the command instead cleans up your desktop.

If you're like me, you have taken great pains to place icons carefully in specific places on your desktop. Cleaning up your desktop destroys all your beautiful work and moves all your perfectly arranged icons around.

Arrange

The command beneath Clean Up says Arrange (see Figure 3-29), if you're viewing icons, or Sort List (see Figure 3-30), if you're viewing a list.

I'm going to talk about Arrange first. Choosing Arrange by Name causes icons in the active window (or on the desktop if no windows are open or active) to magically rearrange themselves into alphabetical order.

Choosing Arrange by Date Modified causes icons in the active window (or on the desktop if no windows are open or active) to magically rearrange themselves, with the most recently modified icon at top left and the icon modified longest ago at bottom right.

Figure 3-29:
The View menu's Arrange menu item is available only when the active item (a window or the desktop) contains icons or buttons.

Use this view for folders with lots of documents in them. That way, the ones you used most recently will be listed first. If that gets confusing, you can easily switch to the list view for a second to find things alphabetically.

Choosing Arrange by Date Created causes icons in the active window (or on the desktop if no windows are open or active) to magically rearrange themselves, with the most recently created icon at top left and the icon created longest ago at bottom right.

Choosing Arrange by Size causes icons in the active window (or on the desktop if no windows are open or active) to magically rearrange themselves in descending order by size, with the largest item at top left and the smallest item at bottom right.

Choosing Arrange by Kind causes icons in the active window (or on the desktop if no windows are open or active) to magically rearrange themselves in this order from top left to bottom right: applications in alphabetical order, documents in alphabetical order, and then folders in alphabetical order.

Choosing Arrange by Label causes icons in the active window (or on the desktop if no windows are open or active) to magically rearrange themselves in the order in which labels appear in the File menu's Labels submenu, with icons in each label group arranged alphabetically.

Sort List

If you're viewing a window containing a list, the command beneath Clean Up says Sort List (see Figure 3-30).

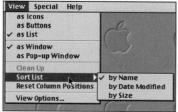

Figure 3-30:
If the active window contains a list (instead of icons or buttons), you see the Sort List command instead of Arrange.

As you may expect, these items sort the contents of the active window.

Here's a shortcut for changing between sorting orders in list views: Notice how the appropriate column title is highlighted in Figure 3-31 — how Name is dark and Date Modified, Size, and Kind are not. This highlight tells you which list view is in use.

Figure 3-31:
This window is sorted by name, as evidenced by the word *Name* highlighted at the top of the window.

Name	Date Modified	Size	Kind
▷ Apple Extras	Yesterday, 10:03 AM	—	folder
▷ Applications	Sat, Jul 25, 1998, 7:48 AM	—	folder
▷ Assistants	Sat, Jul 25, 1998, 7:47 AM	—	folder
▷ Documents	Today, 10:08 AM	—	folder
▷ Internet	Sat, Jul 25, 1998, 7:48 AM	—	folder
▷ Mac OS Read Me Files	Sat, Jul 25, 1998, 8:23 AM	—	folder
▷ MyStuff	Sat, Jul 25, 1998, 7:45 AM	—	folder
▷ System Folder	Yesterday, 10:05 AM	—	folder
▷ Utilities	Sat, Jul 25, 1998, 9:17 AM	—	folder
▷ Web Pages	Thu, Jul 23, 1998, 8:09 AM	—	folder

Spawn — 10 items, 557.1 MB available

Now for the shortcut: You don't need to use the Sort List submenu to switch between list views. Instead, just click directly on the column title, and the window's view changes. Go ahead, give it a try. The only proviso is that you must be in a list view in the first place (the column titles don't appear in icon views). In Figure 3-32, I've clicked the Date Modified column; the window is now sorted with the most recently modified items on top.

In other words, clicking the title of the column is the same as using the Sort List submenu, only faster and easier.

Figure 3-32:
I've clicked
Date
Modified at
the top of
the window;
as a result,
this window
is now
sorted with
the most
recently
modified
items at
the top of
the list.

Name	Date Modified	Size	Kind
Documents	Today, 10:08 AM	—	folder
System Folder	Yesterday, 10:05 AM	—	folder
Apple Extras	Yesterday, 10:03 AM	—	folder
Utilities	Sat, Jul 25, 1998, 9:17 AM	—	folder
Mac OS Read Me Files	Sat, Jul 25, 1998, 8:23 AM	—	folder
Applications	Sat, Jul 25, 1998, 7:48 AM	—	folder
Internet	Sat, Jul 25, 1998, 7:48 AM	—	folder
Assistants	Sat, Jul 25, 1998, 7:47 AM	—	folder
MyStuff	Sat, Jul 25, 1998, 7:45 AM	—	folder
Web Pages	Thu, Jul 23, 1998, 8:09 AM	—	folder

Spawn — 10 items, 557.1 MB available

Reset Column Positions

You don't know this already, but you can change the order in which columns appear by clicking the title of the column and then dragging it to a new position. The only rule is that the Name column always appears first. Go ahead and try it. I can wait. . . .

The reason I give you this information here and now is that the Reset Column Positions is a sort of Undo for changes you make in this manner. So if you move the columns around and decide that you don't like the new arrangement, you can use this command to put them back the way they were.

View Options

The View Options command applies to the active window. If no window is active, it applies to the desktop. If icons or buttons are active when you choose View Options, you see a window like the one in Figure 3-33. If a window using list view is active, you instead see a window like that shown in Figure 3-34.

In View Options for icons and buttons (see Figure 3-33), choosing None for your icon arrangement turns off the invisible grid; choosing Always snap to grid turns it on; and choosing Keep arranged forces the Finder to constantly clean up the window according to the criteria you choose from the pop-up menu (by Name in Figure 3-33).

The Icon Size control enables you to choose between small and large icons.

Figure 3-33:
View
Options for
icon or
button
views.

View Options for lists (see Figure 3-34) has different controls. The Use relative date option intelligently substitutes "yesterday" and "today" for numerical dates. Calculate folder sizes does just what its name implies — it enables you to see how much stuff is in each folder when you look at it in list view. The Show Columns check boxes govern which columns appear in the active window.

Finally, the Icon Size control enables you to choose between small, medium, and large icons in your lists. For my money, I think the smallest ones make windows appear noticeably faster; your mileage may vary.

If you have the Calculate folder sizes option turned on in View Options, the icons in the active window, including folder icons, will be sorted in descending order from biggest to smallest when you sort by size.

If you don't have Calculate folder sizes turned on, icons other than folders will be sorted by size, with all folders — regardless of their size — appearing at the bottom of the list.

Figure 3-34:
View
Options for
the list
view.

Though sorting by folder size may seem convenient, I recommend that you keep this option turned off, as I believe that Calculate folder sizes makes the Finder feel a bit sluggish. If you really need to know how big a folder is, select it and use the File⇨Get Info command (keyboard shortcut Command-I).

Finally, if you want View Options to apply to all folders, use the Finder Preferences window. Conversely, if you want them to apply only to the active window, use View Options.

Something Special in the Menu Bar: The Special Menu

The Special menu is a repository for a group of unrelated functions that don't really fit in any of the other menus: cleaning up (rearranging) icons; emptying trash; erasing and ejecting disks; and the Restart, Shut Down, and Sleep commands, to be precise.

Interestingly, only the Eject Disk command has a keyboard shortcut. One explanation may be that you wouldn't want to accidentally erase a disk or restart or shut down your Mac with something as easy to do as pressing the wrong key combination.

Empty Trash

I've already talked about the Trash (just last chapter, as a matter of fact). And I talked about it earlier in this chapter when I showed you the Get Info box.

I've said it before and I'm going to say it again: Use this command with a modicum of caution. After a file is trashed and emptied, it's gone. (Okay, maybe Norton Utilities can bring it back, but don't bet the farm on it.)

Eject Disk and Erase Disk

See Chapter 2 for more information than you need on ejecting and erasing disks.

Sleep

Sleep puts your Mac and monitor into a state of suspended animation complete with lower power consumption. Waking up from sleep mode is much faster than restarting. You can control when your Mac goes to sleep automatically with the Energy Saver control panel, discussed in Chapter 12.

Restart

The Restart command shuts down your Mac briefly and then starts it back up. Why do you need such a thing? Every so often, your Mac acts wonky. By wonky, I mean that things don't seem to work right. You can't launch a program that used to launch fine. You can't rename an icon. You can't use the keyboard. Or something. That's when to use Restart.

You see, computer problems often disappear when you clear the computer's memory, which is one of the things that occurs when you restart.

One of the best pieces of advice I give people when they call me in a panic is to restart their Macs and try it again. At least half the time, the problem goes away and never comes back after restarting. I'm a little paranoid about things going wrong, so I often restart my computer in the middle of the day, just in case something is *about* to go wrong. It couldn't hurt.

Sometimes when your Mac gets really wonky, you may be unable to choose Special⇨Restart for one reason or another. If you can't because the cursor won't move, or for any other reason, try pressing the Command and Option keys while you press the Escape (Esc) key. If things aren't too messed up, you should see a dialog box asking if you're sure you want to force the current application to quit. You do. Your Mac is so wonked that you had to resort to the Command-Option-Escape technique, so click the Force Quit button. If it works, the current application (or the Finder) quits. If you're in the Finder, it relaunches itself automatically. You lose any unsaved changes in the application that you quit, but you may regain the use of your Mac. If you do, immediately save any documents you have open in other applications and restart. *The Force Quit command leaves your Mac in an unstable state, and you should always restart as soon as possible after using it.* After, of course, saving any unsaved documents.

If that trick doesn't work, try pressing both the Command and Control (Ctrl) keys while you press the Power-On key (the one with the little left-pointing triangle on it). This technique forces your Mac to restart. Unfortunately, it doesn't work all the time or on all Macintosh models. But it usually does.

If Command-Control-Power-On doesn't work for you, look for the reset and interrupt switches on the front or side of your Mac and press the reset switch, which is the one with a triangle. This technique also forces your Mac to restart. Unfortunately, not all Macs have these switches.

If you're still having problems and still can't choose Special⇨Restart, turn the power off by using the power switch and leave your Mac off for at least ten seconds before you try to start up again.

Shut Down

Shutting down is the last thing you do at the end of every session at your Mac. When you're all done using the machine, choose Special⇨Shut Down or press the Power key and click the Shut Down button that appears.

Because I ragged on endlessly in Chapter 1 about how important the Shut Down command is, I'm not going to do it again.

Use it or lose it.

Not Just a Beatles Movie: Help and the Help Menu

One of the best things about all Macs since System 7 has always been its excellent online help. And Mac OS 8.5 has online help, in abundance.

Balloon Help is still available, but Mac OS Help goes it one (actually, a few) better.

Help Center

Choose Help⇨Help Center to open the Help Viewer.

Show Balloons

The Help⇨Show Balloons command turns on Balloon Help. When Balloon Help is on, pointing at almost any item on the screen causes a little help balloon to pop up and explain it (as shown in Figure 3-35).

After you choose Show Balloons, the command in the Help menu changes to Hide Balloons until you choose it again, at which time the command changes back to Show Balloons. And so on.

Figure 3-35:
Balloon
Help in
action.

I rarely use Balloon Help myself, but if you're relatively new to the Mac, you may find it helpful. Most applications include Balloon Help, so don't forget that you can turn balloons on in programs as well as in the Finder and most Apple-supplied programs.

Mac OS Help (Command-?)

In the beginning, not very much help was built into your Mac. In fact, before System 7, you had none. System 7 introduced Balloon Help, and it was good. Well, actually, it was kind of lame, and not that many developers implemented it at first, but it was better than nothing.

After most software did start including Balloon Help, Apple raised the bar in System 7.5 with Apple Guide, an interactive step-by-step guidance system for accomplishing tasks on your Mac. But developers didn't cotton to it, so Apple Guide was replaced yet again with an HTML-based Help system (that is, one that was created the same way you'd create a Web page) called *Mac OS Help.*

Having Mac OS Help is like having a consultant at your side. But nothing opens your eyes quite like a demonstration, so here's how to have your new assistant, Mac OS Help, answer a question for you:

1. **Choose Help from the Help menu (or use the keyboard shortcut Command-?).**

2. **After the Mac OS Help window appears, click the little button that looks like a house and then click the underlined item called Mac OS Help (unless you want help with AppleScript, in which case you choose AppleScript Help).**

   (You can find more information about AppleScript in Chapter 13.) The Mac OS Help system window appears, ready for use (see Figure 3-36).

3. **Click any item in the list on the left.**

   I clicked the one marked Shortcuts and Tips in Figure 3-37. A list of topics magically appears on the right.

4. **Click any item on the right to find out more about it.**

   That's it. You're done.

5. **Close Mac OS Help.**

You can also type a word into the little box at the top and click the Search button to find help on a particular topic.

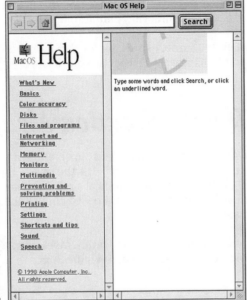

Figure 3-36:
Mac OS
Help —
your new
assistant.

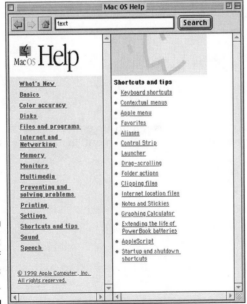

Figure 3-37:
A list of
shortcuts
and tips.

About the only thing you need to know to use Mac OS Help is that underlined items are hot links. Click any underlined item to find out more about it.

Mac OS Help is an excellent resource, especially for those of you who are new to the Mac. I urge you to explore it further at your leisure.

Apply Yourself: The Application Menu

Last but not least is the Application menu (at least for menus in the menu bar; I talk about contextual menus in a moment). It's the one in the upper-right corner. Because all of this menu's functions are related, I'm going to skip describing its commands one at a time and try to convey the gestalt of the Application menu instead.

If the Finder is the active application, the Application menu displays a little Mac OS icon and the word "Finder," as shown in Figure 3-38.

Figure 3-38: The Application menu as it appears when I'm in the Finder.

10:28 AM   Finder

If another application is currently active, a little version of that application's icon (and its name) appears in the Application menu instead (see Figure 3-39).

Figure 3-39: The Application menu as it appears when I'm in Microsoft Word.

10:30 AM   Microsoft Word

The Application menu enables you to choose which program you want to use. As with windows, only one application is active at a time. Because Mac OS 8.5 allows you to open more than one application at a time (if you have enough RAM), the Application menu is one of the ways to switch between all currently running applications and the Finder. (I discuss the other methods near the end of this section.)

If a program is running, its name appears in the Application menu; the Finder's name always appears in it. In Figure 3-40, I have two programs running in addition to the Finder: Microsoft Word and Adobe Photoshop.

Figure 3-40:
The Application menu itself.

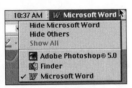

If the Finder is currently active and you want to switch to Microsoft Word, choose its name in the Application menu. Microsoft Word's menus appear in the menu bar, and if a document's open (or an untitled new document), its window becomes the active window.

To switch back to the Finder, you choose Finder in the Application menu. Piece of cake, right?

Wrong. When you switch back to the Finder, Microsoft Word's document window may obscure items on the desktop. Finder windows aren't a problem — they float to the front. But icons on the desktop may be covered.

This situation is where the Hide and Show commands come into play. You could switch back to Microsoft Word and quit that program, but you have an easier way to free up desktop real estate. Choose Hide Others from the Application menu, and the Microsoft Word windows and toolbars are hidden from view. Microsoft Word is still running, but its window or windows and toolbars are hidden from view.

To make Microsoft Word visible again, choose Show All from the Application menu.

Open any application and play around with the Hide and Show commands on the Application menu. They're easier to understand after you play with them a little.

A new feature in OS 8.5 is the capability to "tear off" the Application menu and have it appear as a floating window. To tear the menu off and place it elsewhere on-screen, click the menu. Then, while still holding down the mouse button, move the cursor to the middle of the screen. The menu "tears off" and becomes a floating window, as shown in Figure 3-41. This window is always the frontmost window and is available regardless of which program you're currently using.

Figure 3-41:
The
Application
menu turns
into a
window
after being
"torn off."

They're Sooo Sensitive: Contextual Menus

Context-sensitive menus are a neat new feature introduced in Mac OS 8. A contextual menu lists commands that apply to the item the cursor is over. Contextual menus appear in windows, on icons, and most places on the desktop when you hold down the Control key and click (see Figure 3-42).

If you click inside a window but not on any icon, the contextual menu contains actions you perform on a window (see Figure 3-43).

Figure 3-42:
The
contextual
menu after
you Control-
click a
document
icon; notice
that only
actions that
apply to a
document
icon
appear.

Figure 3-43:
The contextual menu after you Control-click a window; notice that only actions that apply to a window icon appear.

Notice how a contextual menu for a document (refer to Figure 3-42) differs from the contextual menu for a window (refer to Figure 3-43). That's why they call 'em contextual. Actions appear in contextual menus only if they make sense for the item you Control-click.

Don't believe me? Control-click the desktop (that is, click somewhere that's not in any window and not on any icon) and you see a contextual menu with different commands (see Figure 3-44).

Get in the habit of Control-clicking items. Before you know it, using contextual menus becomes second nature to you.

Figure 3-44:
The contextual menu for the desktop.

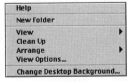

Chapter 4

Polishing the Apple (Menu)

. . . .

In This Chapter

▶ About this computer (yours)

▶ Desk accessories

▶ Those interestingly named folders in the Apple menu

▶ Customizing your Apple menu

▶ A deep, dark secret

. . . .

*T*he Apple menu is beneath the little Apple logo, an apple with a bite taken out of it, that graces the upper-left corner of your screen. It gets its own chapter because, unlike the menus I discussed previously, it's entirely configurable by you, the user. This menu embodies one of the finest features of the Mac — the capability to create your own customized file-launching and folder-accessing environment.

Mac OS 8.5, like all versions since 7.5, supports hierarchical submenus, which power users have loved in the form of Now Software's NowMenus and other similar programs for years. Finally everyone else can see what the power-user elite have been raving about for so long. Submenus in the Apple menu are fantastic!

So I show you the basics of configuring *your* Apple menu in this chapter, but I'm telling you in advance: I'm saving the really cool tricks for Chapter 11.

Before I talk about how to customize your Apple menu, I describe the stuff that's already in it: *desk accessories,* the little miniprograms (Jigsaw Puzzle, Calculator, and so on) that Apple thoughtfully stuck in your Apple menu along with several special folders. In all fairness, I also show you how to use the essential and useful desk accessories such as the Scrapbook and the Chooser, so don't think that all desk accessories are lame. Only most of them are.

Oh, and one last thing: At the end of this chapter, I let you in on a deep, dark secret that you probably figured out already.

About This Computer (Yours)

Before we do anything, let me tell you a bit about the Apple menu's only permanent item, About This Computer.

The first item on every Apple menu (at least if the Finder is the active application) is the About This Computer command. Take a peek at it from time to time — it tells you how much of your memory (RAM) is currently being used, how much of it is real RAM and how much of it is virtual memory, which programs are using it, and how much is left for programs yet to be launched. Those are good things to know. It also tells you what version of the System software is running.

In Figure 4-1, you can see that my System software is using 17.8MB of RAM (random access memory).

Figure 4-1:
A wealth of
information
about this
computer.

 17.8MB of RAM is a lot for System software. But I'm running all the options Mac OS 8.5 has to offer — QuickDraw 3D, QuickDraw GX, QuickTime VR, File Sharing, AppleScript — the whole shebang. In Chapter 14, I show you how to turn this stuff off (or get rid of it completely), as well as give you advice on when you can safely do so. For now, just accept that your System software probably uses somewhat less RAM than mine does.

In Figure 4-1, the Jigsaw Puzzle application is using 516K, and SimpleText is using 528K. The bars to the right of the programs' names and numbers are especially meaningful. The right part of each bar reflects the amount of memory the program has grabbed (and corresponds to the number just to the left of the bar). The highlighted part of the bar shows how much of that memory the program is actually using at the moment. My System software looks like it's using all its allocation; SimpleText looks like it's using less than a third. Jigsaw Puzzle seems to be using about two-thirds.

 What? You aren't willing to accept "about two-thirds" as an answer? Sigh. Okay. To find out *exactly* how much RAM Jigsaw Puzzle is using, choose Help⇨Show Balloons and then point at the bar for Jigsaw Puzzle. What you ought to see is shown in Figure 4-2.

Figure 4-2:
Jigsaw
Puzzle is
using
exactly
357K of the
516K it
requested
when I
opened it.

Why is the information in the About This Computer window important? First, you can see how much RAM is left (the Largest Unused Block) for launching additional programs. I have approximately 109 megabytes (wow!), but I have a lot of RAM (128MB of real RAM, plus 1 additional megabyte of virtual memory). If you try to launch a program that requires more RAM than the Largest Unused Block at any given time, your Mac politely informs you that it doesn't have enough memory to launch this program.

The other thing that's important is that I can see that SimpleText gobbled up 512K when I launched it, but it's using only 128K of its allocation at this time. (I found that out by using the Balloon Help tip.) So it's grabbing about 400K of precious RAM and not using it.

What can I do about it? Well, I can tell SimpleText to grab less RAM next time I launch it. Here's how:

(Oops. Almost forgot. If SimpleText is open, quit before performing the following procedure. An application can't be running when you adjust its Preferred Memory Size.)

1. **Select the SimpleText icon.**

2. **Choose File⇨Get Info or use the keyboard shortcut Command-I.**

   The SimpleText Info window appears (as shown in Figure 4-3).

3. **Choose Memory from the pop-up menu in the Info window.**

4. **Change the Preferred Size from 512K to a smaller number, somewhere between the Minimum and Suggested Size.**

5. **Close the Info window.**

The change doesn't take effect until the Get Info window closes.

Figure 4-3: Reduce the Preferred Size from 512K to a lower number (but not lower than the Minimum Size above it).

When I say "a smaller number," it's not because I don't want to tell you what number to use. But it's not a precise science. I don't know how big the documents you open with SimpleText are, and that's what determines how much RAM it needs. Try 256K. If you someday discover that you can't open a document due to low memory (your Mac tells you so), increase this number a bit — to 384K or even 450K. It still saves you a little over the old setting of 512K.

Don't perform the preceding procedure haphazardly. Most programs run better with their Preferred memory set *higher* than the suggested size. But (and it's a big but) if you're short on RAM for other programs and you can see that a program is only using a fraction of the RAM that it requests, you can probably reduce its Preferred size at least a little and maybe a lot.

From the Desk (Accessories) Of . . .

You use items in the Apple menu the same way that you use any menu item — click the Apple and drag down to the item. After you release the mouse button, the item opens. If the item is a folder, it has a submenu; you can see its contents by dragging down until the folder is highlighted and stopping. Don't release the mouse button, or the folder pops open. To choose an item in the submenu, drag to the right.

If you haven't modified your Apple menu, it probably looks something like the one in Figure 4-4.

Ignoring the folders for now (I talk about them after I ridicule a few desk accessories), take a look at each desk accessory in turn.

Figure 4-4:
A standard
issue,
unconfigured,
fresh-from-
the-installer
Apple
menu.

Technically, only a few of the items in the Apple menu are desk accessories (known affectionately as DAs), special types of miniprograms that are a little different from regular applications and are a holdover from System 6 and earlier. The rest are regular old applications. Even so, most people prefer the programs Apple sticks under the Apple menu as desk accessories, and so do I. Desk accessories are basically miniapplications, and they're discussed further along with control panels and extensions in Chapter 14.

Profile THIS: Apple System Profiler

Apple System Profiler was new in Mac OS 7.6. It's a little program that gives you information about your Mac. What a concept. If you're curious about things such as what processor your Mac has, or what devices are on its SCSI bus, give it a try. Poke around the Select menu and check it out if you like; this little puppy is benign and won't hurt anything.

If you ever have occasion to call for technical support for your Mac, software, or peripherals, you're probably going to be asked to provide information from Apple System Profiler. So don't get rid of it just because *you* don't care about this kind of stuff.

Sounds good to me: AppleCD Audio Player

Next on the Apple menu is the AppleCD Audio Player. It's a little program you use to play regular old stereo CDs on your CD-ROM drive (see Figure 4-5). Just pop your David Garza CD into the CD-ROM drive, select AppleCD Audio Player from the Apple menu, and then click the Play button. Your room is filled with the mellow tones of Austin's own Dah-veed.

Figure 4-5:
AppleCD
Audio
Player is a
slick remote
control
program for
playing
audio CDs
in your
CD-ROM
drive.

You may need to plug a pair of amplified stereo speakers into the stereo output jacks on some external CD-ROM drives. If you have an internal CD-ROM drive, you may need to select Internal CD from the Sound Input pop-up menu in the Monitors & Sound control panel before you hear music through your Mac's built-in speaker. Finally, you must have the Audio CD Access extension in the Extensions folder within your System Folder for the AppleCD Audio Player to function.

Because the internal speakers in most Macs suck, a good pair of multimedia speakers is a good investment; then you can rattle the walls when you slap that David Garza CD in your drive.

A whole chapter (see Chapter 14) talks about every item in your System Folder and whether you need it. It also explains what an extension is, in case you're wondering. In any event, it should be obvious to you even now that this program isn't much use if you don't have a CD-ROM drive.

A calculated risk: Calculator

The Calculator has been in the Apple menu as long as I can remember, and it hasn't changed one iota since it was introduced. (All right, it got a spiffy new icon when System 7 first arrived, but that's the extent of it.) Figure 4-6 shows what the ol' Calculator (still) looks like.

The Calculator DA is the *pixel* (for picture element, the little dots that make up your screen) equivalent of the cheesy calculators that cheap companies give away — or the kind you see at the grocery store for $1.99. The Apple Calculator does have one feature that makes it different from all those Taiwan specials: Cheap calculators don't require a four-figure investment in computer equipment.

Figure 4-6:
The
ancient-yet-
venerable
Calculator
DA.

I'm kidding, of course. Even though it's looking a little long in the tooth (Hey, Apple — how about a facelift for the old fellow? Maybe some pastel colors? More graceful-looking buttons? A paper tape? And a Clear Entry button instead of only Clear All?), it still comes in handy more often than you might expect. For example, my wife used it to balance our checkbook for years (till she got hooked on Quicken).

The Calculator DA works just like a real calculator. Use the numeric keypad on your keyboard; the keys correlate to their on-screen counterparts.

Unfortunately, the Calculator lacks all but the most basic features. As noted, it doesn't have a paper tape, a Clear Entry key, or even a single memory recall. There are shareware and commercial calculators galore, with features galore. If you need a calculator DA, almost anything you can buy or download is better than the Calculator DA that comes with Mac OS 8.5.

Be choosy: Be a Chooser user

The Chooser is a desk accessory that enables you to choose at least two things: which printer to use and which computer(s) to share files with.

If you click a printer icon on the left side of the window, all the printers available on the network appear in a list on the right side of the window (see Figure 4-7).

Figure 4-7:
The
Chooser.

The Chooser is also where you choose other Macs to share files with. If you click the AppleShare icon on the left side of the Chooser, every Mac on your network that has file sharing turned on appears in the list on the right.

Finally, the Chooser is also where you create desktop printer icons, but because there's an entire chapter on printing and yet another one about file sharing. I think you know enough about the Chooser to hold you till you get to them.

Digital Color Meter

Digital Color Meter is a desk accessory (introduced with Mac OS 8.1, I believe) that enables you to point (using the cursor) at anything on the screen and discover its RGB (Red Green Blue) values. I find it useless, and the Mac OS installer doesn't install it on all Macs, but if you're in the graphic arts, you may need it someday for something. I can't imagine what but you may. So leave it alone for now, okay?

Finder of lost files: Find File (again)

Choosing Apple⇨Find from the menu bar is the same as choosing File⇨Find in the Finder. (Try saying that fast three times.) The only advantage this DA has is that, because it's in the Apple menu, you can choose it even if the Finder isn't currently the active application. If you've forgotten how Find File works, read Chapter 3.

Fakin' it with Graphing Calculator (Power Macs only)

I still have no idea what this thing is really supposed to do. I do enjoy running its demos for my friends and pretending I do, though. If Graphing Calculator appears in your Apple menu, here's how to fake it. Choose 3D Surfaces from the Demo menu. You should see something like Figure 4-8.

Click the Stop button and then use your mouse to spin the graph. Mumble something half-intelligibly about "PowerPC processors and real-time 3D surface mapping capabilities." I guarantee you're going to impress your friends.

Figure 4-8:
The 3D
Surfaces
demo in
Graphing
Calculator.

Better than puzzles of old: It's Jigsaw Puzzle

Better than the old 15-numbers-in-16-squares puzzle of System software of old, the Jigsaw Puzzle is only a little less lame. It's a jigsaw puzzle. Click the pieces to move them around (see Figure 4-9).

Figure 4-9:
It's a jigsaw
puzzle.
What did
you expect?

One cool thing is that you can paste another picture onto the puzzle and that picture becomes the jigsaw puzzle. It's kind of fun. Here's how to do it:

1. **Select any picture in a graphics program, word processor, or SimpleText (what I used).**

2. **Choose Edit➪Copy.**

3. **Choose Apple⇨Jigsaw Puzzle.**

4. **Choose Edit⇨Paste.**

In Figure 4-10, I've pasted my own picture into Jigsaw Puzzle.

And there you have it — a new puzzle for you to solve. This technique works with any picture you can copy to the Clipboard, and also with icons (see the preceding chapter for information on copying and pasting).

Figure 4-10:
Paste a new picture, get a new puzzle.

The key to all your fonts: It's Key Caps

Want to know what every character in a font looks like? Or where the funny optional characters such as ´, ®, ©, æ, and ™ are hidden on your keyboard? Sounds like a job for Key Caps, a modest little desk accessory that shows you a lot about your installed fonts.

If you're not sure what a font is, choose Apple⇨Key Caps. You see something like Figure 4-11.

Figure 4-11:
The Key Caps DA shows you all the cute characters in your fonts.

The items in the Key Caps menu are your fonts. When you pull down the Key Caps menu you see a list of your installed fonts. To see what a particular font looks like, choose it in the Key Caps menu and type a few words. They appear in the white text entry box at the top of the Key Caps window. If you want to see what those words look like in another font, choose that font from the Key Caps menu.

Of course, you could do the same thing in any program that has a font menu. In fact, you can do more because Key Caps displays the font only in a single size, 12 points; other programs enable you to change the size as well as the font, and you can also apply character styles such as bold, italic, and outline.

So what good is Key Caps? It's the easiest way to find special symbols. Just open Key Caps, choose a font, and hold down the Option key. Key Caps displays the special symbols and characters on the keyboard. For example, to type ™ in your document, hold down the Option key and press the 2 key on your keyboard. Instant ™.

What Key Caps doesn't show you is how to create diacritical marks such as acute accents and umlauts. To type them, follow these instructions:

- To type a grave accent (`), press Option-` and then type the character. So to accent an *e,* you press **Option-`** and then type **e**. It comes out looking like this: è. (The ` key is usually in the top row to the left of the 1 key.)

- To type an acute accent (´), press Option-e and then type the character. So to accent an *e,* you press **Option-e** and then type **e**. It comes out looking like this: é.

- To type a circumflex (^), press Option-i and then type the character. So to put a circumflex over an *i,* you press **Option-i** and then type **i**. It comes out looking like this: î.

- To type a tilde (~), press Option-n and then type the character. So to put a tilde over an *n,* you press **Option-n** and then type **n**. It comes out looking like this: ñ. I'm pretty sure that the *n* is the only character you can put a tilde over; I tried to put it over other characters, but they came out looking like this: ~b.

- To type an umlaut (¨), press Option-u and then type the character. So to put an umlaut over a *u,* you press **Option-u** and then type **u**. It comes out looking like this: ü, as in Motley Crüe.

Browse yer local area net with Network Browser

If your Mac is on a local area network, you can view a list of available network servers using the Network Browser in your Apple menu. You can also use the Network Browser to connect to listed servers and create a list of favorite servers for quick access.

If you want to know more about Network Browser than I've told you, open Mac OS Help and search for **Network Browser**. You find a ton of interesting stuff that I don't have room for here.

Take note of the Note Pad

Note Pad is a handy, dandy little note-taking utility that lets you store gobs of unrelated text items without saving a zillion different files all over your hard disk. Everything that you type into Note Pad is automatically saved in the Note Pad File, which is in your System Folder. Figure 4-12 shows Note Pad in action.

Figure 4-12: Note Pad is a handy little program for jotting random thoughts and phone numbers.

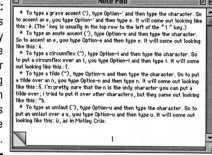

Note Pad uses a page metaphor. Click the dog-ear corner at bottom left to change the page or choose File⇨Go to Note and type the page number of the note that you want to go to.

The Note Pad in Mac OS 8.5 has several improvements over Note Pads of old. Most welcome is the Find command. And its window is resizable and has scroll bars. (Can you believe it took Apple until System 7.5 to add scroll bars and make its window resizable?) Finally, the pages seem to hold a lot more text than older versions. Oh, and you can choose a font in the Preferences dialog box; the older Note Pads gave a choice of Geneva or Geneva.

You can print notes, and Note Pad (like almost every Mac application ever made) includes full support of Cut, Copy, or Paste, so you can easily get text in and out of Note Pad by using the Clipboard.

Some people prefer Note Pad to Stickies (you read about Stickies in a second), some people use both, and some people use neither. For a freebie, Note Pad is relatively well equipped. If you have a lot of random thoughts that you'd like to type, you might want to leave it open all day (it only uses a little RAM). It's also a good spot for frequently dialed phone numbers.

Remote Access Status

A component of ARA (Apple Remote Access). See Chapter 8.

The not-so-scrappy Scrapbook

The Scrapbook is like the Note Pad, but you use it to store graphics, text, and sounds. Instead of pages, the Scrapbook uses an item metaphor. You move from item to item by using the scroll bar in the lower part of the Scrapbook window (see Figure 4-13).

Figure 4-13:
The Scrapbook is a storage repository for graphics, sounds, and text; you control it with the Cut, Copy, Paste, and Clear commands.

To put something into the Scrapbook, copy it to the Clipboard; then open the Scrapbook and choose Edit⇨Paste or use the keyboard shortcut Command-V. The pasted item will become the item before the current item. So if you're looking at item 1 when you paste, the pasted item becomes item 1, and the former item 1 becomes item 2, and so on.

Here are the various ways to use the Scrapbook:

✔ To remove an item from the Scrapbook and use it elsewhere, choose Edit⇨Cut or use the keyboard shortcut Command-X. This action removes the current item from the Scrapbook and places it on the Clipboard for pasting into another document.

✔ To use a Scrapbook item in another document without deleting it, choose Edit⇨Copy or the keyboard shortcut Command-C. Then open a document and choose Edit⇨Paste.

✔ To delete a Scrapbook item forever, choose Edit⇨Clear or use the keyboard shortcut Command-B. Doing so deletes the item from the Scrapbook without placing it on the Clipboard.

You can't always paste a picture or sound into a document. The determining factor is the kind of document that you're trying to paste into. For example, you can't paste a picture into cells in spreadsheets or most fields in databases. And you can't usually paste a sound into a graphics file.

If you try to paste an inappropriate item into a document, your Mac either beeps at you or does nothing. If nothing happens when you paste, assume that the document can't accept the picture or sound you're trying to paste.

You can paste text into the Scrapbook, but it's probably easier to paste it into the Note Pad where you can select only a portion of it or edit it. After text is pasted into the Scrapbook, it can't be selected or edited, so if you want to change it, you'll have to copy and paste the entire chunk of text into an application that supports text editing (such as Note Pad, SimpleText, or a word processor).

If you want to replace the old version of an item in the Scrapbook with a changed version, you have to copy the new version to the Clipboard and then paste it into the Scrapbook. Don't forget to delete the old version by scrolling until it appears and choosing Edit⇨Clear (Command-B) to delete it.

SimpleSound

It's a simple little DA for recording your own alert sounds. You need to have a proper microphone; contact your nearest Apple or clone dealer for details. Just open SimpleSound, click the Add button, the Record button, and then the Save button, and just like that you have a new beep sound.

SimpleSound has one other feature: Its Sound menu enables you to choose between CD Quality, Music Quality, Speech Quality, and Phone Quality sound. Frankly, I can't tell the difference, even using excellent amplified speakers.

Don't be stuck up: Use Stickies

Stickies, which were new in System 7.5, are electronic Post-It Notes for your Mac. They are akin to the Note Pad; they're a slightly different but no less convenient place to jot notes or phone numbers. Stickies are shown in Figure 4-14.

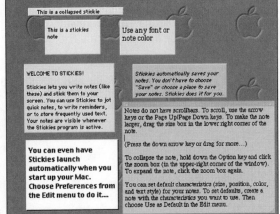

Figure 4-14: Stickies are the electronic equivalent of Post-It Notes.

Stickies are nothing if not flexible. They can be moved around on-screen (just drag 'em by the title bar). They can display text in any font you desire. They can be collapsed by Option-clicking their grow boxes. They can be any color you like (if you have a color monitor, of course). You can import and export text files. And, of course, you can print Stickies.

As with the Note Pad, anything that you type on a Sticky is saved automatically as long as you keep that note open. But when you close a note (by clicking its close box, choosing File⇨Close, or using the keyboard shortcut Command-W), you lose its contents forever. Fortunately, Stickies gives you a warning and a second chance to save the note in a separate file on your hard disk.

If you like to live dangerously, you can turn the warning off by choosing Edit⇨Preferences and unchecking the Confirm Window-Closing option. In the Preferences dialog box, you can also tell Stickies to save all notes every time you switch to another application (safer), set the zoom box so that it collapses the window without the Option key, and set whether Stickies should launch automatically at startup (if you check this item, Stickies creates an alias of itself and puts it in your Startup Items folder).

Those interestingly named folders in the Apple Menu

There are a handful of folders in your Apple menu spread out amongst the desk accessories. You may see little triangles to the right of their names (if you don't, I'll show you how to turn them on in a minute). The triangles indicate that these folders have hierarchical submenus and will reveal their contents when you pull down the Apple menu and drag the cursor onto them. Submenus are a newish feature, introduced with System 7.5, though commercial programs such as NowMenus and shareware programs such as MenuChoice have provided this functionality since the early days of System 7.

To select an item in the submenu, drag to the right and highlight it, as shown in Figure 4-15.

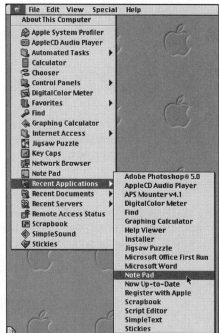

Figure 4-15:
A
hierarchical
submenu.

To choose Note Pad in the Recent Applications folder (refer to Figure 4-15), click the Apple, drag down until the Recent Applications folder is highlighted, drag to the right and down until Note Pad is highlighted, and then release the mouse button.

What is a control panel, anyway?

Control panels are little programs that you use to adjust and configure your Mac. Each one has one or two specific functions — set the Mac clock (Date & Time), change menu blinking (General Controls), configure memory (Memory), adjust the mouse (Mouse) and keyboard (Keyboard), and so on.

Control panels go in the Control Panels folder inside your System Folder. The Installer automatically creates an alias of the Control Panels folder and puts it in your Apple menu for you when you install Mac OS 8.5.

If you get a new control panel (many screen savers and other utilities are control panels), simply drag it onto the System Folder icon, and Mac OS 8.5 automatically puts it in its proper place, the Control Panels folder. (Incidentally, Mac OS 8.5 is smart about extensions, fonts, and sounds as well. If you drag an extension, font, or sound onto the System Folder icon, Mac OS 8.5 puts it in its proper place automatically.)

There's a whole chapter on control panels and how to configure them (see Chapter 12), so I'm leaving it at that for now.

If you don't see the little triangles to the right of your folders, here's how to turn them on:

1. **Choose Apple⇨Control Panels.**
2. **Open the Apple Menu Options control panel.**
3. **Click the On radio button, as shown in Figure 4-16.**

Now that you know how submenus work, I'm going to talk about the five or six folders you may see in your Apple menu.

Figure 4-16:
Turning on the hierarchical submenus in the Apple Menu Options control panel.

Apple Menu Options

Submenus
● On   ○ Off

☑ Remember recently used items:

Documents: 30

Applications: 30

Servers: 5

The Control Panels folder

As previously noted, the Installer creates an alias of the Control Panels folder and puts it in your Apple menu so that you always have access to your control panels, even when you're using an application other than the Finder. Before submenus were introduced (1994), you had to choose the Control Panels folder from the Apple menu. That action would automatically switch you to the Finder (if you were in another application) and open the Control Panels folder's window. Then you had to open the icon for the control panel manually. Ugh. Mac OS 8.5, with its marvelous submenus, is much nicer.

Recent Applications, Recent Documents, and Recent Servers

I'm discussing these three Apple menu items together because they're related and work the same way.

If you don't see them in your Apple menu, open the Apple Menu Options control panel (choose Apple menu⇨Control Panels⇨Apple Menu Options) and check the Remember recently used items check box (refer to Figure 4-16). This action will create the folders in your Apple Menu Items folder as soon as you open an application, document, or server. If you never open a server (access another Macintosh over a network), the Recent Servers folder is never created.

Even if you do see these items in your Apple menu, you may want to use the Apple Menu Options control panel to change the number of applications, documents, and servers that the folders will remember. I find that 30 is a good number on my big 20-inch monitor — enough to ensure that the application or document (I rarely use the server folder) that I am looking for is still there, but not so many that the submenu scrolls off-screen.

These three folders track the last *x-many* applications, documents, and servers that you opened. Each time you open one of these three types of icons, the System makes a mental note of it and then creates an alias of that application, document, or server and pops it into the appropriate folder in your Apple Menu Items folder. The System also limits the number of items in each folder based on the Apple Menu Options control panel's settings. So when you open your 31st application, the oldest application alias in the Recent Applications folder disappears.

Why are these folders useful? Often the document or application that you're looking for is one you had open earlier in the day or yesterday. These special folders in the Apple menu keep recently used items handy. Chances are, if you used it recently, you'll want to use it again soon. If so, look in one of these folders. (**Hint:** Use the submenu — it's faster.)

Automated Tasks

The Automated Tasks folder contains a collection of useful AppleScript scripts. AppleScript is the Mac's internal scripting language. Scripts can perform many Macintosh tasks that would take several steps to perform manually, such as turning File Sharing on and off, changing the number of colors that you see on your monitor, and adjusting the speaker's volume. Many people refer to what a script does as a *macro*.

AppleScript is kind of neat, and it's included with Mac OS 8.5 at absolutely no charge. If you're the kind of person who likes to climb under the hood and get your fingers dirty, there's a whole chapter (see Chapter 13) about AppleScript, the scriptable Finder, and tips on creating your own scripts. Don't miss it.

Favorites

The Favorites folder contains aliases of — what else? — your favorite files. If you use a particular program, document, or even folder more than a few times a day, you should add it to your Favorites for easy access.

To put an item into *your* Favorites folder, select it in the Finder and then choose File⇨Add to Favorites (or Control-click the item and choose Add to Favorites from the contextual menu).

Conversely, to get rid of an item from your Favorites folder, choose Apple Menu⇨Favorites. The Favorites folder opens, and you can drag the unwanted item to the Trash.

The Favorites folder in your Apple menu is an alias of the actual Favorites folder, which lives right inside your System Folder. Don't believe me? Open the System Folder and look for yourself!

Roll Your Own: Customizing Your Apple Menu

Do you remember Figure 4-4, way back there at the beginning of the chapter? Can you say "Boooorrrring"?

The Apple menu is fully configurable. Whatever is in the Apple Menu Items folder appears in the Apple menu. It's that simple.

So start transforming your Apple menu from a dull repository for barely useful software to a turbocharged powerhouse that enables you to open any file in seconds. (You finish the transformation in Chapter 11.)

Just open your Apple Menu Items folder (it's in your System Folder) and get ready to rock.

Before you do anything else, choose View⇨by Name. Now the Apple Menu Items folder's contents reflect the order that they appear in the Apple menu.

Doing the right thing with your desk accessories

As you've seen, most of the desk accessories are pretty lame. You probably won't use most of them very often. We're going to rearrange your Apple menu now so that desk accessories don't take up so much space while preserving your ability to open them quickly. Here's how:

1. **Open the System Folder by double-clicking its icon (or by single-clicking its icon to select it and then choosing File⇨Open or pressing the keyboard shortcut Command-O).**

2. **Open the Apple Menu Items folder (it's in the System Folder) and create a new folder inside it.**

   To create a new folder, choose File⇨New Folder or press Command-N.

3. **Name the new folder Desk Accessories.**

4. **Select all the icons in the window *except* the folders (see Figure 4-17).**

   You have two ways to do this: the easy way and the hard way. Easy way first: Press Command-A (or drag a selection box around the entire contents of the window) to select all the icons; then hold down the Shift key and click each folder. Hard way: Click Apple System Profiler, hold down the Shift key, click AppleCD Audio Player, hold down the Shift key, click Calculator, hold down Shift key, and so on until all the nonfolder icons are selected.

   This step illustrates one of the Finder's finer points. You can extend or unextend your selection by using the Shift key. In other words, if you hold down the Shift key and then click an icon, it is added to or subtracted from the selection; if you don't hold down the Shift key when you click an icon, only that single icon is selected.

5. **Drag these icons onto the Desk Accessories folder that you created in Step 2.**

   After you release the mouse button, all the desk accessories, applications, and aliases that aren't folders move into the Desk Accessories folder.

Figure 4-17:
Select all
the icons
except the
folder and
folder alias
icons and
drag them
into the
Desk
Accessories
folder.

6. Pull down your Apple menu and revel in your handiwork.

The menu should now look like the one in Figure 4-18.

Figure 4-18:
Your Apple
menu is
now a lean,
mean, file-
launching
machine.

Putting your stuff into the Apple menu

That last trick was pretty easy, wasn't it? Try one more thing before you move on. Why not add your favorite applications — the programs you use most often — to the Apple menu? Here's how:

1. **Find a favorite application on your hard disk, select it, and make an alias of it (by choosing File⇨Make Alias or Command-M).**

2. **Move the alias to the Apple Menu Items folder.**

3. **Repeat Steps 1 and 2 for any additional applications that you want to appear in your Apple menu.**

An even easier way to add something to your Apple menu is hiding right there in the Automated Tasks submenu. Just select the item that you want to add to the Apple menu in the Finder and then choose Apple Menu⇨ Automated Tasks⇨Add Alias to Apple Menu. It's that simple.

My Deep, Dark Secret

I can't go on with this charade any longer. I confess: The screen pictures you've been looking at aren't from my real hard disk at all. They're from a hard disk called Spawn that I borrowed from Apple to create the screen shots for this book. When I start up using my real hard disk, my Mac looks *totally* different.

I'm a power user. I've got my Mac souped up and tricked out to the max. I've got strange icons in the menu bar. I've got a Trash alias behind the Apple menu (hidden in this shot). A slot machine is in my control strip.

I didn't want to confuse you, so I wrote the book using the Spawn hard disk, a disk that had nothing on it except Mac OS 8.5-related stuff. It makes for much cleaner screen shots so that I can avoid explaining every last difference between your Mac and mine. For the record, my Mac really looks like what you see in Figure 4-19.

I'll just point out a few highlights. First, I have a 20-inch Sony Trinitron monitor. The clock and telephone in the menu bar enable me to look at my appointments or phone book file without launching my calendar or contact database program (Chronos Software's excellent Consultant). The CC icon next to the Application menu is for Conflict Catcher, a kind of Extensions Manager on steroids from Casady & Greene (see Chapter 12). The slot machine in my control strip is shareware. Finally, an alias of my Trash can is hiding behind the Apple menu so that I don't need to drag trash as far.

Figure 4-19:
My Mac.

I have three hard disks: Bootman (internal) and Spawn and Sid (both external).

There. I feel better having gotten that off my chest.

P.S.: By the time you read this book, I'm going to be running the final released version of Mac OS 8.5 — in case you noticed that I was running OS 8.1 in Figure 4-19.

Chapter 5

Save Yourself Heartache: Master the Save and Open Dialog Boxes

Mark my words, this may well be the most important chapter in this book. If you don't understand the Open and Save dialog boxes, the doohickeys that appear when you choose File⇨Open or File⇨Save in most programs, you'll never quite master your Macintosh. Yet mastering these essential techniques is perhaps the biggest problem many users have. I get more phone calls that begin, "Well, I saved the file, and now I don't know where it went."

This chapter is the cure. Just pay attention, and it'll become crystal clear. And keep saying to yourself, *"The Save and Open dialog boxes are just another view of the Finder."* I explain in a moment.

Nested Folders and Paths (It's Not as Bad as It Sounds)

Before I get started, I need to remind you that you work with Open and Save dialog boxes within applications. I assume that you know how to launch your favorite application and that you know how to create a new document.

For the rest of this chapter, I use SimpleText as the sample application. SimpleText comes with Mac OS 8.5, so you should have it too. In fact, you've probably already used SimpleText to read any Read Me files that came with Mac OS 8.5. (If you can't find a copy, Command-F gives you the Find dialog box. Search for Simple.)

So if you want to follow along, keystroke by keystroke, launch SimpleText and use File⇨New to create a new document. Type a few words in your document, like "All work and no play makes Jack a dull boy." Or something like that. (Forgive me, Stephen King.)

Switch from SimpleText to the Finder (you remember how). You may find the next part easier if you hide SimpleText (you know how to do that, too!) while you work in the Finder. If you've forgotten how to do either, pull down the Application menu, the one at the far right; everything you need is right there.

1. **Open your hard disk's icon and create a new folder at root level (that is, in your hard disk's window). Name this folder Folder 1 to reflect the fact that it's one level deep on your hard disk.**

2. **Open Folder 1 and create a new folder in its window. Name this folder Folder 2 to reflect the fact that it's two levels deep on your hard disk.**

3. **Open Folder 2 and create a new folder in its window. Name this folder Folder 3 to reflect the fact that it's three levels deep on your hard disk.**

You should now have a set of nested folders looking something like Figure 5-1.

Figure 5-1:
Nested folders, going four levels deep.

Let me make this perfectly clear: Stuff *inside* Folder 3 is four levels deep. Folder 3 itself is three levels deep. Folder 2 itself is two levels deep, but stuff inside Folder 2, such as Folder 3, is three levels deep. And so on. Got it?

What's important here is that you are able to visualize the *path* to Folder 3. To get to Folder 3, you open Spawn, open Folder 1, open Folder 2, and then open Folder 3. Remember this concept. You need it in the next section when you look at the Save dialog box.

 An easy way to see the path to any open folder is to Command-click its name in the title bar of its window (hold down the Command key before you press the mouse button). This action displays a drop-down path menu for that folder starting at the desktop level, as shown in Figure 5-2.

Figure 5-2:
The drop-down path menu for Folder 3 appears when you press its name in the title bar while holding down the Command key.

This path menu is *live,* which means that you can choose another folder from it by sliding the cursor to the folder's name and releasing the mouse button.

Try out this feature with Folder 3. Command-click its name in the title bar, move the cursor down until Folder 1 is highlighted, and then release the mouse button. Folder 1 pops to the front and becomes the active window. Try to remember this shortcut, as Command-clicking title bars can save you lots of time and effort.

Okay, our preparatory work in the Finder is through. Use any of the techniques you know to make SimpleText the active application. And don't forget what that path to Folder 3 looks like.

Save Your Document Before It's Too Late

Okay, back in SimpleText, it's time to save your masterpiece. Choose File⇨Save (Command-S). This command brings up the Save dialog box (shown in Figure 5-3). Don't panic. These dialog boxes are easy as long as you remember that they're just another view of the folder structure in the Finder.

Figure 5-3: The Save dialog box for Simple- Text after clicking the Desktop button.

When the Save dialog box appears, the first thing I want you to do is click the Desktop button to view the icons on your desktop.

Let's talk about the Save dialog box for a moment. It contains that other view of your hard disk I talk about earlier. You're looking at the icons on your desktop right now. You know that they're the icons on your desktop because the active item is the desktop. Its name appears on the drop-down menu at the top and center.

In programs other than SimpleText, the Save dialog box may look slightly different because it contains additional options. Don't worry. The Save dialog box always *works* the same, no matter what options are offered. When you can navigate with the SimpleText Save dialog box, you can navigate with any program's Save dialog box. So don't worry if the one you're used to seeing doesn't look exactly like Figure 5-3; just follow along.

Click Spawn (that is, your hard disk, whatever its name is) in the scrolling list (known as the *file list box*) and then click the Open button or press the Return or Enter key on your keyboard. (In all dialog boxes, the Return or Enter key activates the default button, which is the one with the heavy border around it.) Double-clicking Spawn will open it as well.

Open Folder 1 the same way. Open Folder 2 the same way. Open Folder 3 the same way. Your Save dialog box should look like Figure 5-4.

Figure 5-4:
If you save now, the document will be saved into Folder 3 and named *untitled*.

In other words, you navigate folders in the Save dialog box the same way you navigate folders in the Finder: by opening them to see their contents.

In the Save dialog box, the name at the top in the drop-down menu is the name of the active item (a folder, disk, or the desktop). Think of the active item in a Save dialog box as the active window in the Finder. That's where your file is saved if you click the Save button. This concept is important. The file is always saved in the active folder (or disk or the desktop) — the folder (or disk or the desktop) whose name appears at the top of the dialog box in the drop-down menu.

To make comprehension easier, think back to when I asked you to remember the path to Folder 3 in the Finder. Now look at the current path to Folder 3 in the Save dialog box by clicking the drop-down menu. Like the drop-down path menu in the Finder (Command-click the window's name in the title bar), the drop-down menu in the Save dialog box is also live, so if you slide the cursor down to another folder (or Spawn or the desktop), that item becomes the active item. (See Figure 5-5.)

Figure 5-5:
The drop-down menu shows the path to the current folder.

The Save (and Open) dialog boxes treat disk icons and the desktop the same as they treat folders. Though they're not really folders, you can save items to the desktop or root level (your hard disk's window).

You always move through the hierarchy in the same way. The desktop is the top level. When you're at the desktop level, you can see all mounted disks and any folders on the desktop. If you open a disk icon, you see its folder structure. You always navigate up and down the tree. Your most deeply nested folders are at the very bottom; the desktop is at the very top.

If you have more than one disk mounted, make sure that the disk name, which appears in the top right next to a little disk icon (hard disks have a hard disk icon; floppies have a floppy disk icon), is correct. If it's not, navigate back up to the desktop level and choose the correct disk.

Get into the habit of noticing the disk name in the Open and Save dialog boxes if you often have multiple disks mounted. Nothing is more frustrating than saving a file to the wrong disk and not being able to find it later.

Your file is saved to the active item in the drop-down menu when you click Save. In other words, when the desktop is the active item (as it is in Figure 5-3), your document is saved on the desktop if you click the Save button. When Spawn is the active item, your document is saved in the Spawn window if you click the Save button. When Folder 3 is the active item, your document is saved in Folder 3 if you click the Save button.

1. **In the Save dialog box, navigate to Folder 3; that is, make Folder 3 the active item.**

2. **When Folder 3 appears as the active item, select the word "untitled" and type in a more descriptive name. (I called mine Love Letter to Lisa.)**

3. **Click the Save button (or press the Return or Enter key).**

That's it. If you switch to the Finder and open up Folder 3 (if it's not already open), you can see that the file is saved right there in Folder 3.

Congrats. That's all there is to it. You now know how to navigate in a Save dialog box.

Remember the path I asked you to remember, the one you saw when you Command-clicked the name in the title bar of Folder 3's window? Just remember that the path in the Save dialog box's drop-down menu (shown back in Figure 5-5) is the same.

If that information makes sense to you, you're golden. If you're still a little shaky, go back and try the exercise again and keep trying to understand the relationship between the three folders that you created (one inside the other inside the other) and the drop-down path menus you see when you

Command-click Folder 3's title bar or click its name in the drop-down menu in the Save dialog box. Keep reviewing the illustrations. Eventually it'll just click, and you'll slap yourself in the head and say, "*Now* I get it."

Don't read on until you get it. This idea of paths and navigating is crucial to your success as a Macintosh user.

There's a little more, but if you get it so far, you're home free.

The rest of what you should know about Save dialog boxes

One thing you need to know is that the file list box and the file name field are mutually exclusive. Only one can be active at a time. You're either navigating the folder hierarchy or you're naming a file. When a Save dialog box first appears, the file name field is active, ready for you to type a name (as shown on the right in Figure 5-6).

Figure 5-6: The file list box is active on the left; the file name field is active on the right.

Active File List Box — Inactive File List Box

Inactive File Name Field — Active File Name Box

Notice the border around the file list box when it is active. Also notice how the bottom button changes from Open to Save when the file name field is active. You can read more about this phenomenon in a few pages.

When you want to navigate, click anywhere in the file list box to make it active. In Figure 5-6, this box is beneath the active item (Spawn), which contains several folders. When you click anywhere in the box, it becomes active and displays a double-line border around it. If you type something while the file list box is active, the list scrolls and selects the folder that most closely matches the letter(s) you typed. Go ahead and give it a try. It's easier to experience than explain.

For what it's worth, you can also type the first letter or two in any Finder window to select the icon closest alphabetically to the letter or letters you typed.

When the file list is active, the letters that you type do not appear in the file name field. If you want to type a file name, you have to activate the file name field again in order to type in it. Here's how:

Regardless of which box or field is active at the time, when you press the Tab key on your keyboard, the other becomes active. So if the file name field is active, it becomes inactive when you press Tab, and the file list box becomes active. Press Tab again and they reverse — the file name field becomes active again.

If you don't feel like pressing the Tab key, you can achieve the same effect by clicking either the file list box or the file name field to activate them.

Try it yourself and notice how visual cues let you know which is active. When the file list is active, it displays a border; when the file name field is active, the file list has no border and the file name field is editable.

The buttons

There are five buttons in SimpleText's Save dialog box: Eject, Desktop, New Folder, Cancel, and Open/Save. The first four are straightforward and almost explain themselves, but the fifth requires a bit of concentration. I'll describe them all (except for the radio buttons, which are application-specific).

Ejector seat

The Eject button is only active when an ejectable disk is selected in the file list box. It's mostly used to save a file to a different floppy than the one currently in the drive. Use the Eject button to eject that floppy so that you can insert another. When you insert a floppy disk, it becomes the active item automatically. You can tell because its name appears in two places (see Figure 5-7):

✔ At the top right of the Save (or Open) dialog box above the buttons

✔ In the drop-down menu above the file list box

Do it on the desktop

The Desktop button takes you rocketing up the hierarchy of folders to the very top level, as high as you can go. When you click the Desktop button, the desktop becomes the active folder (I know that the desktop isn't really a folder, but play along) in the Save dialog box. From here, you can navigate your way down into any subfolder.

Figure 5-7:
The floppy
disk auto-
matically
becomes
the active
item.

If you get lost in a Save (or Open) dialog box, the best thing to do is click the Desktop button and start from the top (the desktop), which should make it easy to find your way to the folder you desire. Just remember to navigate down through folders in the same order you would in the Finder.

Something new: The New Folder button

This button is a nice touch. If you click the New Folder button, a new folder is created inside the active folder in the Save dialog box. You can then save your document into it. Not every program has this button; in fact, many don't. So don't get too used to it.

What usually happens is that you don't think about needing a new folder until the Save dialog box is on-screen. And in most Save dialog boxes, you can't do a thing about it.

What I do in these cases is to save my file on the desktop. Later, when I'm back in the Finder, I create a new folder in the proper place on my hard disk and then move the file from the desktop to its folder.

That's an 86: Cancel

The Cancel button dismisses the Save dialog box without saving anything anywhere. In other words, the Cancel button returns things to the way they were before you brought up the Save dialog box.

The keyboard shortcut for Cancel is Command-period (the Esc key sometimes works, too). I've said it before and I'll say it again: Command-period is a good command to memorize. It cancels almost all dialog boxes, and it also cancels lots of other things. If something is going on (for example, your spreadsheet is calculating or your database is sorting or your graphics program is rotating) and it's taking too long, try Command-period. It works (usually).

The Open/Save button: The exception to the rule

If you've been paying extra-careful attention to the illustrations, you've no doubt noticed that the button near the bottom sometimes says Save and other times says Open. I even called your attention to it a few pages ago. So? What gives?

In particular, how do you save something when there's no Save button (see Figure 5-8)?

Say I want to save the file Love Letter to Lisa in Folder 1. I navigate my way to Folder 1. I see it at the top in the drop-down menu. I'm ready to save it, but there's no Save button, as is the case in Figure 5-8.

Figure 5-8:
How do I
save when
this is what
you see?

That's because Folder 2 is selected in the file list box, and if a folder is selected in the file list box, the button says Open, not Save. To deselect Folder 2, click anywhere in the file list box except on Folder 2 or press the Tab key. When Folder 2 is no longer selected in the file list box, the Open button becomes the Save button, and you can now save. (See Figure 5-9.)

I know. It doesn't really make sense, but that's how it works. Try it a couple of times. It's not as straightforward as other parts of the Mac interface, but once you get it, you get it for life.

I could have just as easily pressed the Tab key instead of clicking. The net result would be exactly the same — the Open button would change to the Save button.

Figure 5-9:
The Open
button
changes to
the Save
button,
which
allows me
to save
Love Letter
to Lisa in
Folder 2.

If this little section confuses you, look again at Figures 5-8 and 5-9. Folder 1 is where I want to save the file. But there's no Save button in Figure 5-8 because a folder, Folder 2, is currently selected. When I click anywhere in the file list box (anywhere except on Folder 2) or press the Tab key on my keyboard, Folder 2 is deselected, the Open button changes into the Save button, and I can save the file named Love Letter to Lisa in Folder 1.

If you still aren't sure what all this stuff means, try it. It's not particularly intuitive, but it's relatively easy to get the hang of.

1. **Select Folder 2 in the file list box of the Save dialog box. (Folder 1 is the active folder.)**

2. **Click the file list box anywhere but on Folder 2. Notice the Open or Save button before and after you click.**

3. **Press the Tab key. Notice the Open or Save button before and after you press Tab.**

When the button says Save and you click the button or press Return or Enter, the file is saved in Folder 1. When the button says Open (because Folder 2 is selected) and you click the button or press Return, you move down one level and Folder 2 becomes the active folder.

Got it?

It Looks Like Save and It Acts Like Save, So Why Is It Called Save As?

The Save As command, which you can find in the File menu of almost every program ever made, lets you save a file that's already been saved and give it a different name.

Why might you want to do that? Let's say you have two sisters, Jodie and Zelda. You write Jodie a long, chatty letter. You save it as Letter to Jodie. Now you decide you want to send it to Zelda, too, but you want to change a few things. So you change the part about your date last night (Zelda isn't as liberated as Jodie) and replace all references to Steve (Jodie's husband) with Zeke (Zelda's husband). Aren't computers grand?

You've made those changes to Letter to Jodie, but you haven't saved again since you decided to make the changes. So now the document on your screen is actually a letter to Zelda, but its file name is still Letter to Jodie. Think of what would happen if you were to save now.

Save early, save often = no heartache

This is as good a time as any to talk about developing good saving habits. Needless to say, saving your work every few minutes is a very good idea.

Here's my advice:

✔ Always save before you switch to another program.

✔ Always save before you print a document.

✔ Always save before you stand up.

If you don't heed this advice and your Mac crashes while switching programs, printing, or sitting idle (which, not coincidentally, are the three most likely times for it to crash), you lose everything you've done since your last save.

Command-S is the keyboard shortcut for Save in almost every program I know. Memorize it. See it in your dreams. Train your finger muscles to do it unconsciously. Use it (the keyboard shortcut) or lose it (your unsaved work).

I'll tell you: If you save now, the file named Letter to Jodie will reflect the changes you just made. The stuff in the letter that was meant for Jodie will be blown away and replaced by the stuff you said to Zelda. If you save now, the file name Letter to Jodie will be inaccurate.

That's what Save As is for. If you use Save As now (it's a different command from Save — look on the File menu and see), you get a Save dialog box where you can type in a *different* file name. You can also navigate to another folder, if you like, and save the newly named version of the file there.

Now you have two files on your hard disk — Letter to Jodie and Letter to Zelda. Both contain the stuff they should.

That's what Save As is for.

Open (Sesame)

You already know how to use the Open dialog box; you just don't know you know yet.

Using the Open dialog box

Guess what? If you can navigate using a Save dialog box, you can navigate using an Open dialog box. They work exactly the same except for a couple of very minor differences.

First, there's no file name field. Of course not. This dialog box is the one you see when you want to open a file! There's no need for the file name field 'cause you're not saving a file.

There's also no New Folder button. You don't need it when you're opening a file. (It sure comes in handy when you're saving a file, though, doesn't it? Sure wish every program had one.)

Anyway, that's it. Those are the differences. Navigate the same way as you would in a Save dialog box. Don't forget your mantra, *"The Open and Save dialog boxes are just another view of the Finder."*

Figure 5-10 shows two different ways of viewing the same file. The Open dialog box, at top, has navigated to the file Love Letter to Lisa in Folder 3. I clicked the drop-down menu in the Open dialog box to show you the path to the file Love Letter to Lisa.

Below the Open dialog box is the Finder view of the path to the file Love Letter to Lisa.

Figure 5-10:
The Open dialog box, like the Save dialog box, is just a different view of the Finder.

If you aren't 100-percent comfortable with the relationship between the two views, please go back and try the hands-on exercises earlier in this chapter again. Please. Keep reviewing the pictures and instructions until you understand this concept. If you don't, your Mac will continue to confound and confuse you. Do yourself a favor — don't read any further until Open and Save dialog boxes feel like the most natural thing in the world to you.

A really big show — Show Preview

Okay, something else about the Open dialog box is different. As you can see in Figure 5-10, the Open dialog box for SimpleText has a check box called Preview. What does this little box do? It lets you create little previews for PICT files, which are the type of files created by many popular graphics programs. Click the check box and then click the Create button when a PICT file is highlighted in the file list. After a moment, a little picture will appear (see Figure 5-11). From now on, every time that file is highlighted in an Open dialog box, its preview picture automatically appears (as long as the Show Preview check box remains checked).

Figure 5-11:
The Preview area in this Open dialog box shows a small picture of what the file MOS85-FD. 0511.pict looks like.

As you might guess, previews are a nice feature to have. Many graphics programs include previews in their Open dialog boxes. At least one, Adobe Photoshop, creates a custom icon for its documents that reflects their contents when it saves them.

Unfortunately, you have to be in the icon view, which you know I dislike, to see these icons. Still, they're pretty cute.

Weird folder or file names

Every so often, you see some weird folder names — such as Move & Rename or Network Trash Folder or Desktop DB or DF or VM Storage — in the Open dialog box, but you don't see these folders when you look at the corresponding windows in the Finder. Don't worry. It's perfectly natural.

Here's what's going on:

Move & Rename and VM Storage are invisible files. You aren't supposed to see them. The System uses them to keep track of stuff that you don't need (or want) to know about. They're invisible when you look in your hard drive's window, but they show up in some applications' Open dialog boxes. This anomaly is known as a *bug*. You shouldn't be able to see those files. Just ignore them, and they won't bother you. If you're lucky, you won't even see them on your Mac (many people don't).

The last thing you need to know

Selectively displaying certain items in Open dialog boxes is a feature of most applications. When you use a program's Open dialog box, only files that the program knows how to open appear in the file list. In other words, the program filters out files that it can't open, so you don't see them cluttering up the Open dialog box. Pretty neat, eh?

On the other hand, not seeing every item in an Open dialog box can be a little disconcerting when you're trying to envision the correlation between the Finder and the Open dialog box. Just remember this: Stuff you see in the Finder doesn't always appear in the Open dialog box. That's why I showed you the Save dialog box first. It always includes everything. In a Save dialog box, items that you can't select appear grayed out, but they do appear. Open dialog boxes usually show only files that you can select and open with the current application.

So . . . if you know something is in a particular folder but you can't see it in the Open dialog box, consider that possibly the program you're using isn't capable of opening that kind of document (not every program can open every document).

Mac OS Easy Open, a standard part of the Mac OS, can often allow one program to open documents created by another program. If you can't see the document in the Open dialog box, quit the current program and find the file in the Finder (that is, open the folders it's in). When you open the document in the Finder, Mac OS Easy Open will kick in and offer you a list of programs on your hard disk that can open that particular type of document.

New-Style Open and Save Dialog Boxes?

One other thing. Really. Then you're done with opening and saving stuff. That thing is this: Mac OS 8.5 has a new style of Open and Save dialog boxes. The new-style dialog boxes are moveable, are resizeable, have the little expansion triangles like windows in the Finder do, and include buttons for shortcuts, recent items, and favorites. Though they look a little different (see Figure 5-12), they work pretty much the same as I describe in this chapter.

That's the good news. The bad news is that I don't know of any programs at present (Summer 1998) that use them. The reason is that programs need to be updated (revised/upgraded/rewritten/and so on) to display the new style of dialog boxes for opening and saving. And none that I know of have yet. In fact, even the programs Apple supplies with OS 8.5, such as SimpleText, PictureViewer, and MoviePlayer, use the old style of dialog boxes.

I did find one place you can look at a new-style Open dialog box — in the Fix Alias dialog box. To see it for yourself:

1. **Create a folder.**
2. **Make an alias of it.**
3. **Drag the original folder to the Trash and empty the Trash.**
4. **Double-click the alias.**
5. **Click the Fix Alias button.**

You should see something that looks like Figure 5-12.

Best of all, you'll be seeing a lot more like it as third-party software programmers update their software to use this nifty new Mac OS 8.5 feature.

Figure 5-12: A new-style Open dialog box. Notice the buttons at the top right. They are (left to right) shortcuts, recent stuff, and favorites.

Part II
Making It Purr

In this part . . .

The chapters in this part show you how to perform important hands-on tasks. But don't get all worked up: This stuff is easy. In fact, I think of this part as "The Lazy Person's How-To Guide."

Chapter 6 deals with how to organize your Mac. You discover, among other things, how to do routine file-management and navigating tasks the easy way.

Next is the how-to-print chapter, Chapter 7. It includes info on how to decipher Print options and plenty of other hows and whys that will help you become a modern-day Gutenberg.

In Chapter 8, you find out how to share. Files, that is. It's easy, it's convenient, it's free, and it beats the heck out of sneakernet.

Finally, there's a wonderful chapter (numbered, conveniently enough, 9) on how to manage memory (and other seemingly complicated arcana) — an easy-to-understand, almost jargon-free primer on how the whole memory thing works.

Chapter 6

File Management Made Simple

In This Chapter

▶ Using Launcher (or not)

▶ Getting yourself organized (or something like it)

▶ Using aliases

▶ Working with spring-loaded folders

I n Chapters 1 through 5, I detail for you the basics about windows and icons and menus. In this chapter, you apply that knowledge as you begin a never-ending quest to discover the fastest, easiest, most trouble-free way to manage the files on your Mac.

I can help. I'm not a doctor, but I play one in books and magazines. I've been wrangling with the Macintosh interface for more than ten years now, and I've learned a lot about what works and what doesn't — at least what works for me. This chapter will spare you at least part of the ten-year learning curve.

Remember, I'm talking about Mac OS here. And I'm talking about developing your own personal style. There is no right way to organize your files, no right way to use aliases, no right way to use the Apple menu, and no right way to use drag-and-drop. The only thing for sure is that these features are useless if you don't use them.

Please take the time to understand these wonderful features. They make your Mac so much easier to use. I'll show you how, and it's *easy*. After absorbing that info, you'll have all the ammunition you need to create your own personal Macintosh experience: a Mac environment designed by you, for you.

Launcher (Or Not)

Launcher is a control panel, introduced in System 7.5, that creates a window in the Finder with single-clickable icons that *launch* (open) frequently used files.

If you don't see Launcher, choose Apple menu⇨Control Panels⇨Launcher. If you want Launcher on all the time, choose Apple menu⇨Control Panels⇨ General Controls and click the box marked Show Launcher at system startup.

The advantage of Launcher is that the icons in the Launcher window can represent items in many different folders on your hard disk. (See Figure 6-1.)

Figure 6-1:
Launcher makes frequently used items available in a single convenient window, even if the items are in different folders as shown.

So Launcher, at least in theory, saves you time by saving you from rooting through folders every time you need one of those items.

Launcher is easy to configure. Just drag anything you want to add to the Launcher window onto the Launcher window.

Here's what happens when you drag an icon onto the Launcher window: Your Mac creates an alias of that icon and places that alias in the Launcher Items folder, which you'll find in your System Folder. (See Figure 6-2.)

Figure 6-2:
If an item's alias is in the Launcher Items folder, the item appears in the Launcher window.

If you want something to appear in the Launcher window, put an alias of it in the Launcher Items folder or drag its icon onto the Launcher window. To remove an item, hold down the Option key and drag it to the Trash. That's it. The whole enchilada.

Well, almost the whole enchilada. I feel obligated to mention one other feature. You can create categories for Launcher by creating folders in the Launcher Items folder and starting their names with the bullet character (•, which you create by pressing Option-8). This creates categories with different buttons for different stuff, as shown in Figure 6-3.

Figure 6-3: The secret for creating categories in Launcher is folders that start with a bullet.

For what it's worth, I couldn't find anything about Launcher in my Apple manual, but I got a great demo of this trick by searching for *Launcher* in Mac OS Help. Yet another reason for you to check out Apple's cool new Help system.

I think I've been objective up to this point. Now I'll tell you why I think Launcher stinks:

- ✔ It doesn't float in front of other Finder windows, so it's easy to lose behind other windows.

- ✔ It has only an icon view, so it wastes valuable screen real estate. (**Hint:** You can change the size of the icons by Command-clicking anywhere on the Launcher window except on an icon. But its smallest buttons are still larger than the smallest buttons you can have in Finder windows.)

- ✔ It can't be chosen from the Application menu.

- ✔ It's no different from a regular window in View as Button mode except for the stupid categories feature.

✔ Like the stupid View as Buttons view, Launcher uses single clicks to open icons, a clear violation of *Macintosh Human Interface Guidelines,* the bible of Macintosh interface design.

Gasp. So why did Apple start including Launcher, first with Performas and now in OS 8.5? And why, after ten years of rabid insistence that double-click means *open,* did Apple change its mind?

My take on it is that Apple is afraid that new users are too stupid to grasp the concept of double-clicking to open a file. And too stupid to realize that you can do everything Launcher does and more by customizing your Apple menu (as you can see later in this chapter).

I don't think you're that dumb. I say get rid of the lame-o Launcher. (See Chapter 14 for complete instructions on shuffling Launcher off this mortal coil.) And, for the most part, I eschew the Button views mostly on the grounds that it's too easy to accidentally open something by single-clicking it.

With what I present in this chapter, you can instead create your own customized environment, which I promise will let you find and launch items faster and more flexibly than Launcher or the clunky Button view.

On the other hand, if for some unfathomable reason you *like* Launcher or even the Button view, by all means enjoy them. Launcher doesn't use all that much disk space or RAM, so there's no great advantage to trashing it.

No advantage, that is, besides never seeing Launcher again (which I consider a big advantage). If a single-click file launcher tickles your fancy, there are plenty of excellent commercial and shareware utilities that make Launcher seem even crummier.

Getting Yourself Organized (Or Something Like It)

I won't pretend to be able to do this task for you. Organizing your files is as personal as your taste in music. You develop your own style with the Mac. So in this section, I give you some food for thought, some ideas about how I do it, and some suggestions that should make organization easier for you, regardless of how you choose to do it yourself.

And it's root, root, root for the root level

Root level refers to the window you see when you open your hard disk's icon. It's the first level down in the hierarchy of folders. How you organize the root level is a matter of taste, but let me try to give some guidance.

KISS: Keep It Simple, Stupid

I find that less is more when it comes to organizing files and folders. I try to use the simplest structure that meets my needs. For example, if I have more than a handful of icons at root level, I begin to look for ways to reorganize. I shoot for no more than ten items at root level; fewer is better.

At the very least . . .

Root level must contain the System Folder. It won't work properly if you put it somewhere else (like in another folder or on the desktop). Beyond that, what you place on the root level is up to you.

I think most people should start with two other folders, Applications and Documents, at the very least, but even these don't *have* to go at root level. The desktop is an equally good place for them, as you can see in a later section.

A full install of Mac OS 8.5 leaves a bunch of folders at root level in addition to your System Folder. To keep things tidy, create a new folder at root level called Mac OS 8.5 Stuff and put these folders inside it, as shown in Figure 6-4.

Figure 6-4:
Reducing
clutter on
your hard
disk with a
Mac OS 8.5
Stuff folder.

Documentary evidence: The Documents folder

Remember, you don't need to have a Documents folder, but if you do, here are some tips for organizing it:

- ✔ Don't create subfolders (within the Documents folder) until you need them.
- ✔ Creating a bunch of empty folders because you think that you might need them someday is more work than creating them when you need them. You end up opening an empty folder when you're looking for something else — a complete waste of time.

✔ I recommend saving everything in the Documents folder for a week or two (or a month or two, depending on how many new documents you save each day). Once a decent-size group of documents has accumulated in the Documents folder, take a look at them and create logical subfolders to put them into.

✔ Let your work style decide file structure.

You should create the subfolders based on a system that makes sense to you. Here are some ideas for subfolders:

✔ By type of document: Word-Processing Documents, Spreadsheet Documents, Graphics Documents

✔ By date: Documents May-June, Documents Spring '97

✔ By content: Memos, Outgoing Letters, Expense Reports

✔ By project: Project X, Project Y, Project Z

When things start to get messy and you start noticing some folders bulging (that is, filled up with tons of files), subdivide them again and use a combination of the methods I just mentioned.

For example, if you start by subdividing your Documents folder into four subfolders — Memos, Expense Reports, Letters, and Other Documents (as shown in Figure 6-5) — a few months later, when those folders begin to get full, you might subdivide them in one or more ways, as shown in Figure 6-6.

Figure 6-5:
A
Documents
folder
containing
four
subfolders.

The folder called Other Documents hasn't required subdividing yet, as it only contains four items so far.

The point is that your folder structure should be organic, growing as you need it to grow. Let it happen. Don't let any one folder get so full that it's a hassle to deal with. Create new subfolders when things start to get crowded.

How full is too full? That's impossible to say. If I find more than 15 or 20 files in a single folder, I begin thinking about ways to subdivide it. On the other hand, some of my subfolders that contain things I don't often need, such as

Figure 6-6:
The same
Documents
folder
several
months
later,
with new
subfolders
for three of
the original
four
subfolders.

my Correspondence 1992 folder, contain more than 100 files. Because I don't use the folder all that much (but want to keep it on my hard disk just in case), its overcrowded condition doesn't bother me. Your mileage may vary.

After almost ten years of growth, my Documents folder contains only about 20 subfolders, most of which contain their own subfolders. (See Figure 6-7.) Being a nonconformist, I call my Documents folder Stuff.

Figure 6-7:
My
Documents
folder
and its
subfolders.

Other folders at root level

You can follow this same philosophy for other folders at root level, sub-dividing them as needed. If you use a particular folder a great deal, move it from the Documents folder to root level or to the desktop (more about that in a few pages) to make it easier to use. For example, if you write a lot of letters, keep your Correspondence folder at root level or on the desktop. And so on.

The only thing I want to caution you against is storing stuff in the System Folder that doesn't belong there. There's no harm in it, but the System Folder is already the repository for many files used by the System software and by applications. For most people, the System Folder is the most crowded folder on their disk, so sticking items that don't belong in it would only cause further clutter. Word-processing documents and spreadsheets (and indeed almost all documents) don't belong in the System Folder. You know how the file system works. Create a folder somewhere else for your documents.

Other than that, the only rule is that there are no rules. Whatever works for you is the best way. And don't forget Find File if you lose something!

Apply here: The Applications folder

I recommend having an Applications folder for all your programs. The best place for this folder is either at root level or on the desktop. Your Applications folder can also be subdivided when the need arises. Given what I do for a living, I have a lot of programs, so my Applications folder has subfolders for business programs, graphics programs, writing tools, utilities, toys, and online (modem) stuff, as shown in Figure 6-8.

Figure 6-8: My Apps folder contains six subfolders.

It'll probably be a while before you need so many subfolders — unless you're like me and try a lot of new software. Either way, organize your applications the same way you organize your documents — in a way that makes sense to you. Follow this advice, and I promise that you'll always be able to find what you're looking for.

The Greatest Thing Since Sliced Bread: Aliases

When System 7 first arrived several years ago, many of its features were heralded as breakthroughs. But of these features, none has proved to be more useful than the alias.

An *alias* is a quick-opener for another file. With aliases, a file can seem to be in two (or more) places at once. When you create an alias of a disk, file, or folder, opening its alias is the same as opening the item. And an alias takes up only the tiniest bit of disk space.

Why is this feature so great? First, it lets you put items in more than one place, which on many occasions is exactly what you want to do. For example, keeping an alias of your word processor on your desktop and another in your Apple menu is convenient. You may even want a third alias of it in your Documents folder for quick access. Aliases let you open your word processor quickly and easily without navigating into the depths of your Applications folder each time you need it.

Here's another example: If you write a memo to Fred Smith about the Smythe Marketing Campaign to be executed in the fourth quarter, which folder does the document go in? Smith? Smythe? Marketing? Memos? 4th Quarter?

With aliases, it doesn't matter. You can put the actual file in any of the folders and then create aliases of the file and place them in all the other folders. So whichever folder you open, you'll be able to find the memo.

Finally, many programs need to remain in the same folder as their supporting files and folders. Some programs won't function properly unless they are in the same folder as their dictionaries, thesauruses, data files (for games), templates, and so on. Ergo, you can't put those programs on the desktop or in the Apple Menu Items folder without impairing their functionality.

Icons on the desktop

How about a little hands-on training? You can create an alias for your favorite application and put it on the desktop, a very good place for it.

1. **Find your favorite application — ClarisWorks, Microsoft Word, Myth: The Fallen Lords, whatever — and select its icon, not the folder that it's in. Be sure to select the program's icon.**

2. **Choose File⇨Make Alias or press Command-M, as shown in Figure 6-9.**

   An alias of the application appears right next to the original. The alias's file name will be the same as the original's, except that it is in italics and has the word *alias* appended at the end.

Figure 6-9:
Make an
alias of
your very
favorite
program.

3. **Drag the alias onto the desktop and move it to a convenient place.**

   Under your hard disk icon is one prime location. (See Figure 6-10.) Along the bottom of the screen is another.

Figure 6-10:
Right under
your hard
disk icon is
an excellent
place to put
a frequently
used alias.

There. You've just made it easier to use your favorite program. Next time you need your favorite program, just open its alias right there on your desktop instead of opening several folders and cluttering up your screen.

Frequently used folders or documents are good candidates for aliases on the desktop. In fact, any icon you use more than a couple of times a day is a good candidate for an alias on the desktop.

Remember, aliases don't take up much disk space (a measly 3K or 4K each), so there's no penalty for making an alias and later deciding that you don't like it. Big deal. Drag it to the Trash.

The temporary alias theory

I use a lot of *temporary* aliases on my desktop. When I first create a file, I save it in its proper folder inside my Documents folder somewhere. If it's a document that I plan to work on for more than a day or two, such as a magazine article, I make an alias of the document (or folder) and put it on the desktop. When the article is done and I've submitted it to my editor, I trash the alias. The original file is already stashed away in its proper folder.

With bigger projects like books, which have multiple subfolders of their own, I keep an alias of the parent folder on the desktop for easy access. When I submit the last chapter, the alias goes into the Trash.

Incidentally, a similar technique can be used without the aliases. Just save all your new documents on the desktop (click the Desktop button in the Save dialog box or use the shortcut Command-D). Later, when you're done with them, you can file them away in their proper folders.

My point is that the desktop is an excellent place for the things that you need most often. Whether you use aliases of documents or save the actual files on the desktop until you figure out where you want to store them, the desktop is a fine place for the things you use most. Keep frequently used programs on the desktop forever and use the desktop as a temporary parking place for current projects.

Whatever you do, I encourage you to do it on the desktop.

What a drag it is not to drop

Macintosh drag-and-drop deals with dragging text and graphics from one place to another. But there's another angle to drag-and-drop, one that has to do with documents and icons.

You can use drag-and-drop to open a file using a program other than the one that would ordinarily launch when you open the document. This concept is easier to show than to tell, so follow along on your own computer:

1. **Make a screen shot picture of your desktop by holding down the Command and Shift keys and pressing the 3 key. Command-Shift-3 takes a picture of your desktop.**

2. **You hear a cute snapshot sound, and a document called Picture 1 automatically appears in your hard disk's root level window. Open it.**

3. **Assuming that there's a copy of SimpleText on your hard disk, SimpleText launches and displays Picture 1.**

   But you don't want to use SimpleText. SimpleText can open and display a picture file but can't make changes to it. You want to open the picture with a program that can edit it. What do you do? Use drag-and-drop.

4. **Quit SimpleText.**

5. **Drag the icon for Picture 1 onto the alias of your favorite program that you created earlier. Figure 6-11 shows how I made changes to Picture 1.**

If the alias of your favorite program didn't get highlighted when you dragged Picture 1 on top of it, or if dragging Picture 1 onto the alias launched the program but didn't open Picture 1, then your favorite program isn't capable of opening picture files.

Figure 6-11:
After dragging Picture 1 onto the Photoshop icon, I was able to make a few minor changes to it. . . .

Your solution if your favorite program can't open Picture 1: Get a different favorite program. Just kidding. The solution is to try dragging Picture 1 onto other program icons (or aliases of program icons) until you find one that opens it. When you do, you might want to put an alias of that application on the desktop, too.

What happens if you don't have a copy of SimpleText on your hard disk when you try to open Picture 1? Mac OS Easy Open kicks in and offers you a choice of other programs that can open it. (See Figure 6-12.)

Figure 6-12:
Mac OS
Easy Open
lets you
choose
from
compatible
applications
if you try to
open a
document
created by
a program
you don't
have on
your hard
disk.

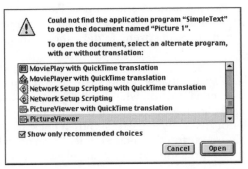

When I trashed SimpleText and tried to open Picture 1, Figure 6-12 is what I saw. In a more technical book, I'd go on to explain about file type and creator codes and how they have to do with which program gets launched when you open a document. But this is *Mac OS 8.5 For Dummies,* so I won't.

Suffice it to say that Mac OS 8.5 is smart enough to figure out which applications on your hard disk can open what documents and offer you a choice. Earlier versions weren't that smart.

Spring has sprung: Meet your nifty new spring-loaded folders

Speaking of dragging and dropping, Mac OS 8.5 has a new wrinkle that makes dragging and dropping less of a drag: the useful and usable spring-loaded folders. Spring-loaded folders make folders spring open temporarily when you hold an item over them.

To turn on spring-loaded folders and give them a try:

1. **Make the Finder the active application.**

2. **Choose Edit⇨Preferences.**

3. **Click the General tab at the top of the window; then click the spring-loaded folders check box.**

4. **Set the Delay Before Opening slider to Short (at least for this demo).**

Now grab an icon in the Finder, any icon, and drag it onto the System Folder icon. Don't release the mouse button. There. See how the System Folder springs open automatically when you hold an icon on top of it? That's spring-loaded folders in action.

If you can stand more excitement, drag the icon you're holding onto the Preferences folder (or any other subfolder in the System Folder) without releasing the mouse button. That folder springs open. Finally, without releasing the mouse button, drag the icon away from any windows or folder icons or drag it into the menu bar. All sprung folders should magically spring shut.

One other nice thing about spring-loaded folders is that you can use them without even dragging any icons. Just do what I call a "one-and-a-half-click" on any icon when spring-loaded folders are turned on. To do this, click once on the target icon (folder or disk only, please) and then click again quickly, but do not release the mouse button the second time. If you keep holding the button down, the cursor turns into a magnifying glass and you can cruise through your folders, spring-loaded style. (See Figure 6-13.)

Figure 6-13:
A click and a half gives me the magnifying glass cursor that indicates that I'm browsing via spring-loaded folders.

Smart Apple menu tricks

Remember when I called the Launcher lame earlier in this chapter? Here's something way better. I talk a bit about the Apple menu in Chapter 4; now I show you how to make it work for you.

First, make sure that you've turned the wonderful submenus on in the Apple Menu Options control panel. If you don't see little black triangles to the right of all the folders in the Apple menu, they're not turned on.

Now do something useful. Make a file launcher that enables you to open every file on your hard disk from a single Apple menu item.

The hard-disk-alias-in-the-Apple-menu trick

1. **Select your hard disk icon and make an alias of it by selecting your hard drive and choosing File⇨Make alias or by using the shortcut Command-M.**

2. **Put the alias of your hard disk in the Apple Menu Items folder (which is in your System Folder).**

3. **Pull down the Apple menu and admire your handiwork.**

If having your hard drive on the Apple menu is too overwhelming for you, consider putting an alias of your Documents folder or your Applications folder in the Apple menu. It's easy, it's fast, and it's convenient. Get in the habit of putting frequently used items (it's not just for desk accessories and folders anymore) in the Apple menu. You'll be glad you did.

A quick trick for adding an alias to the Apple menu

1. **Select the icon of the item that you want to appear in the Apple menu.**

2. **Choose Apple menu⇨Automated Tasks⇨Add Alias to Apple Menu.**

This script automatically creates an alias of the selected item and puts it in the Apple Menu Items folder.

The old alias-of-the-Apple-Menu-Items-folder-on-the-desktop trick

Are you growing fonder of your Apple menu? You should be. It's a great resource and it's easy to customize. If you find yourself customizing yours a lot, make an alias of the Apple Menu Items folder and put it on your desktop for easy access.

If you make frequent changes to your Apple menu, this tip saves you at least one step. And here's another tip: You can also put an alias of the Apple Menu Items folder in the Apple menu so that you can select it even if a window is covering the alias on your desktop.

When you put an alias of the Apple Menu Items folder in your Apple menu, it won't have subfolders, which makes sense when you think about it. If it had subfolders, they would create an endless loop.

By the way, I reveal some more very cool Apple menu tricks in Chapter 11.

Chapter 7

Publish or Perish: The Fail-Safe Guide to Printing

- -

- -

*P*rinting is like being. It just is. Or at least it should be. It should be as simple as pressing Command-P and then pressing the Return or Enter key. And usually that's how it is. Except when it isn't, and printing turns into a raging nightmare.

You won't be having any nightmares. If you get your printer and printing software configured properly, printing is simple as can be. And that's pretty darn simple.

So this is a chapter about avoiding nightmares. I go through the entire process as if you just unpacked a new printer and plugged it in. If you upgraded from an earlier version of Mac OS and are able to print with Mac OS 8.5 already, you can probably skip some of the steps. The objective here is to familiarize yourself with the printing process from start to finish.

One thing I suggest is that you read the documentation that came with your specific printer. There are hundreds of different printer makes and models available for the Mac, so I may contradict something that your printer manual says. If you run into this discrepancy, try it the way the manual says first. If that doesn't work, try my way.

Another thing you need to know is that every application can use its own custom print and Page Setup dialog box. Though many look like the ones in this chapter, others don't. For example, the Print and Page Setup dialog boxes for Microsoft Word include choices I don't cover in this chapter, such as Even or Odd Pages Only, Print Hidden Text, and Print Selection Only. If you see commands in your Print or Page Setup dialog boxes that I don't explain in this chapter, they're specific to that application and should be explained in its documentation. I use Apple's SimpleText program for this demonstration.

Don't forget about Balloon Help and Mac OS Help. Many programs support these excellent Apple technologies; they can be the fastest way to figure out a feature that has you stumped.

I'll get started then. In previous editions of this book, I said, "Begin by connecting the printer to the Printer port on the back of your Mac (with both the Mac and the printer turned off, of course — but you knew that, didn't you?)." These days I have to change it to "Begin by connecting the printer to the *appropriate* port. . . ." That's because these days printers don't always connect to the Printer port. Some printers connect to the Ethernet port. Others connect through the USB port. So read the instructions that came with your printer and plug it into the appropriate hole in your Mac.

If you don't have a cable (and many Apple printers don't come with cables), contact your printer manufacturer and ask where it is. Plug the printer into an outlet. Turn it on. If the printer came with software, install it on your hard disk, following the instructions that came with the printer. That's it.

Ready, set, print!

Ready: Choosing a Printer in (What Else?) the Chooser DA

The path to printing perfection begins with the humble Chooser DA. In earlier versions of the Mac OS, it was a necessary evil, but with Mac OS 8.5's desktop printers, you'll use it once to set up your printer, and under ordinary circumstances, you'll rarely use it again.

Many of the steps involving the Chooser require that the printer be turned on and warmed up, so if yours isn't, it should be. Do that now so that you can choose a printer.

From the Apple menu, grab the Chooser. The Chooser desk accessory opens. If you have previously chosen a printer, its icon is selected when the Chooser opens; if you've never printed before, the Chooser appears with no printer icon selected.

The Chooser is also where you choose network connections. You will see an icon for AppleShare and may also see one for your fax modem. Don't mess with them yet. I talk about File Sharing in the next chapter.

If no icon is selected in your Chooser, click the printer icon that matches your printer. If you have an Apple printer, one of the icons should match it. If you have an Apple printer and none of the icons match your printer, try clicking the one that sounds most like your printer.

If you have a non-Apple printer, see its manual for instructions on installing printer drivers for your printer. Or try clicking one of the Apple printer drivers. (If it's a laser printer, try LaserWriter 8; if it's an inkjet, try the StyleWriter 1200.)

Most of the icons in the Chooser represent *printer drivers.* Printer drivers translate between your Mac applications and your printer, ensuring that what you see is what you print. Technically, a printer driver is a special piece of software called a Chooser extension. When you drag a printer driver onto your System Folder, Mac OS 8.5 automatically places it in the Extensions folder for you. As long as a printer driver is in the Extensions folder, you should see an icon for it in the Chooser.

If you have a printer made by someone other than Apple, you may want to contact the manufacturer about getting the latest, greatest driver. Many printer manufacturers are offering new drivers with enhanced functionality. If you have a modem, you may find new drivers for your printer on America Online or the Internet. Check with your printer manufacturer for details.

Apple printer drivers are installed automatically when you install the Mac OS. You remove them by dragging them from the Extensions folder to the Trash. It's perfectly safe to remove printer drivers for printers that you never intend to use. Removing unneeded printer drivers can free up more than a megabyte of hard disk space.

Now I want to get down to business. The left side of the Chooser should be displaying a selection of printer icons; the right side of the Chooser should be displaying either your printer's name (see Figure 7-1) or a pair of icons (see Figure 7-2).

If you've never used a printer with Mac OS 8.5, you may see a warning box that says, "If the printer you wish to use has not been set up, please click the Setup button." If that happens, do what it says. If there's an "Auto Setup" button there, use it.

Figure 7-1:
The Chooser DA as it appears when you select an AppleTalk printer.

Figure 7-2:
The right side of the Chooser DA as it appears when you select a serial printer.

If you have an AppleTalk printer

If you have an AppleTalk printer, click your printer's name on the right side of the Chooser to select it — even if only one name appears, as shown in Figure 7-1.

If you have a serial printer

If you have a serial printer, you'll see two icons on the right side of the Chooser instead of a printer name. Choose whichever port — Printer or Modem — the printer cable is connected to on the back of your Mac.

If you have a SCSI, Ethernet, USB, or server-based printer

If you have a SCSI, Ethernet, USB, or server-based printer, you're on your own. What you see on the right side of the Chooser depends on the printer's manufacturer or your server's setup. I couldn't beg or borrow one, so I don't know what you'll see. With luck, you'll figure it out.

My printer is a Hewlett Packard LaserJet 4ML, a compact, inexpensive 300-dots-per-inch PostScript AppleTalk laser printer. I've had the HP for more than three years now and it has performed like a champ. At some point I plan to upgrade to a 600- or 800-dpi printer, but it's not mission-critical as long as the faithful HP keeps chugging along.

The AppleTalk Active/Inactive radio buttons

Okay. Here's something I can help you with. Should AppleTalk be active or inactive? My answer: Inactive unless you need it.

How do you know if you need AppleTalk? Well, for starters, if you're on a network and use File Sharing, you need it. If your printer is an AppleTalk-only printer (many are), you need it. If you're in neither of these situations, you probably don't need AppleTalk. There's no reason to keep it turned on if you don't need it.

If in doubt, just give it a try. You'll know if your printer works with AppleTalk inactive if your printer spits out a page.

That's it for the Chooser. Go ahead and close it. A desktop printer will be created automatically on your desktop for the printer you chose. I talk much more about those desktop printers later in the chapter. For now, just know that if for some strange reason you hate it, you can trash it later. (But, much like the proverbial bad penny, it'll keep coming back every time you select a printer in the Chooser.)

Before you close the Chooser . . .

I go through the rest of this exercise using my printer, an AppleTalk printer, as the example. If you have a different kind of printer — a serial, SCSI, or server — and you can print to your printer at this point (close the Chooser, open a document, and choose File⇨Print — if the document comes out of the printer, you can print to your printer), everything in the rest of the chapter should work the same for you.

Set: Setting Up Your Page with Page Setup

The hard part is done. Now you should be able to print a document quickly and easily. Right? Not so fast, bucko. Though you may not need it right this second, you need to know about the Page Setup dialog box.

Almost every program that can print a document has a Page Setup command on its File menu. Some programs call it Page Setup and others call it Print Setup. (Print Setup is the quaint, old-fashioned term, more popular in the System 6 era than today.) Either way, this dialog box lets you choose paper type, page orientation, scaling percent, page flipping, and page inverting.

The Page Setup dialog box should look like Figure 7-3.

Figure 7-3:
The Page
Setup
dialog box.

Paper type

The objective here is to choose the type of paper currently in the paper tray of your printer or the type of paper that you're about to feed manually.

To do so, click the Paper pop-up menu (see Figure 7-4) and choose the type of paper you plan to use for your next print job.

Figure 7-4:
Choosing a
paper type
in the Page
Setup
dialog box.

Page Setup dialog box settings remain in effect until you change them. So if you are printing an envelope this time, don't forget to change back to US Letter before trying to print to letter-size paper.

Page orientation

Page Orientation lets you tell the printer whether the page you're about to print is a portrait-oriented (letter, longways) or landscape-oriented (spreadsheet, sideways) page. (See Figure 7-5.)

Figure 7-5:
Portrait
(left) and
landscape
(right)
pages.

The Page Setup dialog box offers a choice of portrait or landscape, as shown in Figure 7-6.

Figure 7-6:
Portrait
(left) and
landscape
(right)
orientation
buttons in
the Page
Setup
dialog box.

Scale

The Scale control (see Figure 7-7) lets you print pages bigger or smaller than their size on the screen.

Figure 7-7:
The Scale
control lets
you enlarge
or reduce
your image
for printing.
This setting
(200%)
doubles the
size of my
printout.

Just type a new value into the text entry box, replacing the number 100 (200 in Figure 7-7). In old-style Page Setup dialog boxes, you can also use the arrow buttons on the screen to change the value.

The range of scaling is 25 percent to 400 percent. If you try to enter a higher or lower number, your Mac beeps at you and changes it automatically to the closest acceptable number. Nice touch.

To see the statistics on the left in *your* Page Setup dialog box, just click the dog. Click again to see them in centimeters.

PostScript options

But wait, there's more. The Page Setup dialog box offers two additional sets of options if you choose PostScript Options from the pop-up menu (see Figure 7-8) — Visual Effects and Images & Text.

Figure 7-8: PostScript Options in the Page Setup dialog box.

Visual Effects

Flipping the page vertically or horizontally merely requires that you check the appropriate check box. The dogcow on the miniature page reflects your choices. (See Figure 7-9.)

Figure 7-9: The miniature page featuring Clarus the Dogcow (Moof!) provides visual feedback for your choices of Visual Effects.

The tail of the dogcow

The dogcow has appeared in the Page Setup dialog box since time immemorial. He is a kind of unofficial Macintosh mascot. His name, they say, is Clarus. His bark, they say, is *Moof.*

As you can see in Figure 7-9, Clarus is more than just a mascot. He's an elegant way to give you visual feedback on your choices. Look at Figure 7-9. It works.

Checking the Invert Image option inverts your page, making light areas dark and dark areas light, like a photograph negative.

Note that this option generally uses a lot of toner or ink. And printing a large number of inverted pages could cause a laser printer to overheat or an inkjet printer to clog. So use this feature sparingly.

I suppose that the Invert Image option is useful for creating artsy effects or making negative images of documents that will be printed to film. I've never used it in the 12 years I've used a Mac.

Image & Text

These next five options are thrilling. I could spend two pages explaining them, but I'm going to invoke another weasel-out (see Chapter 1) and tell you to look at the Balloon Help to find out what they do.

To do that, while the Page Setup PostScript Options dialog box is on the screen, choose Show Balloons from the Help (question mark) menu and point at each of the five check boxes, as shown in Figure 7-10.

Figure 7-10:
Balloon Help explains these five check boxes almost as well as I could. It'll save a tree (part of one, at least), too.

LaserWriter 8 Page Setup   8.6b3

PostScript™ Options

Visual Effects:
☐ Flip Horizontal
☐ Flip Vertical
☐ Invert Image

Image & Text:
☑ Substitute Fonts
☑ Smooth Text
☑ Smooth Graphics
☐ Precision Bitmap
☐ Unlimited Down

When this checkbox is selected, the printer substitutes the Times font for New York, Helvetica for Geneva, and Courier for Monaco, producing higher-quality text.

One last thing . . .

Most programs also offer their own Page Setup choices. To see them (if your program offers them, of course), choose the program from the pop-up menu below the words "LaserWriter 8 Page Setup." Photoshop and Microsoft Word have them (see Figures 7-11 and 7-12); SimpleText doesn't.

Figure 7-11:
Photoshop's
Page Setup
choices.

LaserWriter 8 Page Setup   8.6b3

Adobe Photoshop® 5.0 ◊

Screen...   Border...   ☐ Calibration Bars   ☐ Labels
Transfer... Bleed...   ☐ Registration Marks ☐ Negative
Background... ☐ Caption   ☐ Corner Crop Marks   ☐ Emulsion Down
                          ☐ Center Crop Marks   ☐ Interpolation

Cancel   OK

Figure 7-12:
Microsoft
Word's
Page Setup
choices.

LaserWriter 8 Page Setup   8.6b3

Microsoft Word ◊

Custom...   No custom page size selected.   Margins...
                                                           Print...
Apply Size and Orientation To: Default...
Whole document ◊

Cancel   OK

The Print Dialog Box: Printing to Most Printers

Now I come to the final step before that joyous moment when your printed page pops out of the printer. It's the Print dialog box, and it's the last thing standing between you and your output.

Though most of you will see Print dialog boxes that look like the ones in this chapter, others won't. The features in the Print dialog box are strictly a function of the program with which you're printing. Many programs choose to use the standard-issue Apple dialog boxes as shown in this chapter, but others don't. If a feature isn't explained in this chapter, chances are it's a feature that's specific to the application that you're using and should be explained in that program's documentation.

Your printer is chosen in the Chooser. Your page is set up in Page Setup. If, up to this point, you haven't been working with a document that you want to print, find one now and open it because it's time to . . .

1. Choose File⇨Print (Command-P).

One of the best things about the Mac is that Apple has published a set of guidelines that all Mac programs should use. Consistency among programs is one of the Mac's finest features. Notice how 99 percent of all programs have Open, Close, Save, Save As, Page Setup, Print, and Quit commands in their File menus and Undo, Cut, Copy, and Paste commands in their Edit menus. That's the kind of thing *Macintosh Human Interface Guidelines* recommends.

According to Apple's guidelines, the Print command should always appear in the File menu, which is good. *Macintosh Human Interface Guidelines* also says that the keyboard shortcut Command-P should be reserved for plain text (the way Command-B is often used for bold and Command-I for italic). This is bad.

Fortunately, software developers listened to Apple about the first item and ignored Apple about the second, so Command-P is almost always the shortcut for the Print command in the File menu.

Every so often you come across a program that doesn't follow these conventions, but I'd say at least 90 percent of commercial Mac programs put the Print command in the File menu and use Command-P for its keyboard shortcut.

The point is that there is a slight chance that Step 1 won't work for you. If the Print command is on a different menu, if there is no Print command, or the keyboard shortcut is anything but Command-P, you'll have to wing it.

Then write the software company a brief note mentioning that they *could* make things easier on everyone by putting the Print command in the proper place and using the generally-agreed-upon keyboard shortcut.

Anyway, the Print dialog box appears. It looks like Figure 7-13 when it first appears.

The Print dialog box has a pop-up menu that offers seven options. (See Figure 7-14.) I go through these options and their suboptions one at a time.

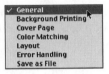

Figure 7-13:
The general
Print
dialog box.

Figure 7-14:
The Print
dialog box's
pop-up
options
menu.

The Print⇨General dialog box

The choices you make in the Print⇨General dialog box are

- ✔ How many copies to print
- ✔ Which page numbers to print
- ✔ Automatic or manual feed paper
- ✔ Which printer to use for this print job
- ✔ Destination: printer or PostScript file
- ✔ Whether to save these settings permanently

Try pressing the Tab key and watching what happens. The active field jumps to each of the text fields in the dialog box in rotation. Shift-Tab makes the active field jump backward. Try it; you'll like it.

Copies

How many copies do you want to print? The Print dialog box defaults to one copy in most applications, so you'll probably see a 1 in this field when the dialog box appears. Assuming that's the case, don't do anything if you only want to print one copy. If you want to print more than one copy of your document, select the 1 that appears in the Copies field and type in a new number. (See Figure 7-15.)

Figure 7-15:
To print 13 copies, replace the 1 with 13.

Pages

Which pages do you want to print? All of them? Or just some? This option is easy. If you want to print your entire document, click the All radio button. If you only want to print a specific page or range of pages, type their numbers in the From and To text entry boxes.

For example, say you have a ten-page document. You print the whole thing and then notice a typo on page 2. You fix the typo and then print only page 2 by typing a 2 in both the From and To fields, as shown in Figure 7-16.

You can type any valid range of pages into the From and To fields.

Figure 7-16:
Here's how to print only the second page of a document.

Pages: ◯ All
⦿ From: 2   To: 2

Paper source

Your choices are Paper Cassette or Manual Feed for your first page or all your pages.

If you plan to use the paper in your printer's paper tray, choose Cassette. If you plan to feed a single sheet, choose Manual Feed.

If you want the first page to come from one place and the remaining pages to come from another, click the appropriate radio button and make the appropriate choices from the pop-up menus.

It's that simple.

Destination: Printer or PostScript file

The pop-up menu in the dialog box's upper-right corner lets you choose to print to your printer or create a PostScript file on disk instead. When you choose File, the Print button becomes a Save button. When you click the Save button, a standard Save dialog box appears.

Save Settings

This button saves the current settings and makes them the default for future print jobs. If everything is just as you like it, click this button and all future print jobs will use these settings.

The Print⇨Background Printing dialog box

Choosing Background Printing from the Print dialog box's pop-up menu lets you turn background printing on or off and set a print time if you so desire. (See Figure 7-17.)

Figure 7-17:
The Print
dialog box's
Background
Printing
options.

Print in foreground or background

Background printing has been around for a while. It's the thing that allows you to continue using your Macintosh while it's printing. Wonderful stuff.

It didn't used to be that way. In the bad old days, in the pre–System 6 era when there was no background printing, you sat and waited until the printing was done before you could use your Mac again.

Under Mac OS 8.5, background printing is turned on unless you specifically turn it off. You may notice your Mac feeling a little twitchy or jerky when a document is printing in the background. That's normal. Ignore it. After a while, you hardly notice it at all. And it's much better than the alternative — being unable to work until your print job is done.

Print time

To set a printing time for your document (see Figure 7-17), click the radio button next to your desired print time priority. Here's what the priorities mean:

- ✔ The Normal option prints the document now. If other documents are in the print queue, it takes its place behind documents printed before it.

- ✔ The Urgent option prints the document now and places it ahead of any documents in the print queue.

- ✔ The Print at option lets you choose a specific time. When you click its radio button, you can adjust the time and date.

- ✔ The Put Document on Hold option lets you prepare a document for printing but not print it at this time.

The Print⇨Cover Page dialog box

Clicking the Before Document or After Document radio button (see Figure 7-18) adds a page at the beginning or end of your print job. The cover page contains your name, the program and document names, the date and time, and the printer name. In other words, a page that looks pretty much like this:

User: Bob LeVitus
Application: Microsoft Word
Document: Great American Novel
Date: Wednesday, Aug 12, 1998
Time: 3:54:02 PM
Printer: HP LaserJet 4ML

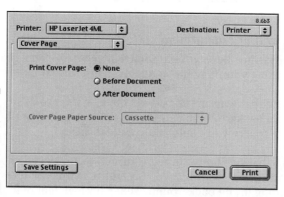

Figure 7-18:
The Print
dialog box's
Cover Page
options.

I may have used this feature once in the past ten years. I suppose if you're on a network sharing a printer, you may have a reason to waste trees by printing useless pages with hardly anything on them. But unless you must have a cover page, leave the None button selected and save a tree.

The Print⇨Color Matching dialog box

Here's where you choose from Black and White, Color/Grayscale, or ColorSync Color Matching for your output. (See Figure 7-19.) Use your best guess.

Figure 7-19:
The Print dialog box's Color Matching options.

The Print⇨Layout dialog box

Choose the number of pages per printed sheet and whether or not you prefer a border. (See Figure 7-20.)

Figure 7-20:
The Print dialog box's Layout options.

The Print⇨Error Handling dialog box

This dialog box provides options in case a PostScript error occurs; leave it alone unless you have a reason to change it.

The Print⇨Save As File dialog box

These options let you save your file as a PostScript file on disk. One pop-up menu lets you choose between raw PostScript and several flavors of Encapsulated PostScript. Another pop-up menu lets you include no fonts, all fonts, or only nonstandard fonts. (Nonstandard fonts are fonts other than the ones the Install Mac OS program installs.) Choose whichever setting is appropriate for the recipient of your document.

The safest bet is to include all fonts, just in case. The downside to this solution is that the PostScript file will be much larger than the original. For example, a SimpleText file of mine uses only 5K of disk space in its original form (that is, saved as a SimpleText document). When I save it as a PostScript file with all fonts included, it grows more than tenfold, requiring a whopping 80K of disk space.

Several things can inflate the size of the PostScript file. Including all fonts adds a lot of K. High-resolution images add a lot of K. And long documents use a lot of K. It's common for color artwork or page layout documents printed to disk as PostScript files to be larger than a high-density floppy disk. So if you plan to save a PostScript file to your hard disk and then copy it to a floppy disk, you may have to use a backup or compression utility to segment the file so that it will fit on several floppy disks. Or use a Zip disk or some other high-capacity storage option.

I can't tell you much about the PostScript Level and Data Format choices; ask the people to whom you're sending the file if they have a preference.

One last thing . . .

StyleWriter and StyleWriter II users, as well as users of other inkjet printers and/or non-PostScript printers, may see slightly different versions of the Print and Page Setup dialog boxes. The differences should be minor enough not to matter.

Desktop Printers

Desktop printers are unique and a huge improvement over earlier printing schemes; the new architecture for printing makes the entire experience easier.

What is a desktop printer, anyway?

A desktop printer is an icon on your desktop that represents a printer that is connected to your computer. It's created automatically when you select a printer in the Chooser DA. To print a document, drag its icon onto a desktop printer. (See Figure 7-21.)

In Figure 7-21, when I release the mouse, Great American Novel will print.

Figure 7-21:
Drag and
drop
printing
with
desktop
printer
icons.

Technically, Microsoft Word, the application that created the Great American Novel document, will launch, and its Print dialog box will open automatically. Click the Print button, or press Return or Enter, and the document will print and then Word will quit automatically.

What if Word isn't available? If you have a translator that can open Word documents, you see a dialog box where you can choose another application. If you don't have a compatible application or translator, you see an error message telling you that the document cannot be opened.

You create new desktop printers with the Chooser desk accessory.

Using desktop printers

Before I talk about using desktop printers, I need to tell you why you should use desktop printers. Three words: They save steps. Rather than open a document, choose File⇨Print, and diddle around in the Print dialog box, you can drag that document onto a desktop printer, click Print (or press Return or Enter), and then go out for a Jolt cola or whatever. In a word, it's easy. No muss, no fuss. Just drag and drop and click (or press), and in a few moments, paper starts popping out of your printer.

So basically, you use desktop printers by dragging documents onto them. As long as the application that created the documents is available, they'll be printed after you click Print (or press Return or Enter) with no further ado.

Another handy use for desktop printers is to create desktop printers for special kinds of print jobs. For example, create one for envelopes that uses the landscape, manual feed, and black and white settings. Create another for grayscale portrait mode printing. And so on. Just drag your file onto the appropriate desktop printer (be sure to give it a descriptive name) and you avoid all those messy adjustments in the Page Setup and Print dialog boxes.

But there's more to using desktop printers than just drag-and-drop. When you select a desktop printer (by single-clicking it), a new Printing menu appears in the menu bar, as shown in Figure 7-22. To view the print queue, open the desktop printer icon. (In case you forgot, you open an item by double-clicking its icon or by selecting its icon and choosing File⇨Open [Command-O].)

Figure 7-22:
The
Desktop
Printer
window and
menu.

You'll notice a set of tape recorder–like icons in the Desktop Printer window. From left to right, these are Stop the Print Queue, Start the Print Queue, Set the Print Time for the Selected Item or Items, and Delete the Selected Item from the Queue. Also note that you can click any of the column heads — Document Name, Pages, Copies, or Print Time — to change the sorting order of the items in the list.

In Figure 7-22, three Microsoft Word documents are in the queue. Chapter 1 is currently printing. Clicking the stop button would suspend the printing of Chapter 1 until I chose to resume. Clicking the delete button would permanently remove Chapter 1 from the printing queue, and it would never print.

So what do the menu commands do?

✔ **Start Print Queue and Stop Print Queue** are like the Play and Pause buttons on your VCR. To pause the printing process and be able to resume where you left off later, choose Stop Print Queue. To resume, choose Start Print Queue.

✔ **Change Setup** lets you choose another PPD (PostScript Printer Description) file for this printer.

✔ **Show Manual Feed Alert** lets you decide whether or not your Mac pauses to ask you to insert a sheet of manual feed paper before a manual feed print job. A check mark beside this item means it's turned on.

✔ **Set Default Printer** lets you decide, if you have more than one printer attached, which one will be the default printer (that is, the one that's selected when you choose Print) in the Print dialog box.

One last thing about these here desktop printers: You can choose your desktop printers from the pop-up menu in the Print dialog box! That's right, the Print To pop-up menu in the Print dialog box gives you a choice of any printer that appears on your desktop. No more trips to the Chooser! Hooray!

What is QuickDraw GX? (And Should I Use It?)

Here's Apple's pitch about QuickDraw GX from when System 7.5 was the rage several years ago: "QuickDraw GX is setting the stage for the next generation in graphics. QuickDraw GX greatly extends and expands the graphics capabilities of the Macintosh, creating a new standard for desktop graphics computing and reaffirming the place of Macintosh as the premier publishing platform in the personal computer industry. It offers significant improvements to all customers, from generalist users to publishing professionals."

Here's Apple's pitch today: "Prompted by our new dual OS strategy — Mac OS and Rhapsody — Apple has reevaluated the graphics and printing architectures of Mac OS. Beginning with Mac OS 8 and QuickDraw GX 1.1.6, Apple provides a unified operating system printing architecture, standard- izing on classic (non-GX) QuickDraw printing and printer drivers. With the unified printing architecture, QuickDraw GX printer drivers and QuickDraw GX printing extensions will not be supported in Mac OS 8.5 and future Mac OS releases."

Basically this means that QuickDraw GX is dead and the only people who need it are those who have QuickDraw GX–specific programs. You know who you are. Otherwise (that is, most of you), don't even bother installing it.

Font Mania

To a computer user, *font* means typeface. Although professional typographers will scream, I'll go with that definition for now.

Each font looks different. Tens of thousands of different fonts are available for the Macintosh. You can buy single fonts and font collections anywhere you can buy software. Plenty of shareware and public domain fonts are also available from online services and user groups. Some people have thousands of them.

How to install fonts

This is a very short section. To install any font except a Type 1 font, drag it onto your System Folder icon. To install a Type 1 font, drag all of its files — the "printer font(s)" and the "screen font" — onto your System Folder. Note that there may be more than one printer font file with your Type 1 font.

When you drag any font onto your System Folder icon, your Mac asks if you want to place it in the Fonts folder. Click OK. When you click OK, the deed is done and the font is installed.

To remove a font, drag it out of the Fonts folder (which is in the System Folder). After a font is installed, it appears in the Font menu of all your applications.

You can store fonts anywhere on your hard disk, but a font is only available in an application if it's in the Fonts folder when you launch that application.

Type formats

You need to know about four different kinds of fonts:

- *Bitmap* fonts, unlike other font formats, come in different sizes. You need a separate bitmap file for each size of the font that you want to display or print.

- *TrueType* fonts come with Mac OS 8.5. They are the Apple standard issue and are in wide use on Macs as well as on Windows machines. These fonts are scaleable, which means that there is only a single outline for the font, and your Mac makes it bigger or smaller when you choose a bigger or smaller font size in a program.

- *Type 1* fonts, sometimes referred to as PostScript Type 1 fonts, are the standard for desktop publishing on the Mac. Tens of thousands of Type 1 fonts are available (and not nearly as many TrueType fonts exist).

  Type 1 fonts come in two pieces, a bitmap font suitcase and a second piece, called a printer font. Some Type 1 fonts come with two, three, or four printer fonts. They usually have related names.

- *TrueType GX* is the latest font format. Very few of these were ever produced, and with GX dead, probably few more will ever be.

Font advice in brief

You don't need to know a thing about font types. Really. When you get a font, just drag it (or all of its parts) onto your System Folder icon.

If you have a lot of fonts and need help managing them, try Adobe's ATM Deluxe.

Chapter 8

File Sharing for the Rest of Us

● ●

In This Chapter

▶ What is file sharing?

▶ Users and groups and guests

▶ Access and privileges

▶ The actual act of sharing

▶ Remotely sharing

▶ A few other things you ought to know

● ●

Computer networking has a well-deserved reputation for being complicated and nerve-wracking. The truth is, there's nothing scary or complicated about sharing files, folders, and disks (and printers, for that matter) among computers. As long as the computers are Macintoshes, of course.

If you have more than one computer, file sharing is a must. It's fun, it's easy, and it's way better than SneakerNet. (SneakerNet, of course, being "the moving of files from one computer to another via floppy disk or other media such as Zip, Jaz, or SyQuest," according to the Dr. Macintosh Unabridged Dictionary.)

Your Macintosh includes everything you need to share files and printers. Everything, that is, except the printers and the cables. So here's the deal: You supply the printers and cables, and I supply the rest.

This chapter is kind of unusual. I don't show you how to actually share a file until the next-to-the-last section. The first four sections provide an overview and tell you everything you need to know to share files successfully. Trust me, there's a method to my madness. If you try to share files without doing all of the required prep work, the whole mess becomes confusing and complicated — kind of like networking a pair of PC clones.

So just follow along and don't worry about why you're not sharing yet. You'll share soon.

What It Is

Macintosh file sharing lets you use files, folders, and disks from other Macs on the network as easily as if they were on your own local hard disk.

Devices connected directly to your computers, such as hard disks or CD-ROM drives, are *local*. Devices you access (share) over the network are *remote*.

File sharing also lets any computer on the network access (if you desire) your files, folders, and disks as easily as if they were on someone else's local hard disk.

Finally, file sharing lets you link programs on your computer to programs on other computers. Why would you want to do that? You'll find out.

For our purposes, a *network* is two or more Macs connected by LocalTalk-compatible cables or via Ethernet.

This chapter assumes you're working on a small network, the kind typically found in a home or small business. There are also huge corporate networks, spaghetti-like mazes with thousands of computers and printers connected by cable, phone, infrared link, and ISDN, complete with confusing-sounding hardware such as routers and hubs and hublets and transceivers and netmodems. That kind of network *is* complicated, even if the computers are Macs. And, of course, this chapter isn't about that subject.

If you're part of a mega-monstrous corporate network and you have questions about your particular network, talk to the P.I.C. (person in charge, also known as your network administrator).

If you're trying to *build* one of these mega-networks, I regret to inform you that you'll need a book a lot thicker than this one.

Portrait of a LocalTalk Network

This chapter describes my office network. It consists of two Macintoshes and a network laser printer. (By the end of the chapter, that's not all I'll be sharing, if you know what I mean.)

This two-person network is merely an example. In real life, a network can and often does have dozens or hundreds of users. Regardless of whether your network has two nodes or 2,000, the principles and techniques in this chapter are the same.

My little network looks like what's shown in Figure 8-1.

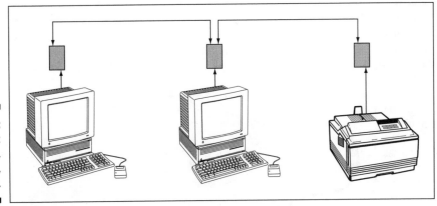

Figure 8-1:
Left to right:
My Mac,
Lisa's Mac,
the printer.

The black lines between the devices are cables; the gray box near each device is a connector. You need one connector for each device and enough cable to run between them. We happen to use the Apple LocalTalk Locking Connector Kits (part number M2068) and Apple Locking Cable Kits (M2066). LocalTalk connectors look something like Figure 8-2.

We could have used PhoneNet connectors from Farallon/Netopia instead of the Apple connectors. The big difference is that PhoneNet connectors use regular telephone cord from Radio Shack (or Target or anywhere) instead of expensive Apple Locking Cables. PhoneNet connectors are also less expensive than Apple LocalTalk connectors. Finally, PhoneNet connectors perform as well as (if not better than) Apple's LocalTalk connector. So why did I use the Apple cables? Because they were here. They came with my loaner computer. If I were paying my own money, I'd have gone with PhoneNet instead.

When discussions of networks take place, you're likely to hear the words AppleTalk, EtherTalk (or Ethernet), TokenTalk, and/or LocalTalk bandied about with great regularity. The first three are *protocols,* a kind of language networks speak. The last, LocalTalk, is a collection of wires and connectors. I talk more about this aberration in a moment.

Support for the AppleTalk protocol, and for LocalTalk, is built into every Mac. Your Mac includes all the software and ports that you need to set up an AppleTalk network; all you have to provide are LocalTalk-compatible cables and connectors (such as the Apple or Farallon/Netopia products I mention earlier).

LocalTalk is an aberration. It's not a protocol even though it sounds like one. In the old days, Apple referred to both the wires and the protocol as AppleTalk. Then one day a few years ago, Apple decreed that AppleTalk was a protocol and LocalTalk was the wires and connectors.

Figure 8-2:
The plug
coming out
the far side
goes into
the modem
or printer
port of your
Mac. The
two holes
(ports) on
the near
side are
where you
connect
your Apple
Locking
Cables.
(Don't
laugh —
I drew
this picture
myself!)

I suppose disassociating the protocol and the wires makes sense. Still, LocalTalk sounds like a protocol (AppleTalk, EtherTalk, TokenTalk), even though it's not. Anyway, LocalTalk refers to the physical connections that an AppleTalk network uses.

Got it? AppleTalk, EtherTalk, and TokenTalk are protocols, the languages that the network speaks. LocalTalk is a collection of physical parts — connectors (LocalTalk connectors), ports (like the modem or printer port), and cables (LocalTalk-compatible cables) — that hook the machines together.

Getting Turned On

The first thing to do is turn AppleTalk on. No network activity can take place until it's on.

1. **Open the Chooser (Apple menu⇨Chooser).**

2. **Click the Active radio button to turn on AppleTalk. (See Figure 8-3.)**

Figure 8-3:
Click the
AppleTalk
Active radio
button in
the Chooser
desk
accessory.

3. **Close the Chooser by clicking its close box in the upper-left corner or by choosing File⇨Close (Command-W).**

4. **Open the AppleTalk control panel (Apple menu⇨Control Panels⇨ AppleTalk) and choose the appropriate connection from the pop-up menu. (See Figure 8-4.)**

Figure 8-4:
Choose the
appropriate
connection
from the
AppleTalk
control
panel's
pop-up
menu.

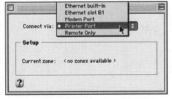

If you're using a small network, that's all there is to getting started.

If your network has multiple zones, you also have to choose a zone at this time.

Zones are mini-networks connected together. When a network gets to about 50 users, zones help network managers keep network traffic under control. If you have zones, there's probably somebody around to ask if you need to know more.

5. **Close the AppleTalk control panel by clicking its close box in the upper-left corner or by choosing File⇨Close (Command-W).**

Setting Up File Sharing

Okay. AppleTalk is on, and you're ready for a quick game of Name That Mac before you turn file sharing on.

Get a network identity

1. **Choose Apple menu⇨Control Panels⇨File Sharing.**

   The File Sharing control panel opens. (See Figure 8-5.)

Figure 8-5:
The File Sharing control panel for Lisa's Mac.

2. **Type in all three pieces of information in the Network Identity section at the top: your name, a password, and a name for your Mac.**

   - **Owner Name:** This one should be self-explanatory — type your name.

   - **Owner Password:** Your password can be any combination of up to eight letters and numbers. When you click anywhere outside the Password field, the letters or numbers in your password turn into bullets, as shown in Figure 8-5.

   - **Computer Name:** Select a computer name that's unique and memorable. Lisa's Macintosh is a better choice than Mac.

You can press the Tab key to move from field to field in the File Sharing control panel.

Turn file sharing and program linking on

File sharing and program linking each have a Stop/Start button. It's a toggle: If it's turned on, the button reads "Stop." If it's not turned on, the button reads "Start." Turn file sharing and program linking on, if they're not on already, by clicking each section's Start button.

The status of file sharing and program linking appears to the right of their buttons, as shown in Figure 8-5. Both are presently on. How do I know? The buttons read Stop, and the status boxes to the right of the buttons say that they're on.

You want your File Sharing control panel to look like Figure 8-5, so if file sharing and program linking aren't on, click their Start buttons. (Click each one once.) In other words, if *your* buttons say Start, click them. If they say Stop, don't click them.

Program linking lets certain Macintosh programs exchange information with other programs. Programs implement linking in various ways, and not all programs can link. See the documentation that came with your program to see if linking is supported and how to use it.

There is no penalty for turning program linking on, so I keep it running — even though I can't recall ever using it — in case I need it someday. You allow or disallow program linking for specific users in the Users & Groups control panel (more on that subject in a second).

If program linking is not on (in the File Sharing control panel), other users on your network cannot program link even if the Allow user to link to programs on this computer check box is checked in the appropriate user window of the Users & Groups control panel.

Users and Groups and Guests (Oh My!)

Macintosh file sharing is based on the concept of users and groups. Shared items — disks or folders — can be shared with no users, one user, or many users. Other people's access to items on your local hard disk is entirely at your discretion. You may configure your Mac so that nobody but you can share its folders and disks, so that only one other person can share its folders and disks, or so that many people can share its folders and disks. People who share folders and disks are called *users*.

Users

Before you can go any further, you need to create user identities for the people on your network. You perform this little task with the Users & Groups control panel. I'm going to demonstrate on Lisa's Mac:

1. **Open the Users & Groups control panel (Apple menu⇨Control Panels⇨Users & Groups).**

   A Users & Groups window appears, as shown in Figure 8-6. If you haven't previously created users or groups, two users appear in the window:

   > **Owner:** Lets you configure sharing for the owner of your Mac, the person whose name appears in the Owner Name field of the File Sharing control panel. This icon should have your name on it.

   > **Guest:** Lets you configure a guest account for your Mac.

Figure 8-6:
The Users
& Groups
window.

2. **Click the New User button to create a new user.**

3. **Rename the new user something meaningful.**

4. **When you create a new user, you have the option of assigning a password. If network security is unimportant to you (if only people you trust use the network), it's okay to leave the password field blank. You can also use the Allow user to change password check box to give your new user more control over his or her password. If you leave this box unchecked, the owner of the Mac has control over this user's password.**

5. **Click the Users & Groups window and then open the item with your name on it (the name that you typed in the Owner Name field of the File Sharing control panel).**

6. **Pull down the pop-up menu at the top of the window and choose Sharing.**

7. **Open the new user's item and choose Sharing from the pop-up menu.**

If you arrange things so that you can see both users' windows, you should see something similar to Figure 8-7. Use the following descriptions to determine how to configure the check boxes.

Figure 8-7:
The user privileges windows for Lisa and me.

The check boxes set the privileges of each user. Because Lisa and I are partners and want full access to each other's computers, we check both choices:

- ✔ **Allow user to connect to this computer:** Lets the user connect to this Mac from a remote Mac (as long as he or she knows the proper password).
- ✔ **Allow user to see all disks:** This choice is only available for the owner of the Mac. It means that you can see every file on your hard disk if you connect from a remote machine.

After you close the user window, that user is said to be *registered.* In a forthcoming section, I discuss the three categories of users on the network; registered users are one of the three.

Groups

Groups are a convenient way to deal with a bunch of users at once. In the preceding example, I set privileges for a single user, Lisa. Say I want to create a group so that I can assign the same privileges to everyone in our family: Lisa; our daughter, Allison; and our son, Jacob, who occasionally use our computers; and myself. First, I open the Users & Groups control panel (Apple menu⇨Control Panels⇨Users & Groups). Next, I create new user items for

Allison and Jacob. Then I create a new group (by clicking New Group) and name it LeVitus Family. Finally, I drag the icons for Lisa, Bob, Jacob, and Allison onto the group icon. The group icon inverts as shown in Figure 8-8.

If you open a group window and look inside, you see items representing the individual users. (See Figure 8-9.) Opening one of the user items is the same as opening it in the Users & Groups window. In other words, the Jacob LeVitus item in the LeVitus Family group window is like an alias of the Jacob LeVitus item in the Users & Groups window.

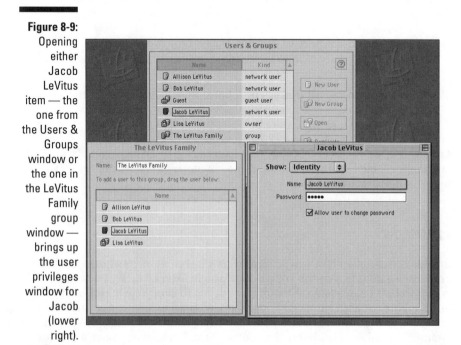

Giving privileges to a group is the same as giving those same privileges to each individual member of the group.

Be our guest

Notice the icon in your Users & Groups window called Guest. The Guest icon represents any users who haven't been assigned individual access privileges. Use this icon to allow or disallow guests to connect to your shared folders or disks. Even when guest access is turned on, no one but you has access to any of your folders or disks until you specifically share them. I talk about assigning access privileges to disks and folders in the next section.

Removing users or groups

To remove a user or group item from the Users & Groups window, drag it to the Trash. It's that simple.

Access and Privileges (Who Can Do What)

Now that file sharing is on and you've created users and/or groups for your networks, you're ready to begin deciding who can use what.

Sharing a folder or disk

To share a folder or disk with another user, take the following initial steps.

1. **Select the folder or disk icon and choose File⇨Get Info (or use the keyboard shortcut Command-I).**

   The Get Info window for the selected item opens. (See Figure 8-10.)

2. **Choose Sharing from the pop-up menu at the top of the window.**

3. **Click the Share this item and its contents check box.**

   If you want to be the owner of the folder, leave the Owner pop-up menu alone (more about ownership in a sec).

Figure 8-10:
The access
privileges
window
for the
Documents
folder on
Spawn.

3. **Choose a user or group from the User/Group pop-up menu. (The LeVitus Family group is shown in Figure 8-10.)**

4. **For the owner and each user or group, choose access privileges from the pop-up menus. Each of the access categories is explained in the following sections.**

You may not see exactly what's in Figures 8-9 and 8-10 on your screen. Well, of course you won't. I'd be surprised if your network's users were named LeVitus. But there are other differences you might see as well:

✔ If you've selected a folder inside another shared folder, the check box at the top says "Use enclosing folder's privileges" instead of "Share this item and its contents."

✔ If you've selected a folder on another computer, the Owner and User/Group areas are text entry boxes, not pop-up menus.

✔ If you've selected a folder that someone else owns, all the pop-up menus are dimmed.

Setting access privileges

The pop-up menus to the right of the Owner and User/Group pop-up menus control the access. In other words, they control who can use what and how much they can use it.

There are three categories of users on the network:

✔ **The owner:** The owner of a folder or disk can change the access privileges to that folder at any time. The name in the Owner Name field of the File Sharing control panel is the default owner of shared folders and disks on that machine. Ownership may be given away (more on that in a moment).

✔ **A registered user or a group:** A registered user has access to shared disks and folders over the network as long as the user or group has been granted access by the folder or disk's owner. A registered user is any user who has an entry in the Users & Groups control panel. A group is nothing more than a bunch of registered users.

✔ **Everyone:** This category is an easy way to set access privileges for everyone at once — the owner, registered users and groups, and guests.

The access privileges pop-up menus (the ones with icons, to the right of the Owner, Registered User, and Everyone items) let you control how much access each type of user has to the shared folder or disk. If you click one, you see the privilege description that corresponds to the icon.

You can choose from four kinds of access for each user or group:

✔ **Read & Write:** A user with read and write access can see, add, delete, move, and edit files just as if they were stored on his or her own computer.

✔ **Read only:** A read-only user can see and use files that are stored in a shared folder, but can't add, delete, move, or edit them.

✔ **Write only (Drop Box):** It's like the label says: A user with write-only access can drop files into your shared folder or disk.

✔ **None:** With no privileges, a user can neither see nor use your shared folders or disks.

Useful settings for access privileges

Here are some ways you can combine access privileges for a folder or disk:

Allow everyone access
Figure 8-11 shows the settings that allow access for everyone on a network.

Allow nobody but yourself access
Figure 8-12 shows the appropriate settings that allow only the owner access.

Allow one person or one group access
Figure 8-13 shows the settings that allow only one person or group (in addition to the owner) access.

Figure 8-11:
Let everyone on the network open, read, and change the contents of this shared disk or folder.

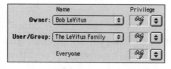

Figure 8-12:
Let nobody except the owner see or use the contents of this shared disk or folder.

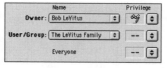

Figure 8-13:
Let the owner and a single user or single group see, use, or change the contents of this shared disk or folder.

Allow others to deposit files and folders without giving them access (a drop box)

Figure 8-14 shows the settings that allow users to drop files or folders without being able to see or use the contents of the disk or folder.

Figure 8-14:
No users can see or use the contents of this shared folder or disk, but they can deposit files or folders of their own in it.

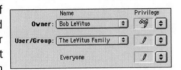

After a file or folder is deposited in a drop folder, the dropper cannot retrieve it, as he or she doesn't have access privileges to see the items in the drop folder.

Read-only bulletin boards

Figure 8-15 shows the settings that let everyone access the contents of the disk or folder without giving them the ability to make changes.

Figure 8-15:
Everyone can open and read the files and folders in this shared folder or disk, but only the owner can make changes.

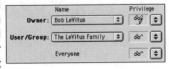

The two other privileges

There are two more items in the access privileges window. At the top, the Can't move, rename, or delete this item check box protects the folder from being moved, renamed, or deleted by users whose privileges would otherwise allow them to move, delete, or rename that folder. (This check box doesn't appear in the access privileges window for disks.)

The Copy these privileges to all enclosed folders option, at the bottom of the access privileges window, does exactly what its name implies. This feature is a fast way to assign the same privileges to many subfolders at once.

The Actual Act of Sharing

Okay, this is the moment you've all been waiting for. You've done everything leading up to the big moment: Sharing is set up, users and groups are registered, and access privileges are assigned.

If you've been following along, you know how to do all of the prep work and more. So make sure that you've shared at least one folder on your hard disk and that you have full access privileges to it. Now go to another computer on the network, and I'll show you how to access that folder remotely.

Interestingly, file sharing doesn't have to be activated on the other machine. A Mac can access shared files over the network even with file sharing turned off. If file sharing is turned off, you can't create users and groups or assign access privileges, but you can access a remote shared disk or folder if you have been granted enough access privileges by its owner, even with file sharing turned off on your Mac.

If file sharing is turned off on your Mac, though, others won't be able to access your disk or folders, even if you've shared them previously.

Connecting to a shared disk or folder

Continuing my little network example, I'm going to access the Documents folder on Lisa's Mac, which Lisa owns but has granted me full access to. (See Figure 8-16.)

On my computer, I choose Apple menu⇨Chooser and then click the AppleShare icon.

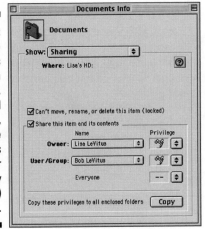

Figure 8-16:
The
Documents
folder on
Lisa's Mac.
I have full
privileges,
so I'm able
to access
this folder
from my
(remote)
computer.

AppleTalk, of course, is active on my machine. If it's not, I won't be able to use the network. While file sharing doesn't have to be turned on for me to access a remote disk or folder, AppleTalk does.

I select Lisa's Macintosh in the Chooser's file server list and then click OK. (See Figure 8-17.)

Figure 8-17:
The
Chooser on
my Mac as I
connect to
Lisa's Mac.

After I click OK, the Connect dialog box appears. Because I'm the owner of this Mac, my name appears in the Name field. I type in my password and then click OK. (See Figure 8-18.)

I now encounter another dialog box where I can select one or more items to use. Because that single folder, Documents, is the only folder on Lisa's Mac that has been shared with me, it's the only one that appears in Figure 8-19.

I click OK, and the Documents icon appears on my desktop, as shown in Figure 8-20.

Figure 8-18:
The Macintosh owner's name appears automatically. Type the correct password, click the Connect button, and you're connected.

Figure 8-19:
The last dialog box before the Documents folder on Lisa's hard disk appears on my desktop.

Lisa's Mac
Select the items you want to use:

Documents

Checked items (☑) will be opened at system startup time.

Cancel   OK
3.8.1b3o1

Figure 8-20:
The Documents icon, which represents a shared folder from Lisa's hard disk, appears on my desktop.

The unique icon for the Documents folder clearly indicates that this is a shared folder accessed over the network. Those are, of course, wires coming out of the bottom of the icon. This icon is what you see whenever a remote disk or folder is mounted on your desktop.

If there are multiple items in the item selection dialog box (refer to Figure 8-19) and you want to select more than one, click the first item, hold down the Shift key, and click once on each item that you want to add to the selection. After you've selected all the items that you want to use, click the OK button, and they are all mounted on your desktop.

Connecting automatically at startup

If I wanted the Documents folder, which is on Lisa's Macintosh, to appear automatically on *my* Mac's desktop every time I turn it on, I would click the check box to the right of Documents in Figure 8-19.

I only expect to use this folder occasionally, so I won't.

Reopening the remote Documents folder quickly and easily

Now that I've mounted Lisa's Documents folder on my desktop for the first time, I can make it easier to use in the future by creating an alias for it. Next time I want to use the Documents folder, I open the alias, and the Connect dialog box appears. I type in my password and the folder appears (is mounted) on the desktop. No Chooser; no other dialog boxes; no muss and no fuss.

If you use remote folders often, mount each one on your desktop, create an alias for each one, and put the aliases in a folder called Remote Folders. Move the Remote Folders folder to your Apple Menu Items folder and you'll be able to mount these remote folders on your desktop almost instantly.

Getting on your own computer from a remote computer

Because Lisa is the owner of her computer, if she walks over to my computer, she can mount her entire hard disk on my desktop. She has checked the Allow user to see entire disk check box in the sharing pane of her user item in the Users & Groups control panel. In other words, after she opened the icon representing herself in her Users & Groups control panel, she gave herself the privilege of seeing her entire disk remotely by choosing the appropriate options.

Anyway, if Lisa were at my Mac and wanted to use her hard disk, she'd do almost the same things that I did to mount the Documents folder on my desktop, with one small difference.

Here's how she'd do it: First, she'd walk over to my Mac. Then she'd select Apple menu⇨Chooser. In the Chooser, she'd select her Macintosh from the list of servers. Now, here's where the procedure is a little different: When the Password dialog box appears, it has the owner's name in it, as shown in Figure 8-18. She would delete the "Bob" part and replace it with "Lisa." Then she would click OK. After typing her password, instead of seeing a list of folders, she'd see her hard disk in the next dialog box. (If Lisa had logged on as a guest or used my name and password, she'd have seen the Documents folder instead of her hard disk in the dialog box.)

Here's a great tip for Lisa. If she plans to use her hard disk while working at my Mac, there's an even easier way. Before she leaves her computer, she should make an alias of her hard disk and copy it to a floppy disk. When she gets to my computer, all she has to do is insert that floppy and open the alias of her hard disk. The Connect dialog box appears, and as long as she types the correct password, her hard disk will mount on my desktop. Neat.

This technique is often called office-on-a-disk. If you work in a largish office and find yourself trying to connect to your hard disk from someone else's computer, carry one of these office-on-a-disk floppies with you at all times.

Disconnecting from a shared folder or disk

When you finish using the shared disk or folder, close any open files or programs on the shared disk or folder and then disconnect using one of these three methods:

- ✔ Select the shared disk or folder icon and choose File⇨Put Away (Command-Y).
- ✔ Drag the shared disk or folder icon to the Trash.
- ✔ If you're done working for the day, choose Special⇨Shut Down. Shutting down automatically disconnects you from shared disks or folders.

A Few Other Things You Ought to Know

That's the gist of it. But you still may want to know about a few more aspects of file sharing. For example, how do I know who is using the network? How do I change my password? How can I unshare a folder or disk? And how do I connect to my shared computer remotely via modem?

The answers to these and other fascinating questions await you. Read on.

Monitoring file sharing

When file sharing is on, you can see what's going on out on the network with the Activity Monitor within the File Sharing control panel. (See Figure 8-21.)

Figure 8-21:
The Activity Monitor portion of the File Sharing control panel tells you what's happening on the net.

A list of connected users appears at the top, and a list of shared folders and disks appears at the bottom. To disconnect a user at any time, select his or her name in the list and then click the Disconnect button. A dialog box appears, asking you how many minutes until the selected user is disconnected. (See Figure 8-22.)

Figure 8-22:
Type in a number and click OK; the user is disconnected after that many minutes have passed.

Type in a number and click OK. When that amount of time has passed, the user is disconnected. The shared disk or folder icon becomes grayed out on the user's desktop, indicating that the item is no longer available. The disconnected user sees a dialog box saying that he or she has been disconnected. (See Figure 8-23.)

Figure 8-23:
If you see
this dialog
box, you've
been
disconnected.

"Lisa's Mac via AppleTalk"

You were disconnected from the file server [9:11 AM on 8/13/98].

OK

In the dialog box shown in Figure 8-22, if you set the number to zero and click OK, the user is disconnected immediately.

The Activity Monitor at the bottom of the screen tells you how much activity there is on the network. If yours is always up in the busy range, you may need to rethink your network strategy.

AppleShare file servers can ease network traffic, and so can hardware add-ons like hubs and routers. If your network appears busy in the Activity Monitor most of the time, you should beef up your network with one or more of the aforementioned items.

Changing your password

You can change your password at any time.

1. **Open the File Sharing control panel (Apple menu⇨Control Panels⇨ File Sharing) from your own computer.**

2. **If the Activity Monitor tab still shows, click the Start/Stop tab to get back to the main file sharing window.**

3. **Delete your old password.**

4. **Type in a new password.**

5. **Close the File Sharing control panel.**

Your new password is now in effect.

Unsharing a folder or disk

To unshare a folder or disk you own, merely select it, choose File⇨Sharing, and uncheck the Share this item and its contents check box. The folder or disk becomes inaccessible over the network as soon as you close the Sharing window.

Logging on remotely via modem

The Mac OS offers Apple Remote Access at no extra charge. It used to be an "additional-cost add-on." This change is a very good thing.

What remote access means is that if you're at another location with a Mac and modem, and your Mac has a modem that's been configured for remote access (I show you how in a moment), you can access your home hard disk from the remote Mac!

Before you can use remote access, you may have to install it. (See Appendix A.) Remote access is usually installed automatically, but if you don't see it on your Mac, you may have to install it manually.

Preparing your Mac for remote access

Preparing your Mac so that you can log onto it remotely is simple. Because remote access uses the same Users & Groups and File Sharing control panels as network file sharing, if you've followed along so far in this chapter, you're almost ready for remote access. You have just one last thing to do:

1. **Open the Remote Access control panel.**

2. **Choose Modem from the Remote Access Menu. The Modem control panel opens automatically.**

3. **Turn your modem speaker on or off by clicking the appropriate radio button (shown in Figure 8-24).**

Figure 8-24:
The Modem
control
panel.

4. **Select your dialing method by clicking the appropriate radio button.**

5. **Leave the Ignore dial tone check box unchecked. (If you can't make things work, try checking it later.)**

6. **Close the Modem and Remote Access control panels.**

That's it! Your Mac is now ready for registered users to access it remotely.

Getting files from your Mac while you're on the road

When you installed Mac OS 8.5, a folder called Mac OS Read Me Files was created on your hard disk. I strongly recommend you read the one called Remote Access Read Me. Go on, do it now. There may be something important in there that isn't in here.

Upon arriving in your remote location, use the Remote Access control panel to make a connection to the hard disk of your home Mac. Launch Remote Access. Fill in the fields for your name, password, and the phone number of the modem connected to your home Mac. (See Figure 8-25.)

Figure 8-25:
Fill in the blanks and then click Connect to mount your home computer's hard disk on this remote computer's desktop.

	Remote Access
▽ Setup	
	⦿ Registered User ○ Guest
Name:	Bob LeVitus
Password:	••••••••
	☐ Save password
Number:	15125556666
Status	
Idle.	
⃝	[Options...] [Connect]

Save this connection, if you expect to use it again, by choosing File⇨Save (Command-S).

If you click the Save my password option, you don't have to type your password when you connect. On the other hand, people who get their hands on this document can connect to your home computer and wreak havoc with your files. So don't check it unless you're certain that you won't misplace the disk with the Remote Access Client document on it.

That's it. Almost. There are two other things you need to know about before you're a Ph.D. in remote access: the Options dialog box and the DialAssist control panel.

The Options dialog box, shown in Figure 8-26, lets you specify whether and when to redial, choose an alternate phone number, and specify whether and when you want to be reminded of your connection if you forget.

Figure 8-26:
Remote
Access's
Options
dialog box.

DialAssist is a control panel that helps you remember and dial complicated phone number sequences. If you choose DialAssist from Remote Access's Remote Access menu (or choose DialAssist from the Control Panels submenu in the Apple menu), the DialAssist control panel opens. (See Figure 8-27.)

Figure 8-27:
The
DialAssist
control
panel
helps you
remember
and dial
stuff like
your credit
card or
long-
distance
access
number.

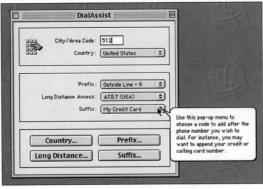

If dialing home involves anything more complicated than dialing a 9 before your phone number — a country code, long-distance access number, credit card number, or whatever — check out DialAssist.

Notice that DialAssist has Balloon Help, so if you need to know more about how a feature works, turn it on. A nice touch.

After you've used DialAssist's pop-up menus to create your custom dialing string, you can preview the results in the Remote Access Client window.

There. That's it! You know how to share files with the best of them, no matter where you are.

Chapter 9

Memory and Other Seemingly Complicated Arcana

- -

- -

The Mac lets the user — that's you — get along fine without knowing much about memory. Many users go through their entire lives with a Macintosh without knowing anything more than "it has 32 megs in it."

On the other hand, a working knowledge of the way your Mac's memory works can be invaluable in getting the most out of your Mac.

In other words, you don't have to know this stuff, but it's likely to come in handy someday. It's not particularly complicated or particularly technical, so it wouldn't hurt to just jump right in.

Baby, Baby, Where Did Our RAM Go?

RAM is the TLA (three-letter acronym) for Random Access Memory. RAM is the special kind of memory in which your System software and applications live while your Mac uses them. System software (including most extensions and control panels) loads into RAM on startup; applications load into RAM when you open them.

Your Mac probably came with 16, 32, or more megabytes of RAM. Depending on what you want to do, that amount may or may not be enough.

If you never plan to do anything more than use a single program that doesn't require a massive amount of RAM (that is, not Photoshop, which requires at least 16MB of RAM) and never plan to use two or more programs at once, a 16-meg Mac may let you squeak by.

If you have 32MB or less of RAM, read this chapter and Chapter 14 very, very carefully. The less RAM you have, the more important it is to manage it wisely.

If you want to keep a word processor, a calendar, a phone book, and a graphics program all open at the same time, a 16MB Mac may not have enough RAM for you. I actually consider 32MB the functional minimum for using Mac OS 8.5 effectively. If you have less RAM than that, I suggest that you use an earlier, less RAM-hungry version of Mac OS.

The simple rule is that the more stuff you want to run at once, the more RAM you're gonna need. If you have programs that require a lot of RAM, you need enough RAM to run them and your System software simultaneously. You also need even more RAM if you want to keep several programs open at the same time.

Go ahead: Add more RAM

You can add more RAM to most Mac models easily and relatively inexpensively. (32MB is going for under $100 today, and 128MB DIMMs can be had for under $400, but prices change quickly, so check around before you buy.)

If you are so inclined, you can install RAM yourself with a minimum of technical skills. Memory comes mounted on cute little printed circuit boards called SIMMs (fancy acronym for Single In-line Memory Module) or DIMMs (fancy acronym for Dual In-line Memory Module) that snap into little printed circuit board–holders inside your Mac. Installing RAM yourself does, of course, void your warranty. (On the other hand, if your Mac is more than 366 days old, it doesn't have a warranty.)

If you are technologically challenged and never want to lift the lid off your Mac (I don't

blame you), you can have RAM installed for you at any Apple dealer. But this service costs significantly more than doing it yourself.

I'm a klutz. I don't repair things around the house. But I've managed to install RAM upgrades in several Macs without incident. It's not terribly difficult, and it doesn't require soldering or other specialized skills. If you can turn a screwdriver, you can probably handle the task.

If you do decide to go the do-it-yourself route, I recommend TechWorks (800-234-5670 or 512-794-8533). Their prices are fair, their support and manuals are superlative, and they offer a lifetime guarantee on every RAM chip they sell.

Essentially, you should remember that three things use RAM:

- ✔ The System and Finder
- ✔ Extensions and control panels
- ✔ Applications

You have no control over the first pair, the System and Finder. That dynamic duo is going to chew up almost 8MB of RAM no matter what you do.

You do, however, have control over extensions, control panels, and applications, and you can use this control to make the most of the memory you have.

Okay. RAM is used *primarily* for three things. Other stuff — PRAM (parameter RAM), debuggers, rdev and scri files — could be rattling around in there, using up small amounts of your RAM. But their impact on the amount of RAM that you have to work with is negligible, so they're not important to this discussion. Besides, most people never need to know what a scri file is.

Sigh. Okay, just this once. A *scri file* is a special kind of extension that automatically loads before all other extensions. The old System Update 3.0 that you should have been using with System 7.1 (but don't need with Mac OS 8.5) is a scri file. So is Speed Doubler 8.

System software memory theory: Where some of the RAM goes . . .

To observe how RAM is being used on your Mac, look at the About This Computer window (Apple menu➪About This Computer).

Figure 9-1 shows a Mac running Mac OS 8.5. No extensions or control panels are loaded. The System software uses 15.4MB of RAM.

Figure 9-1:
Mac OS 8.5
alone,
with no
extensions
or control
panels
loaded, uses
15.4MB of
RAM on
this Mac.

How do you get Mac OS 8.5 alone to load, without loading any extensions or control panels? Easy. Hold down the Shift key during startup until you see the "Extensions Off" message on the Welcome to Mac OS 8.5 screen. Memorize this tip; it's a good thing to know. If you run into memory problems (that is, if you see error messages with the word *memory* in them), starting up with your extensions turned off will enable you to run your Mac so that you can pinpoint problems related to any of your control panels or extensions.

On my Mac (which has 128MB of RAM installed in it), after the System software eats up its share of RAM, 112.5MB of RAM is available for extensions, control panels, and applications.

Your mileage will vary, and you'll probably see a slightly different number on your Mac. Don't worry about it. The System software for each Mac model requires a slightly different amount of RAM.

When I restart my Mac the old-fashioned way, without holding the Shift key down, the extensions and control panels load as usual, and the System software expands to take up a whopping 26.4MB. (See Figure 9-2.) See what I mean about 16MB being the functional minimum? If you only have 16MB of RAM, you have no RAM left available for running applications. That's not good. You'll need more RAM or virtual memory (which I cover soon).

Figure 9-2:
Mac OS 8.5, with its full complement of extensions and control panels loaded at startup, uses 26.4MB of RAM.

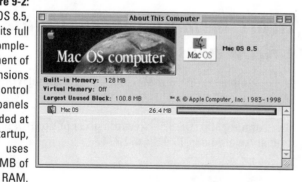

This situation often causes confusion. When you look at the bar for System software in the About This Computer window, it displays not only the RAM used by your System and Finder but also the RAM used by your extensions and control panels that load at startup.

There's no way to tell how much of that bar is the System and Finder and how much is the extensions and control panels. The important thing is that the System software bar tells you how much combined RAM the System, Finder, extensions, and control panels use.

If you're good at math, you can figure out that loading the full complement of Mac OS 8.5 extensions and control panels costs 11MB of RAM.

26.4MB – 15.4MB = 11MB.

On my 128MB Mac, I'm left with slightly more than 100 megabytes available for applications.

You can free up a bit more RAM for applications by turning off extensions and control panels in the Extensions Manager control panel. Read Chapter 14 for details on exactly how much RAM each extension and control panel uses and what happens if you turn them off.

Application memory theory: Where the rest of the RAM goes

If you haven't read the first part of Chapter 4, which explains the About This Computer item in the Apple menu and provides you with your first glimpse of memory management, you should do so now. I discuss a very important technique there — how to adjust Application memory — and I'm not going to waste space repeating it.

Sigh. I guess I have to repeat at least part of it. This *is*, after all, a chapter about memory management.

When you launch an application, the application grabs a chunk of memory (RAM). You can see how big a chunk of RAM it grabs by going back to the Finder after you launch it and choosing Apple menu⇨About This Computer. (See Figure 9-3.)

Figure 9-3:
Microsoft
Word, being
somewhat
of a RAM
hog, grabs
13.3MB of
RAM when
I launch it.

The beginning of Chapter 4 has a lengthy discourse on changing the amount of RAM a program grabs when you launch it and why you may want to do so. If you weren't paying attention, you diddle a program's RAM usage by selecting its icon and either choosing File⇨Get Info or using the keyboard shortcut, Command-I. (See Figure 9-4.)

Figure 9-4:
Microsoft Word grabbed 13.3MB of RAM when I launched it because that's what its Preferred Size was set at (more or less).

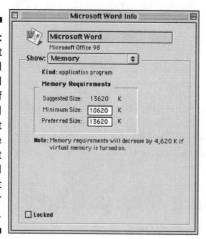

Here's a brief review of what these memory sizes mean:

✔ The Suggested Size is the size the manufacturer of the program recommends. In most cases, the Preferred Size should be set to at least this amount. You can't change the Suggested Size.

✔ The Minimum Size is the smallest amount of memory the program needs to run. It is usually (but not always) slightly smaller than the Suggested Size.

✔ The Preferred Size is the amount of memory the application requests (and gets, as long as there is that much memory available when the application is launched). Your Mac doesn't let you set the Preferred Size lower than the Minimum Size.

When you try to open an application, if the available RAM (Largest Unused Block in the About This Computer window) is less than the Preferred Size but more than the Minimum Size, the program launches. But its performance may be degraded, or you may encounter memory-related errors.

In summation

Make sure that you're clear on this theory stuff before you move on to execution. Three things use RAM: System software (and Finder), extensions and control panels, and applications.

You can make more RAM available for your programs by holding down the Shift key at startup, which disables all extensions and control panels.

You can fiddle with the amount of RAM that a program uses in its Get Info box.

Everything else you need to know about memory involves the Memory control panel, which you're about to meet.

The Shift-key-at-startup technique is wonderful, but it's absolutely absolute. Either your control panels and extensions are on or they're off. The Shift key provides no way to turn some off and leave others on. When they're all off, you lose the ability to share files, the ability to use desktop printers and the CD-ROM drive, and much more.

That's why Apple provides the Extensions Manager control panel. You use it to selectively disable and enable control panels and extensions. As I keep saying, I discuss this dandy tool in Chapter 14, a chapter designed to help you figure out which extensions and control panels you truly need. You can find out how much precious RAM and disk space each control panel and extension uses, and you can also discover how to get rid of the ones that you don't want (both temporarily and permanently).

In other words, Chapter 14 may be the most useful chapter in this book.

Memories Are Made of This: The Memory Control Panel

You configure memory-related functions for your Mac in the Memory control panel, which is in the Control Panels folder. You open the Memory control panel by choosing Apple menu⇨Control Panels⇨Memory.

Here's a look at the Memory control panel's components, which are for the most part unrelated.

Cashing in with the disk cache

The *disk cache* (pronounced "cash") is a portion of RAM set aside to hold frequently used instructions. In theory, if you set a reasonable-size cache, say 5 percent of your total RAM, your Mac should feel like it's running faster. In reality, many people can't tell the difference.

The first important thing to know is that the size of the disk cache is added onto the RAM used by the System software. Therefore, memory assigned to the disk cache is not available for programs to use. In Figure 9-2, the System software is using 15.4MB of RAM. The disk cache is set to 4,096K.

If I increase the size of the disk cache to 8,160K (see Figure 9-5) and restart the Mac, the System software balloons to 30.8MB (see Figure 9-6).

Figure 9-5:
The disk cache is increased to 8,160K; see the results in the next figure.

Figure 9-6:
The System software uses 4.4MB more RAM than before ("before" being Figure 9-2).

Those of you who caught the math thing a few pages ago have certainly noticed that the numbers here don't add up correctly. 30.8MB – 26.4MB = 4.4MB, which does not equal 4,064K (the amount I increased the Disk Cache by) as it should.

The vagaries of RAM usage are well known. The amount of RAM that System software uses changes from hour to hour, seemingly at random. I opened About This Computer three times today and got three different numbers, ranging from a low of 24MB to a high of 30MB.

In other words, RAM usage is not a precise science. Take all numbers in this chapter with at least one grain of salt.

How to set your disk cache

If RAM usage is an imprecise science, telling you how to set your disk cache is imprecise science *fiction.* Bearing that in mind, here's some excellent advice on figuring out the best setting for you.

As I said in the previous section, some people don't notice the speed improvement provided by a larger disk cache. So first you must determine whether you can tell the difference in speed by cranking the disk cache size way up. Here's how to crank up the disk cache size:

1. **Choose Apple menu⇨Control Panels⇨Memory to open the Memory control panel.**

2. **Click the Custom Setting radio button. You'll see a warning that diddling with the Cache size can "severely decrease performance." Ignore it and click the Custom button.**

3. **Click the upward-pointing arrow on the button labeled Cache Size repeatedly until it won't increase any further. (See Figure 9-7.)**

Figure 9-7:
Click the up-arrow repeatedly until it won't go any higher; then click the down-arrow two times.

4. **Click the down-arrow two or three times (so that you leave enough RAM available to open an application).**

5. **Restart your Mac.**

You now have a huge disk cache, larger than you would actually use in real life. But I want you to exaggerate its effects for this experiment.

When your Mac gets back to the Finder, proceed to Step 6.

6. **Open the System Folder, noticing how long it takes for the window to appear completely.**

7. **Close and then reopen the System Folder window, again noticing how long it takes to appear on-screen.**

The difference in speed (the System Folder should have opened noticeably faster the second time) is a result of the increased size of the disk cache.

You should also notice a speed improvement when you scroll through documents. Launch your favorite application and scroll around a document for a while.

If you don't notice any speed improvement in the Finder or in your favorite application, return to the Memory control panel, set Cache Size to its lowest setting (96K or 32K), and be done with it.

If you notice (and like) the speed improvement, you still have a little more work to do. As you may remember, memory assigned to the disk cache is not available for applications. So you want to set the disk cache to the lowest possible number that still feels fast to you.

To lower the disk cache, repeat the preceding steps, lowering the disk cache one click each time. Restart after each change. Then close and reopen the System Folder two times and note the difference in speed the second time. When you begin to notice sluggishness when closing and opening or when scrolling through documents, then you've discovered your threshold. Return to the Memory control panel, increase Cache Size one click, and be done with it.

The old rule about the disk cache is to allow 32K per megabyte of RAM. I've always thought that this suggestion was bunk, as many people can't tell the difference between a 32K disk cache and a 1,024K disk cache. And why should they waste a megabyte of perfectly good RAM? So I've always encouraged people to try the experiment I've just described and see for themselves.

That said, I have to admit that the disk cache in Mac OS 8.5 feels a bit zippier than earlier disk caches. I notice a definite speedup with the disk cache set to 4,096K. Under System 7.1 and earlier versions, the speedup didn't feel as great.

For what it's worth, I'm leaving mine set to the default for my Mac, which is 4 megs (4,096K) for now, and I may even bump it up to 5 or 6 megs. Because I've got oodles of RAM (128MB!), that still leaves me plenty of RAM for applications, so I'm willing to trade a meg or two of RAM for the speedup. Once again, your mileage may vary.

If none of this made sense to you or it seems like too much trouble, click the Default button and be done with it. You can't go wrong using the default settings.

It's not real, it's virtual (memory)

Virtual memory works better in Mac OS 8.5 than ever before.

The truth is that you should have enough real RAM to use your favorite application or applications (if you like to keep more than one program running) comfortably. You should have enough real RAM to open all the documents and programs you need.

If you can't afford that much RAM, consider Connectix RAM Doubler 8, which does what virtual memory does but does it better and faster without using any space on your hard disk, for about $50 (see the "RAM Doubler 8" sidebar). If you can't manage to find $50, virtual memory isn't that bad.

You access virtual memory via the Memory control panel, as shown in Figure 9-8. Just click the On radio button and use the arrows to adjust the total amount of memory you will have after you restart your Mac. (Yes, you have to restart if you want to turn virtual memory on, turn virtual memory off, or change virtual memory settings. Sorry.) In Figure 9-9, after making the appropriate adjustments in the Memory control panel and restarting, my 128MB Mac thinks that it has 200MB.

Figure 9-8:
Making a
128MB Mac
think that it
has 200MB.

Figure 9-9:
After restarting, this Mac acts as if it has 200MB of RAM.

Virtual memory works by setting aside space on your hard disk that acts as RAM. It actually creates a very big, invisible file on your hard disk equal to the amount of virtual memory in use plus all the installed RAM! So if you have a 32MB Mac and want to make it think it has 64MB using virtual memory, you'll have an invisible 64MB file on your hard disk taking up space. For me the cost is even higher — I start out with a 202MB invisible file as soon as I turn virtual memory on.

Figure 9-10 shows how much hard disk space virtual memory is using on my Mac. Of course, I had to know that the file was named VM Storage in order to use Find File to show it, but that's neither here nor there.

Figure 9-10:
One downside of virtual memory: an invisible file on your hard disk taking up 202MB of space.

So now you know that virtual memory eats up some hard disk space, but it does have some benefits. First, virtual memory lets your Mac think that it has more RAM than it actually does. This additional, almost magical RAM is more effective in allowing you to run several small programs than one large program. Second, turning virtual memory on, even if you only set it to add 1MB of virtual memory, allows many applications to run using less RAM on Macs with PowerPC processors.

TIP

Go back and take another look at Figure 9-4. See that little note at the bottom that says "Memory requirements will decrease by 4,620K if virtual memory is turned on in the Memory control panel"? It disappears (and Microsoft Word requires about 4MB less RAM to run) with virtual memory turned on. This tip alone makes it worth turning on VM even if you only set it to 1MB.

For what it's worth, programs also require less RAM under RAM Doubler 8.

Faster than a speeding bullet:
It's a RAM disk

A RAM disk enables you to use part of your installed RAM as a temporary storage device, a virtual disk made of silicon. Using a RAM disk is much, much faster than any other kind of disk and, if you're using a battery-powered Mac, it's much more energy efficient.

Many Macintoshes include a RAM disk feature. To find out if yours is one of them, open your Memory control panel. If you see RAM disk controls like those shown in Figure 9-11, your Mac has the RAM disk feature.

Figure 9-11:
If your Mac
supports the
RAM disk
feature,
you'll see
these
controls
in your
Memory
control
panel.

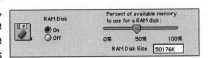

Memory assigned to a RAM disk is not available for opening programs or loading extensions and control panels. So unless you have 64 or more megabytes of RAM, a RAM disk is probably not practical. Even with 64MB, it probably won't be that useful.

RAM Doubler 8

If you need to have more RAM but can't afford the chips, then consider RAM Doubler 8, an alternative virtual memory program from Connectix Corporation. It installs with a single click and magically transforms your 8MB Mac into a 16 or 24MB Mac (or your 32MB Mac into a 64 or 96MB Mac, or whatever). Its speed is much better than that of Apple's virtual memory. It doesn't require a permanent, invisible file on your hard disk, and it works with almost everything virtual memory works with. It's kind of like virtual memory without any of the side effects.

I'd be remiss if I didn't mention that if any single program has its Preferred Size set higher than the amount of free RAM installed in your Mac, performance will more than likely be degraded. Even so, in the same situation, the degradation from Apple's virtual memory will likely be worse. While RAM Doubler 8 is pretty miraculous, even miracles have limitations.

If you like virtual memory, you'll like RAM Doubler 8 even better. Even if you hate virtual memory, you may like RAM Doubler 8. If you need more RAM but can't afford it right now, give RAM Doubler 8 a try. It's the next best thing to real RAM.

Better still, buy 32MB of real RAM. You'll feel better after you do.

RAM disks are wickedly fast while you use them, but they are temporary. When you shut down your Mac (or if the power is interrupted to a non-PowerBook Mac), the contents of a RAM disk are wiped out. In addition, certain kinds of System crashes can erase a RAM disk's contents. The contents of a RAM disk do, however, survive a restart.

Even so, you should never store your only copy of a file on a RAM disk. If you save files on a RAM disk, make sure to copy them to your hard disk every so often — just in case.

Creating a RAM disk

To create a RAM disk, click the On button in the RAM Disk portion of the Memory control panel (refer to Figure 9-11) and drag the slider to choose the percentage of the available memory that you want to use for your RAM disk. Close the control panel and restart your Mac. The new RAM disk appears on your desktop. (See Figure 9-12.)

Erasing a RAM disk

There are three ways to erase the contents of a RAM disk. One, of course, is to shut down your Mac. You'll see a warning that the contents of the RAM disk will be lost; when you click OK, it's gone.

Figure 9-12:
A RAM disk
acts like
any other
disk, only
faster.
Much
faster. With
this setup, I
can kick
your butt at
Myth any
time.

You can also erase a RAM disk by doing one of the following:

- ✔ Selecting the RAM disk's icon and choosing Special⇨Erase Disk
- ✔ Dragging everything on the RAM disk to the Trash and then choosing Special⇨Empty Trash

Resizing or removing a RAM disk

To resize a RAM disk, use the slider in the Memory control panel to choose a new size; then restart your Mac.

The contents of a RAM disk are lost when you resize it, so copy anything important to your hard disk before you resize.

To remove a RAM disk, click the Off button in the Memory control panel and then restart your Mac. The RAM disk must be empty or the Off button is disabled.

Good things to try with a RAM disk

Some applications run a lot faster when they're on a RAM disk. Copy your favorite game to a RAM disk and give it a try.

Your Mac runs screamingly fast if your System Folder is on a RAM disk. You need at least 128MB of RAM to create a RAM disk big enough for most System Folders.

Another thing to try is moving your favorite application to the RAM disk and running it from there. Many applications — including Web browsers — run significantly faster from a RAM disk. And storing your Web browser's cache of recently viewed pages on a RAM disk makes pages appear blazingly fast the second time you visit them. Use your browser's preferences to set the cache on your RAM disk.

And there you have it. More than you really need to know about RAM and your Macintosh!

Part III
U 2 Can B A Guru

The 5th Wave   **By Rich Tennant**

IF BOB DYLAN HAD PURSUED A CAREER IN COMPUTERS

"PUT HIM IN FRONT OF A TERMINAL AND HE'S A GENIUS, BUT OTHER-
WISE THE GUY IS SUCH A BROODING, GLOOMY GUS HE'LL NEVER
BREAK INTO MANAGEMENT."

In this part . . .

1 discuss tips, tricks, and techniques that make using your Mac easier and more fulfilling. More succinctly, this part is about how things work and how you can make them work better.

After two chapters full of tips and tricks, I'll crawl through the Control Panels folder and discuss each and every control panel and its recommended settings.

Moving right along, I'll next delve into automating your Mac using AppleScript, complete with some easy-to-follow info that's guaranteed to get you scripting with the best of them.

Next, in what may be the most useful chapter in the book, I look at every single file installed with Mac OS 8.5. I'll tell you who needs it, how much RAM it uses, how much disk space it uses, and most important of all, how to get rid of it safely if you don't need it.

And finally, I introduce you to the World of the Wide Web, with an introduction to your Internet tools, including the infamous Web browsers from Netscape and Microsoft.

Chapter 10

Sure-Fire, Easy-to-Use, No (Or Low)-Cost Timesaving Tips

● ●

In This Chapter
▶ Flying fingers
▶ In living color — or not
▶ Contextual menus: They're great in context
▶ Getting your Views under control

● ●

Some of what you're about to read has been mentioned somewhere in the first nine chapters already. But this chapter isn't a blatant attempt at upping my page count. No siree. This chapter is here because, by now, you lust for speed.

Now that you understand the basics, if you're normal, you wish your Mac worked faster. (You're not alone — all users wish that their Macs worked faster at some time, even those of us with Power Macintosh G3s.) So in this chapter, I cover things that can make your Mac at least *seem* faster, most of which won't cost you a red cent.

Let Your Fingers Do the Flying

One way to make your Mac faster is to make your fingers faster. Here are a couple of ways:

Use those keyboard shortcuts

I know I've told you this tip already, but the less often you remove your hand from the keyboard to fiddle with the mouse, the less time you waste. Learn to use those keyboard shortcuts. Memorize them. Make your fingers memorize them. The more keyboard shortcuts you use, the faster you can get done with what you are doing. Trust me.

Learn to type better

Learning to type faster may be the very best way I know to make your Mac faster. As a Macintosh consultant and trainer, I get to spend a lot of time with beginners. And almost all of them are lousy typists. When they complain that their computer is too slow, I ask them to perform a task for me. Then I perform that same task for them. I can type about 50 words per minute, and I type without looking at the keyboard. I always accomplish the task in less time; if the task involves a lot of typing, I accomplish it in much less time.

Because you're there and I'm here, I can't provide you with as dramatic an illustration. But trust me, typing fast saves you time at your Mac — a lot. And this speed gain isn't just in word processors and spreadsheets. When you're a decent touch typist, you fly when you use those nifty keyboard shortcuts that I mention so frequently.

Several fine typing programs are out there, and any one of them will do just fine. Most cost less than $30 by mail order and are worth every penny. I happen to like a program called Mavis Beacon Teaches Typing (from The Software Toolworks) for a number of reasons. First, it allows you to choose whether there should be one space or two after a period. The correct answer, of course, is one — at least if you're typing on a Mac.

What? You learned to put two spaces after a period in your high school typing class? Well, you learned wrong, at least if you're going to use a computer. The double space after punctuation is a throwback to the days when typewriters were king and we had no personal computers or printers. Because typewritten text is monospaced (that is, all letters are the exact same width), a double space after a punctuation mark looked better than a single space.

The Mac is not a typewriter

The Macintosh is more of a typesetting machine than a typewriter. So when you use a Macintosh, you should follow the rules of good typography, not the rules of good typewriting. If you want your documents to look truly professional, you need to understand the difference between inch and foot marks (" and ') and typographer's quotation marks (' and ' or " and ") in addition to putting single spaces after punctuation. You also need to know when and how to use a hyphen (-), an en dash (–), and an em dash (—).

In other words, the Mac is not a typewriter. If you want to make your documents look more elegant and professional, get ahold of Robin Williams' excellent book *The Mac Is Not a Typewriter* (Peachpit Press). It's wonderful and easy to understand, and it covers all the stuff I mention (and much more) in great detail.

With the advent of the computer and laser printer, most fonts are no longer monospaced (Courier and Monaco *are* monospaced). Today, on most personal computers, most fonts are spaced *proportionally*. In other words, some characters are wider than others. The width of a space in a proportionally spaced font is just the right size to use a single space after punctuation. A double space looks unattractive.

Mavis Beacon Teaches Typing (or any of the typing programs) can teach you to type significantly faster in just two weeks. If you give it about 30 minutes per day of your undivided attention, you can learn to type quickly without looking down. Mavis Beacon includes timed speed and accuracy drills (see Figure 10-1), as well as a typing game (see Figure 10-2) where you try to type fast enough to keep your computerized opponent's car in the rearview mirror and not ahead of you. The program keeps track of your drills and lets you see graphs and charts of your progress at any time.

Figure 10-1: A typing drill in the Mavis Beacon Teaches Typing program.

Figure 10-2: A game in the Mavis Beacon Teaches Typing program.

The important thing isn't how the typing program works or which program you buy. You simply need to commit the time. Just remember: The easiest way to speed up your Mac is to speed up your fingers. Honest. Trust me, it's not as stupid as it sounds.

End of sermon.

Why Living Color May Not Be So Great

Chances are good that your Macintosh has a color monitor (most do). And chances are also good that you keep that monitor set to the maximum number of colors it supports. That may be a mistake.

Monitor settings

Your screen consists of thousands of square dots (more than 300,000 for the average Mac monitor) known as *pixels* (an acronym of sorts for picture element). Most 13- or 14-inch monitors display a picture that is 640 pixels wide by 480 pixels high — more than 300,000 pixels on the screen for your Mac to deal with. Larger monitors have more pixels; smaller monitors have fewer.

The number of colors that you choose to display on your monitor has a significant impact on how quickly your screen *updates*. The more choices your Mac has to make about the color of each pixel, the longer it takes for the screen to update completely so that you can continue your work.

When I say *update,* I'm talking about the amount of time it takes for your screen to paint all the pixels their proper color or colors after opening or closing an icon or document. For example, when you open a color picture in a graphics application or open a window in the Finder, the screen updates until every element is drawn on-screen in its proper place and in its proper color.

Some people call screen updating *screen redrawing.* It means the same thing: the time you spend waiting for Finder windows to draw themselves completely or the time it takes for documents to appear completely in their windows on-screen. When your screen is updating, you have no choice but to wait for it.

(You might sometimes hear this scourge referred to as *refreshing,* but that term is incorrect in this context. *Screen refresh rate* is a technical term, measured in hertz [Hz], which has to do with the video hardware. Even so, people use the three words — update, redraw, and refresh — more or less interchangeably.)

How quickly your screen updates depends on a few things — mostly CPU speed, hard disk speed, and video circuitry (built-in or on a video card).

You shouldn't find it surprising that much of what's in the rest of this chapter is about making your screen update faster no matter what CPU, hard disk, or video gear you have.

I admit that the faster your Mac is, the less difference the techniques in this chapter will make to your overall performance. If you have a Mac with a G3 chip, try my suggestions out for a while and see if you think they're worth it. Because your Mac has relatively high performance, screen updating is relatively speedy, even with some of the options mentioned in this chapter turned on. You be the judge.

Depending on your video card or built-in video hardware, you can choose from black and white, 4 colors, 16 colors, 256 colors, thousands of colors, or millions of colors.

You choose the number of colors that you want your screen to display in the Monitors & Sound control panel, which is shown in Figure 10-3.

Figure 10-3:
The
Monitors &
Sound
control
panel lets
you choose
the number
of colors
you want to
see on-
screen.

The Power Macintosh G3 (whose Monitors & Sound control panel is displayed in Figure 10-3) has a video card that can display millions, thousands, or 256 colors at once on a 20-inch monitor.

Most Macs today can display a maximum of millions of colors on a 14-inch monitor using built-in video circuitry. And many of these Macintosh models can be upgraded to display thousands or millions of colors on larger monitors by adding an inexpensive VRAM (video RAM) chip.

If you want more colors than your Mac model supports (even with additional VRAM), or you want to use a larger monitor, you may need to purchase a video card that supports that combination of colors and size. Video cards range from a low of a couple of hundred dollars to several thousand dollars. For the big bucks, you can get a superfast, accelerated video card capable of powering a 21-inch monitor set to display millions of colors with bells and whistles such as virtual desktops, hardware zoom and pan, and resolution switching.

If you choose the Black & White option, each pixel on the screen has only two options: to be black or white. If you choose 256 colors, each pixel on-screen can be any of 256 possible colors. If you choose millions of colors, each pixel on-screen can be any one of millions of possible colors. Unfortunately, not all Macs (mine included) offer Black & White as an option these days.

As you may expect, the more choices each pixel has, the more processing time your Mac requires to update the screen. So the more colors you choose in the Monitors control panel, the more sluggish your Mac feels. Scrolling in many programs is much faster if you choose the Black & White option. And in some programs, 256 colors is faster than thousands or millions of colors.

So here's my advice: Unless your application requires color, set your monitor to Black & White (if Black & White is even offered) for maximum performance. When you're using your word processor or spreadsheet, you probably don't need color anyway. Why make your Mac slower if you don't have to?

Use 1-bit color for speed and 8-bit color for games. Use millions of colors only if you need them (for Photoshop, PageMaker, and so on).

In computerese, the number of colors that your monitor displays is often referred to as *bit depth* (or sometimes *pixel depth*). In a nutshell, *bit* is short for binary digit, the smallest unit of information that the computer can understand. The bit depth describes how many bits of information can be sent to each pixel.

Here are the English translations for the most common bit depths:

- ✔ 1-bit means black and white.
- ✔ 8-bit means 256 colors.
- ✔ 16-bit means thousands of colors.
- ✔ 24-bit means millions of colors.

Resolution? It's not just for New Year's anymore

Another setting you can change to improve performance is the *resolution* of your monitor. Most modern monitors and video cards (or onboard video circuitry, depending upon your Mac model) are capable of displaying multiple resolutions on your monitor. You choose these resolutions in the Monitors and Sound control panel.

So here's the deal: The lower the numbers in your resolution, the faster your screen refreshes. 640 x 480 is faster than 832 x 624. 832 x 624 is faster than 1,024 x 768. And so on. That's because, as I mention before, if there are fewer pixels to refresh, they refresh faster.

On the other hand, the speed difference between resolutions these days is relatively minimal. In fact, I can hardly tell the difference between one and the other. So mostly you should pick a resolution based upon your preference rather than which one you think may be faster. That said, if your Mac seems slow at 1,024 x 768, try a lower resolution and see if it feels faster.

Contextual menus: They're great in context

While we're on the topic of speed and shortcuts, don't forget about those delightful new contextual menus. Just hold down the Control key and click any item in the Finder.

My personal fave is the Move To Trash shortcut. That's good. And it has a keyboard shortcut worth memorizing: Command-Delete. That's even better.

A Mac with a view — and preferences, too

The View Options and Appearance windows (shown in Figure 10-5 and accessed via View⇨View Options and Apple Menu⇨Control Panels⇨ Appearance) are other places where your choices affect how quickly your screen updates in the Finder.

The View Options window is, like my old friend the contextual menu, well, contextual. Depending upon what is active when you choose it from the View menu, you see one of two similar versions: folders in icon or button views or the desktop (top left in Figure 10-4) and folders in list view (top right in Figure 10-4).

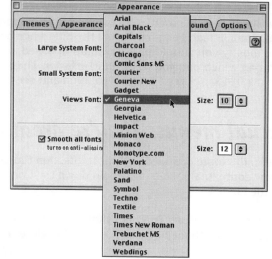

Figure 10-4:
Your choices in the View Option and Appearance windows can make your Mac feel faster.

Geneva: It's not just a city in Switzerland anymore

Let's start with the one speed improvement you can make in the Appearance window (Apple Menu⇨Control Panels⇨Appearance). Using the Geneva font in the Finder is slightly faster than using most other fonts, as Geneva is one of the fonts that your Macintosh stores in its ROM (read-only memory).

One thing's for sure: If you select a third-party PostScript font in an uninstalled size, it will definitely be slower than Geneva 9. And it will look uglier.

Other fonts included in your Mac's ROM include Charcoal and Chicago. But, at least in my humble opinion, both are rather ugly as a Finder view font.

When bigger isn't better

The smaller the icon, the faster the screen updates. In the View Options windows, the little tiny icon on the left is the fastest; the big, horsey-looking icon on the right is the slowest. (In list view, the one in the middle is, of course, in the middle.)

It doesn't pay to calculate folder sizes

I recommend that you deactivate Calculate folder sizes (that is, uncheck or clear its check box) to make the screen redraw faster in the Finder. At least to me, the screen feels like it redraws faster with this feature turned off. This feature is only offered for windows that sport one of the list views, for obvious reasons.

Actually, the Finder is kind of smart about the Calculate folder sizes option. If you try to do anything in the Finder — make a menu selection, open an icon, move a window, and so on — while folder sizes are calculating, the Finder interrupts the calculation and lets you complete your task before it resumes calculating. So, in theory, you should never notice a delay when Calculate folder sizes is on.

Try the Calculate folder sizes option both on and off. I don't know about you, but I find any noticeable delay unacceptable, and I notice a delay when it's turned on, even on very fast Macs. Maybe this feature is just annoying and not actually slowing things down, but I can't stand having it on. If I want to know how big a folder is, I select it and select the Get Info command from the File menu (Command-I).

Getting ahead-er and other stuff

The Show Columns check boxes in the View Options window for list views — Date Modified, Date Created, Size, Kind, Label, Comments, and Version — have a slight impact on screen update speed when you open a Finder window in list view. The fewer items you have checked, the fewer items the Finder has to draw. As a result, the Finder updates windows faster.

The impact of these seven items on screen updating is pretty small, so your choice should be made based on what information you want to see in Finder windows, not on whether choosing them slows your Mac down. Play around with these options if you like, but unless your Mac is very slow, you probably won't notice much difference between on and off.

If you don't need it, turn it off or toss it out

A whole forthcoming chapter is devoted to showing you how to turn off or eliminate Mac OS 8.5 features that you don't need or want. Read it carefully.

Features like AppleTalk, File Sharing, and QuickDraw 3D use prodigious amounts of memory and can also slow down your Mac's CPU. If you don't need 'em, don't let 'em clog up your Mac. Read Chapter 14 carefully and then fine-tune your Mac for the best performance.

What Else Can I Do?

If you've tried every trick in the book (or at least in this chapter) and still think that your Mac is too slow, what can you do? Here are four suggestions:

✔ Get a new, faster model or upgrade yours. Apple keeps putting out faster and faster Macs at lower and lower prices. From time to time, Apple and other venders offer reasonably priced upgrades that can transform your older, slower Mac into a speedy new one.

✔ Get a G3 accelerator. But remember this: An accelerated G3 Mac may not run the next generation of Mac OS, called "Mac OS X." Apple has pretty much said this version of the OS will only run on Apple-branded G3 systems without accelerator cards. So if you want to be with the Mac OS X program, an accelerator card (often referred to as a CPU upgrade) is a bad idea.

✔ Get an accelerated graphics card. Rather than attempting to accelerate your CPU, an accelerated graphics card is designed specifically to speed up one thing: the screen update rate. These things work, blasting pixels onto your screen at amazing speeds. They're extremely popular with graphic arts professionals who would otherwise suffer agonizingly slow screen redraws when working with 24-bit graphics.

✔ Get a new hard disk. Depending on the speed of your Mac, a faster disk may provide a substantial speedup. And if you really crave speed, get a SCSI accelerator and set up a RAID (Redundant Array of Inexpensive Disks) system which stripes your data onto two fast hard drives at once, literally doubling the speed of data access.

Chapter 11

Advanced Techniques for Beginners

- -

In This Chapter

▶ Modifying your Apple menu

▶ Using startup items

▶ Tweaking the Control Strip

- -

*I*n Chapter 10, I show you how to make your Mac faster. In this one, I show you ways to make it better. Indeed, if you haven't guessed already, this chapter is about ways to make your Mac easier to use.

Apple Menu

A customized Apple menu is an absolute must in my book. It's the fastest, easiest, most happening way to manage your Mac. If you don't put your Apple menu to work for you, you're missing out on one of the best things in the Mac OS.

The items in your Apple menu are sorted alphabetically by your Mac, so they appear in alphabetical order in the Apple menu. If you understand how the Macintosh sorts items in a list, you can use this knowledge to your advantage.

Remember, everything in your Apple Menu Items folder appears in your Apple menu.

If you want an item to appear at the top of the Apple menu, precede its name with a number (or a space).

In Figure 11-1, I forced the first four items on the menu to be Spawn (an alias of my hard disk), Documents (an alias of my Documents folder), Desk Accessories (which I created back in Chapter 5), and Control Panels by preceding each one's name with a number. Because the Macintosh sorting algorithm sorts numbers before letters, these items now appear before the first alphabetical entry (Apps) in numerical order.

Figure 11-1:
Controlling
the order of
items in
the Apple
menu with
numbers.

Notice that I chop the word "alias" off the end of my aliases. This is strictly a personal preference; I feel that having that extra five letters tacked onto a file's name is unsightly.

Space cowboy

A second, slightly prettier way to accomplish the same sort is to precede the item names with one or more spaces instead of numbers, as I demonstrate in Figure 11-2.

Figure 11-2:
Controlling
the order of
items in
the Apple
menu with
spaces.

In Figure 11-2, Spawn has four spaces before its name, Documents has three spaces before its name, Desk Accessories has two spaces before its name, and Control Panels has a single space before its name.

Divide and conquer

You can create dividers in your Apple menu using the same principle. Say I want a dividing line after Control Panels. I just use the principles of Macintosh sorting to create a divider line of dashes using an empty folder. (See Figure 11-3.)

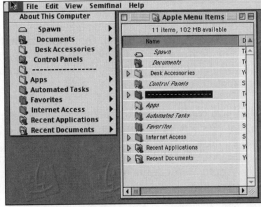

Figure 11-3: An empty folder becomes a divider in the Apple menu.

The divider appears between Control Panels and Apps because hyphens (the empty folder's name) sort after spaces but before letters (or numbers).

Instead of using an empty folder, make an alias of the Clipboard in your System Folder and use it for a divider instead. Using Clipboard aliases makes dividers at least somewhat useful because you can choose one instead of using the Finder's Show Clipboard command. Just create an alias of the Clipboard, rename it ------, and toss it in your Apple Menu Items folder.

There are plenty of interesting characters on your Mac keyboard that you can use instead of spaces to force a specific sorting order. The bullet (•, which you create by typing Option-8) sorts after the Z, so items with names preceded by a bullet sort at the bottom of the list after items starting with a Z. (See Figure 11-4.)

Figure 11-4:
You can
even use
unusual
characters
to reorder
your Apple
menu.

Notice in Figure 11-4 that all the folder aliases in the Apple menu have hierarchical submenus. This feature is what makes all of my organizational tips so great. You can organize your Apple menu so that you can quickly get to any file on your hard disk.

One thing to note is that you can't change the names of the Recent Applications or Recent Documents folders or move them from the Apple Menu Items folder. If you change either one, they'll stop working. In fact, if you do, your Mac creates new Recent Applications and Recent Documents folders and stashes them in the Apple Menu Items folder for you.

Look, Ma, no dividers!

If you want your dividers to look even spiffier, you can make them appear without an icon at all, just like what's shown in Figure 11-5. This trick is strictly cosmetic, but I think it looks cool.

Here's how to make icon-less dividers:

1. **Open any graphics program and use its selection tool to select a patch of white about 1 inch square. Choose Edit⇨Copy to copy the white square to the Clipboard.**

2. **Jump back to the Apple Menu Items folder and select the divider's icon.**

3. **Choose File⇨Get Info (Command-I).**

   The Get Info window for that icon appears.

4. **Click the icon in the Get Info window.**

   A border appears around it.

Figure 11-5:
Look, Ma!
No icons on
my dividers!

5. Choose Edit⇨Paste (Command-V).

The patch of white, which is invisible on the desktop and in the Apple menu, becomes the icon for the divider.

Neat, huh?

All these sorting and organizing tricks are easy after you get the hang of the way the Mac sorts items in folders. And the principles you discover here work in any window.

I use my sorting tricks in most of my folders. In Figure 11-6, I force the most frequently used item (Outgoing Comms '98) to the top of the list by preceding its name with a space, and I force less important items (Books Done.sit, Other Done.sit, HelpFolder Done.sit, and Proposals Done.sit) to the bottom by preceding their names with a grave accent (`).

When you press the tilde key (usually found in the upper-left corner of the keyboard), your Mac types a grave accent (`) if the Shift key isn't down; it types a tilde (~) if the Shift key is held down. The tilde sorts after the Z in the Macintosh sorting scheme. (To be perfectly precise, the tilde sorts after the grave accent, which sorts after the Z.) Figure 11-7 shows other characters that sort after the tilde; these include ™ (Option-2) and • (Option-8). But the accent/tilde is handy, being right there in the corner of my keyboard.

Rather than have me tell you about file sorting, why don't you give it a try for yourself? So go to your Mac right now (unless you've been there all along) and try all the tips you just learned.

If the stuff you've read so far in this chapter is not making sense or not working for you:

Figure 11-6:
Use a
space or a
grave
accent
before a
file's name
to force it to
the top or
bottom of
the list,
respectively.

Figure 11-7:
Option
characters
like °
(Option-
Shift-8), •
(Option-8),
™ (Option-
2), and ∞
(Option-5)
sort after
both Z and
the grave
accent.

1. **Choose View⇨As List.**

2. **Choose View⇨Sort List⇨By Name.**

These sorting tips only work in windows viewed as lists and sorted by name.

If you're in the list view but it's not sorted by name, merely click the word Name under the window's title bar.

Start Up Your Mornings Right

This section presents a pair of techniques for making your Mac start up better. The Startup Items folder tip is the most useful, but the other one, which closes all open windows automatically at startup, can be convenient as well. Both techniques are worth knowing.

Don't overlook the convenience of the Startup Items folder in your System Folder. Everything in this special folder launches automatically at startup.

Think about that for a second. What's the first thing you do after you turn on your Mac and the desktop appears? If your answer begins with the word "Open" or "Launch," you can save yourself some effort by putting an alias of the launched or opened item in the Startup Items folder. It then launches automatically at startup.

If you work with a single database or spreadsheet file every day, why not put an alias of it in the Startup Items folder? Then when you turn on your Mac, that document automatically appears on the screen. Or if the first thing you do each morning is check your e-mail, put an alias of your e-mail program in the Startup Items folder.

You can even put a sound in the Startup Items folder. Thereafter, that sound plays as the Finder appears.

For this trick to work, the sound must be stored in the System 7 sound format. You can tell if a sound is in this common format by opening the sound file. If the sound is a System 7 sound, you will hear it play when you open it. Other sound file formats (such as AIFF, WAV, and so on) do nothing or display an "application can't be found" error message when you open them.

Most sounds floating around Mac circles these days are in the System 7 format.

The Stickies feature is neat to have around all the time. If you put an alias of Stickies in the Startup Items folder, your sticky memos will always be available. (See Figure 11-8.)

Stickies knows that you're likely to want to use it all the time, so it's got a preference setting that not only puts an alias of it in the Startup Items folder, but also makes sure that it launches into the background, making the Finder the active application at startup.

To use this feature, launch Stickies, choose Edit⇨Preferences, and check both the Launch at system startup and ...in the background check boxes. (See Figure 11-9.)

Figure 11-8:
When I start up my Mac, Stickies launches automatically.

Figure 11-9:
Click both Launch at system startup and ... in the background.

Not all programs are as considerate as Stickies; the items in the Startup Items folder launch alphabetically, using that same Macintosh sorting order that I talk about in the previous section. And under ordinary circumstances, the last item to launch would be the active application at the end of the startup sequence.

Stickies can launch itself and then make the Finder the active application.

So if you want the Finder to be the active application at startup and you've got several items in your Startup Items folder, just make sure that Stickies loads last and that you've checked the ...in the background check box in the Stickies preferences.

In other words, precede Stickies' name with a few Zs (or a tilde or bullet) to make it the last item in the list when you view the Startup Items window by name. (See Figure 11-10.)

Figure 11-10:
By making
Stickies
launch last,
you can
take
advantage
of its ability
to make the
Finder
active at
startup.

Control Strip Poker

One relatively new feature that can save you time and effort is the Control Strip, which (if it's turned on in the Control Strip control panel) appears somewhere on your screen.

With the Control Strip, you can adjust your Mac's speaker volume, change monitor bit-depth and resolution, select a printer, and turn file sharing and AppleTalk on and off, all without visiting a control panel or the Chooser.

You can find out more about the Control Strip in Chapter 12, but for now, here are a couple of things you should know:

Control Strip modules live in a folder in your System Folder named (what else?) Control Strip Modules. If a module is in this folder at startup, it appears in your Control Strip on-screen.

Apple provides 17 Control Strip items. (See Figures 11-11 and 11-12.) If you don't want or need some of them, you can delete them (that is, trash 'em) and make your Control Strip even shorter and more efficient. But they're handy if you need to do the things they do.

One last thing: There are many freeware and shareware Control Strip modules available, and some commercial programs even include Control Strip modules. For example, my bookmark program, URL Manager Pro, includes a module that lets me perform a number of bookmark-related actions right from my Control Strip. And my virus program, Virex, has a Control Strip module that lets me scan files for viruses right from the Control Strip.

Figure 11-11:
The full complement of Apple-supplied Control Strip modules as seen in the Control Strip itself.

Figure 11-12:
The full complement of Apple-supplied Control Strip modules as seen in the Control Strip Modules folder.

Chapter 12

Control Tweaks

In This Chapter
▶ Instructions on tweaking every single control panel
▶ Lots of pictures

*T*he Control Panels folder contains (what else?) your control panels. What exactly are control panels? They're usually little mini-programs that control a single aspect of your Mac's operation.

I talk about some of the control panels (Memory, File Sharing) earlier in this book, but because Mac OS 8.5 includes about 30 control panels for most Macs, I go through them one at a time in this chapter, in alphabetical order, describing and suggesting settings for each and every one.

After a brief AppleScript interlude in Chapter 13, I continue this discussion in Chapter 14, "What Can Stay and What Can Go," with a full disclosure of how much memory and disk space each control panel uses and how to remove or temporarily disable ones that you don't need. I even explain why you might want to do this stuff.

I include *no-brainer* settings at the end of many sections for those of you who just want to know how to set the thing and don't care what it does or why. These no-brainer settings are not the gospel, but they're a good place to start. (You can always come back and change them later after you figure out what they are and what they do.)

If your Mac is working the way you expect it to right this second, I implore you to take a moment to note the current settings of any control panel before you change anything. Nothing is more frustrating than changing something and then being unable to change it back to the way it was. So before you change any control panel settings, either write down the current settings or make a screen shot of them so that you can set things straight should the change not suit you. (Command-Shift-3 captures everything on your screen and saves it as a PICT file at root level on your startup disk. You can open the file — named "Picture 1," "Picture 2," and so on — using SimpleText.)

Appearance

Mac OS 8.5's new Appearance control panel replaces the old Color, Windowshade, and Desktop Pictures control panels and adds a couple of twists, including a first-ever opportunity to change the entire look and feel of your Mac using slick new Mac OS 8.5 Themes.

There are six tabs in the Appearance control panel window: Themes, Appearance, Fonts, Desktop, Sound, and Options. Each governs a particular aspect of how your Mac looks and feels. I cover each in turn. But first, you need to understand what a theme is.

A theme is the summation of all the settings you can choose from in the Appearance control panel. So in effect, a theme is how your Mac looks and feels. Among the items in each theme that can be customized are the menu font, the Finder font, the desktop background, sounds, and other stuff.

Mac OS 8.5 may come with a handful of themes, including the bizarre Gizmo (shown in Figure 12-1) and Hi-Tech. Or it may not. Apple hadn't made up its mind when I was writing this book. No big deal: It's just window dressing.

When you have all six Appearance tabs set just the way you like them, click the Themes tab and click the Save Theme button. All your Appearance settings are saved as a theme; you then have the opportunity to name your new theme whatever you like.

Figure 12-1:
The Gizmo
Theme in all
its glory.

Themes

Not much to it. You pick the theme that you like best by clicking it in the Themes tab of the Appearance control panel.

Appearance

Here you can choose specific aspects of how your Mac looks and feels. To wit:

- ✔ The Appearance pop-up menu lets you choose from different appearances. They're hard to describe, so just try them; you'll like them.
- ✔ The Highlight Color pop-up menu lets you choose the color text turns when you select it in a document or in an icon's name in the Finder.
- ✔ The Variation pop-up menu lets you choose the color menu items turn when you select them and also the color of scroll boxes in windows.

Fonts

This is where you choose the fonts your Mac uses in several different places. See Figure 12-2.

The Large System Font pop-up menu governs the font used in all menus and headings (such as the tabs in the Appearance window).

The Small System Font pop-up menu governs the font used in explanatory text and labels.

The Views Font pop-up menu governs the font used in lists and icons in the Finder. Unlike the other two font menus on this tab, you can choose the size of the Views font.

Finally, there is a check box called "Smooth all fonts on screen" and a pop-up menu to select a minimum size for smoothing (sometimes called "anti-aliasing").

Turning on font smoothing may make your Mac feel sluggish. Leave it turned off unless you really like its effect. And if you do turn it on, only smooth sizes 14 and above for minimal impact on your Mac's performance.

Figure 12-2:
The Fonts tab lets you choose the fonts you see in the Finder, as well as turn font smoothing (a.k.a. anti-aliasing) on and off.

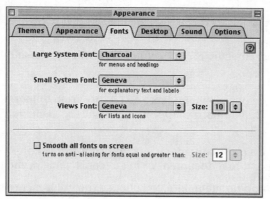

Desktop

The Desktop tab is where you choose a desktop pattern or picture. For background patterns, merely choose one from the list. To have a picture as your desktop background, click the Place Picture button and choose a picture in PICT, JPEG, or GIF format. When the picture or pattern you like best is shown in the preview on the left side of the window, click the Set Desktop button.

Sound

The Sound tab lets you select different sound effects for Finder events such as opening menus, choosing items, dragging, resizing, and so on. (See Figure 12-3.)

Options

This tab controls two aspects of the way windows appear on your Mac. Clicking the Smart Scrolling check box makes scroll arrows in windows double-sided and varies the size of the scroll box depending upon how much of the window contents are hidden.

Clicking the check box called Double-click title bar to collapse windows makes you able to double-click the title bar of any window to roll it up, the same as if you clicked its Windowshade box (upper-right corner of most windows, to the right of the Grow box).

Figure 12-3:
First
choose a
soundtrack;
then
choose
which
sounds you
want turned
on by
checking
their check
boxes.

Much of the functionality of Mac OS 8.5's Appearance control panel was only available via third-party commercial and shareware programs like Wallpaper, Screenscapes, Kaleidescope, Aaron, DeskPICT, and others. It's nice that Apple is finally giving us all this cool functionality for free.

Appearance no-brainer setting: Pick a theme in the Themes tab and then close the Appearance control panel and be done with it.

Don't forget, the no-brainer settings are merely suggestions. For example, if you choose a theme that has sounds attached to it and you discover you hate them, by all means turn them off in the Sound tab.

Apple Menu Options

The Apple Menu Options control panel has two functions:

- ✔ It turns the hierarchical submenus on or off.
- ✔ It lets you specify how many recent documents, applications, and servers your Mac should track.

The first function controls whether or not folders (and aliases of folders as well as disks) in the Apple menu display their contents when you highlight them. Put another way, the Submenus on/off switch (actually, a pair of radio buttons) turns the little triangles on and off. It works while the control panel is open, so try each choice and then pull down the Apple menu to see the results.

The second function requires that you check the Remember recently used items check box. When you do so, your Mac remembers the specified number of documents, applications, and servers for you. You can find the remembered items in the similarly named folders in the Apple menu. (See Figure 12-4.)

Figure 12-4:
The Apple Menu Options control panel and its two offspring: hierarchical submenus in the Apple menu and the Recent Items folders in the middle of my Apple menu.

The Mac remembers these items by creating aliases and putting them in the appropriate Recent Items folder. All three Recent Items folders are in the Apple Menu Items folder.

The Mac uses FIFO (first in, first out) to limit the number of items in each folder according to your choices in the Apple Menu Options control panel. Say you set the number of documents to 20. When you open document 21, document 1 is forgotten. More long-windedly, when you open document 21, your Mac creates an alias for document 21. It then deletes the alias for document 1 so that there are again only 20 items in the folder, as you requested.

All of this stuff is done invisibly, without your knowledge or intervention.

Chapter 12: Control Tweaks

Apple Menu Options no-brainer setting: Submenus: On. Documents: 15. Applications: 15. Servers: 0 (unless, of course, you're connected to a server, in which case it's your call).

AppleTalk

The AppleTalk control panel (see Figure 12-5) lets you choose how and where to network your Mac or Mac compatible. Its main function is to let you select ports — Printer, Modem, Ethernet (if you have it; I do), or Remote Only for dial-in connections, as I discuss in Chapter 8.

Figure 12-5:
The AppleTalk control panel lets you choose where your network connection connects.

But wait, there's more! You can choose Edit⇨User Mode, promote yourself to Administration level, and then password-protect your network settings and much more. If you do that, you'll have access to an Options button that lets you turn AppleTalk on and off. (Big deal. As you surely remember, you can also turn AppleTalk on and off in the Chooser desk accessory.)

Or choose File⇨Get Info (Command-I) to find out more than you need to know about your Mac and its addresses and software version numbers, which may someday come in handy.

Finally, choosing File⇨Configurations (Command-K) lets you create, rename, import, or export your specific configurations.

Most of you will probably use this control panel once and then forget about it forever.

At least now you can say you know what it is and what it does. Don't forget that Mac OS Help is only a keystroke (that would be Command-?) away.

ColorSync

ColorSync is a color-matching technology that ensures color consistency between screen representation and color output. It is of no importance unless you are also using the ColorSync color-matching system on your printing devices and scanners.

I thought not.

So this control panel's settings are totally irrelevant. Nothing good whatsoever will happen if you change them.

ColorSync System Profile no-brainer settings: Don't touch it.

Control Strip

Show or hide the Control Strip by choosing the appropriate radio button in this control panel.

Use the Control Strip's built-in hide and show feature (demonstrated in Figure 12-6) to collapse and expand the strip on-screen. Click the little nub at the bottom of Figure 12-6 to expand it again.

Hold down the Option key and click the roughly triangular nub at the end of the strip to move it around your screen. (*Note:* Your control strip must be touching either the left or right side of the screen. Them's the rules.)

The default keyboard shortcut to hide the control strip completely or bring it back if it's hidden is Command-Control-S. You can change this shortcut to any key combination you like by clicking the Define Hot Key button.

Figure 12-6:
Click at either end of the Control Strip (circled, top) to collapse it to a little nub on-screen (bottom).

Control Strip no-brainer settings: Click the Show Control Strip radio button.

Date & Time

The Date & Time control panel lets you configure your Mac's internal clock, which many programs use, and configure the menu bar clock. (See Figure 12-7.)

Figure 12-7:
Set your
Mac's
internal
clock (and
the menu
bar clock)
in the Date
& Time
control
panel.

To set the date or time

Click the number that you want to change in the Current date or Current time field. The number is highlighted when you click it, and a pair of arrows appears. Increase the selected number by clicking the up arrow; decrease it by clicking the down arrow. You can also use the arrow keys on the keyboard to increase or decrease the number. Or you can type a new number right over the selected number.

Use the Tab key to move from number to number. Month, day, year, hour, minute, second, and AM/PM are selected in sequence when you press the Tab key. If you want to move backward through the sequence, press Shift-Tab. As long as you hold the Shift key down, you'll cycle through the numbers in reverse order as you press Tab.

Time and date formats

You see your choices in the Date or Time Formats dialog boxes anyplace your Mac displays the date and time: in the menu bar, in programs that date- or time-stamp documents, in the Finder (creation and modification dates), and so on.

To change formats, click the appropriate button. The Date Formats dialog box (shown in Figure 12-8) lets you change the punctuation marks in the long date and the dividers in the short date.

Figure 12-8:
The Date
Formats
dialog box.
Apple
thinks of
everything,
doesn't it?

```
┌─────────────────────── Date Formats ───────────────────────┐
│  Region:  U.S.                  ▲▼                          │
│ ┌─ Long Date ────────────┐ ┌─ Short Date ─────────────────┐ │
│ │          Prefix: [    ] │ │  Month/Day/Year    ▲▼       │ │
│ │ [Weekday  ▲▼] [ , ]     │ │  Separator: [ / ]            │ │
│ │ [Month    ▲▼] [   ]     │ │  ☐ Leading zero for day      │ │
│ │ [Day      ▲▼] [ , ]     │ │  ☐ Leading zero for month    │ │
│ │ [Year     ▲▼] [   ]     │ │  ☐ Show century              │ │
│ │ ☐ Leading zero for day  │ └──────────────────────────────┘ │
│ ┌─ Samples ──────────────────────────┐   [  Cancel  ]       │
│ │   Thursday, January 2, 1992         │                      │
│ │       Thu, Jan 2, 1992              │   [    OK    ]       │
│ │           1/2/92                    │                      │
│ └─────────────────────────────────────┘                      │
└─────────────────────────────────────────────────────────────┘
```

You can change the display order of both long and short dates. Use the Weekday, Month, Day, or Year pop-up menu to change the order of the long date; click the Month/Day/Year pop-up menu to choose a different order for the short date.

The Time Formats dialog box lets you choose a 12-hour or 24-hour clock and a bunch of other stuff, as Figure 12-9 shows.

Figure 12-9:
The Time
Formats
dialog box,
which
doesn't
need any
changing.

```
┌─────────────── Time Formats ───────────────┐
│  Region:  U.S.          ▲▼                 │
│ ┌─ Clock ──────┐ ┌─ Format ──────────────┐ │
│ │ ○ 24 hour     │ │ Before noon: [ AM ]   │ │
│ │ ● 12 hour     │ │ After noon:  [ PM ]   │ │
│ │ Noon & midnight:│ │ Separator:  [ : ]    │ │
│ │  ○ 0:00       │ │                        │ │
│ │  ● 12:00      │ └────────────────────────┘ │
│ │               │                            │
│ │ ☐ Use leading zero for hour   [ Cancel ]   │
│ ┌─ Samples ──────────┐                       │
│ │ 12:34 AM    4:56 PM │          [   OK   ]   │
│ └─────────────────────┘                       │
└─────────────────────────────────────────────┘
```

The rest of it

The Daylight Savings Time check box sets the clock forward one hour (checked) or backward one hour (unchecked).

The Set Time Zone button lets you choose your time zone from a scrolling list.

Type the first letter of a big city near you to scroll to that city's name in the list.

Is this thrilling or what?

The Use a Network Time Server check box and server Options button let you synchronize your Mac's clock to a super-accurate time server on the Internet. This function requires a working Internet connection.

I love this new feature. I'm anal about this type of thing and love having my clock be 100-percent accurate. I used to use SetClock (freeware for modems) or Vremya (freeware for TCP/IP connections) to do the same thing, but now I don't have to, thanks to Apple's foresight.

Finally, the Menu Bar Clock On and Off radio buttons and associated Clock Options button let you do all kinds of fun stuff with your menu bar clock (shown in Figure 12-10). You can set the clock to chime on the hour or quarter-hour, and you can select custom fonts and colors.

Figure 12-10:
If you're a tweak freak, you'll have a field day with all the menu bar clock's options.

Apple's menu bar clock is based on Steve Christensen's popular freeware menu bar clock, SuperClock, which many Mac users loved and revered long before Apple began including it back in System 7.5.

Dial Assist

No cop-out, but I cover this little doohickey in clear and loving detail in Chapter 8. I don't want to waste trees, okay?

Energy Saver

Almost all recent Mac models (and the no-longer-sold clones) are said to be *Energy Star compliant* — they can turn themselves off at a specific time or after a specified idle period. If your Mac supports this feature, the Energy Saver control panel is installed when you install Mac OS 8.5. (If your Mac doesn't support this control panel but it was somehow installed and you try to open it, you'll see an error message haughtily informing you that your Mac can't use it. No problemo. Trash the dastardly Energy Saver control panel and be done with it.)

In the top part of the dialog box, you can choose to have your computer go to sleep (a low-power mode) or shut down automatically after so many minutes of idle time (kind of like a killer screen saver).

The first time you restart your Mac after installing Mac OS 8.5, a helpful dialog box tells you that you now have Energy Saver and asks if you'd like to configure it now. Nice, eh?

To turn this feature on, move the slider until the appropriate time displays beneath it. To turn it off, slide the slider to Never. Figure 12-11 shows this little gadget.

Figure 12-11:
To set the idle time before your Mac goes to sleep or shuts down, click the slider and drag.

Click the Show Details button and you'll see two additional sliders to control your display and hard disk sleep patterns separately.

And if you click the Scheduled Startup and Shutdown button at the top of the Energy Saver window, you can choose to have your Mac start up or shut down once at a specific time, or you can set up a recurring shutdown (for example, shut down every day at 11:29 p.m., just in time for Letterman).

If you're not around when one of these shutdowns occurs and you have unsaved work in any application, you'll see a dialog box asking if you want to save your changes. The Mac won't shut down until you click a button in this dialog box. In fact, if you click the Cancel button in this dialog box, the shutdown is canceled along with the Save dialog box.

One last thing: To wake your Mac up from its sleep, merely move the mouse or press any key on the keyboard.

Energy Saver no-brainer settings: Drag the slider to 30 or 45 minutes for sleep (not shutdown); then remember to turn your Mac off manually when you're not going to need it for a while.

Extensions Manager

Extensions Manager is another program that's been around for years as freeware but made its first appearance as an Apple product in System 7.5 and was overhauled extensively for Mac OS 7.6. Extensions Manager lets you turn extensions, control panels, startup items, and shutdown items on and off easily.

I provide a longer, more technical discussion of why you need Extensions Manager, along with some tips, in Chapter 14. For now, here's how you use it.

Extensions and control panels load into memory if they're in the Extensions or Control Panels folders at startup. Without Extensions Manager (or one of its third-party counterparts, such as Casady & Greene's excellent and highly-recommended Conflict Catcher 8), you would have to move an extension or control panel out of its special folder manually and then restart your Mac to disable it — which, as you might guess, isn't much fun.

You still have to restart your Mac, but you can use Extensions Manager to turn individual control panels and extensions on and off without moving them manually.

You can work with Extensions Manager in the Finder by opening its icon or choosing Apple menu⇨Control Panels⇨Extensions Manager. Or you can work with it at startup, before any control panels or extensions load.

To open Extensions Manager at startup, hold down the spacebar on your keyboard until the Extensions Manager window appears. (See Figure 12-12.)

Figure 12-12:
The Extensions Manager window lets you turn control panels, extensions, startup items, and shutdown items off and on at will (at startup).

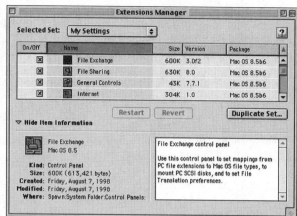

Regardless of which way you open it, you choose which items you want to turn on or off by clicking the box before their name. (An X means the item is turned on.) Your choices remain in effect until you change them in the Extensions Manager window.

You can create *sets,* or groups of extensions and control panels that you want to use simultaneously, with Extensions Manager. To create a set, click items in the list until the ones that you want turned on have Xs and the ones that you want turned off don't. When everything is just the way you like it, choose File⇨New Set. You'll be asked to name the set. After you do, the set will appear in the Sets menu as a custom set along with the preinstalled sets — Mac OS All and Mac OS Base. Sets can be quite convenient, as I explain in Chapter 14.

When you finish making your selections or creating sets, close the Extensions Manager window. If you used the spacebar to open Extensions Manager at startup, your Mac will start up with only the Xed items loaded; if you're in the Finder, click the Extensions Manager's Restart button for your selections to take effect.

The Mac OS Base set turns on only the most essential control panels and extensions, turning off memory hogs like QuickDraw 3D. (See Chapter 14 for details.) Using it may regain some of your precious RAM for other purposes.

You can also turn on or off the entire Extensions, Control Panels, Startup Items, or Shutdown Items folders by clicking the On/Off box next to their names. In other words, turning off the Control Panels folder in Extensions Manager turns off all of your control panels at once. You'll find Duplicate Set, Delete Set, and Rename Set commands in the File menu. They do what they sound like they do.

Finally, if you click an item in the Extensions Manager window (File Exchange is selected in Figure 12-12), some information about it will appear in a box in the lower-right corner of the window. Though Chapter 14 does a more thorough job of explaining this stuff, the little box in the corner will do in a pinch if your copy of *Mac OS 8.5 For Dummies* isn't handy.

File Exchange

The File Exchange control panel, new in Mac OS 8.5, combines the features of two Mac OS 8 control panels, PC Exchange and Mac OS Easy Open.

PC Exchange tab

The PC Exchange tab of the File Exchange control panel manages which Macintosh program launches when you open documents created on that other kind of computer that runs those other operating systems, MS-DOS or Windows. (See Figure 12-13.)

Figure 12-13:
If I open a
DOS or
Windows
document
that has
the .1st
suffix, PC
Exchange
tells
SimpleText
to launch
and open the
document.

Apple throws in this application assignment — .1st documents open in SimpleText — for free. If you'd prefer to read DOS files in a program other than SimpleText, click the application assignment to select it and then click the Change button and choose a new application.

In the Change dialog box, you can change the three-letter suffix, the application program that you want to use to open that type of document, and the type of document.

If you click the Document Type pop-up and nothing happens, the type is set already for that document and you can't change it.

To remove an application assignment, select it by clicking and then click the Remove button.

Double-clicking an application assignment opens the dialog box, just as selecting it and then clicking the Change button does.

The Add button in the PC Exchange control panel brings up the same dialog box as the Change button. To create a new application assignment, make your choices in the dialog box and then click OK.

Finally, click the Mount at startup button to tell PC Exchange you want it to work on other SCSI devices such as external hard drives or Zip, Jaz, or SyQuest drives. If you insert such a disk and it doesn't mount automatically, you can click the Mount Now button.

File Translation tab

The File Translation tab governs the functions that used to be called Mac OS Easy Open (MEO), the enabling technology that lets you choose another application to open a document when you don't have the actual application that created it. If you try to open a document and don't have the application that created it on your hard disk, you'll see a dialog box which allows you to choose a different application to open that document.

If the Translate documents automatically check box isn't checked or if the File Exchange control panel is disabled or deleted, you see an error message telling you that an application couldn't be found for this document instead of the dialog box.

The four check boxes in this tab of the File Exchange control panel manage how the translation dialog box works. (See Figure 12-14.)

If you check the Translate documents automatically check box, the entire process occurs automatically. If you don't have the application available, your Mac will choose another one for you without any further intervention on your part.

Figure 12-14:
The File
Translation
tab of
the File
Exchange
control
panel.

If you check Always show choices when translating files check box, you must confirm your translation preference every time you open a document. In other words, if this item is checked, you will see the "choose an application" dialog box every time you open a file and don't have the program that created it. If you uncheck this option, the second time (and every time thereafter) that you open a document of the same type, it will automatically launch into the alternate program you selected the first time.

If you check the Don't show choices if there's only one check box, you won't see the "choose an application" dialog box if only one program on your hard disk can open the file.

If you check the Include applications on servers option, your Mac will look on all network volumes currently mounted for an application that can open the document.

If you don't have a high-speed network (such as Ethernet or token ring), launching a remote program can take a long, long time. You might want to consider leaving this option off unless you really, really need it.

The Add button lets you link specific types of documents to a particular application manually.

The Remove button deletes the selected link.

File Exchange no-brainer settings: PC Exchange tab — check all three check boxes. File Translation tab — check Translate documents automatically and Don't show choices if there's only one. Uncheck Always show choices when translating files and Include applications on servers in translation choices.

File Sharing

The File Sharing control panel combines the features of two older control panels, File Sharing Monitor and Sharing Setup. This is where you turn File Sharing on and off and find out which items on your local disk are currently being shared, how much network activity there is, and who is currently connected to your hard disk.

I won't waste any more of your time with this one; I cover it in great detail in Chapter 8.

General Controls

This is the big fellow, the granddaddy of all control panels. Figure 12-15 doesn't do it justice.

A whopping six different options are managed by General Controls.

Figure 12-15:
The General
Controls
control
panel is like
six control
panels
in one.

Desktop options

The Show Desktop when in background check box determines whether the Finder shows through in the background when you've got another application open. Unchecking this option makes Finder windows and icons disappear when other programs are active, which means that the only way to switch to the Finder is to choose it from the Application menu. In other words, if you click outside of a word processor window, you don't pop into the Finder.

Checking the Show Desktop when in background option makes it more convenient to return to the Finder from other programs by clicking the desktop or a Finder window, but this feature may be more confusing for beginners.

The Show Launcher at system startup check box governs whether the Launcher is active. I ranted about Launcher in Chapter 6, so I won't bore you with my vitriol. Suffice it to say that I don't find it very useful, but beginners might.

Shut Down Warning

If this check box is checked, you'll see a warning like the one in Figure 1-1 (see Chapter 1) when you restart your computer after a crash, freeze, power interruption, or improper shutdown.

Folder Protection

If the Folder Protection check boxes are checked, items in those folders (System or Applications or both) can't be renamed or deleted.

Insertion Point Blinking

This option sets the speed at which the text insertion point, a flashing vertical line, blinks in documents. Your choices are Slow, Medium, or Fast. I like Medium or Fast because I find it easiest to see the cursor that way. Your mileage may vary.

Menu Blinking

This option controls whether or not menu items flash when you select them, and if they flash, how many times.

Off is the fastest setting.

Documents

This set of radio buttons determines what folder will be active in Open and Save dialog boxes:

- ✔ **Folder that is set by the application:** This option brings up the Open or Save dialog box ready to save or open files in the folder that contains the program you're using or whatever folder that program ordinarily defaults to, often the last folder you opened or saved a file from/to. So if you're using ClarisWorks and you choose File⇨Save or File⇨Open, the list of files you see in the Open or Save dialog box will be the contents of the ClarisWorks folder or perhaps the last folder you saved a file into.

- ✔ **Last folder used in the application:** This option brings up the Open or Save dialog box ready to save or open a file in the last folder you saved to or opened a document from. In other words, your Mac remembers for you. Many programs do this automatically. Clicking this setting makes sure every application does it.

- ✔ **Documents folder:** This option will bring up the Open or Save dialog box ready to save or open a document in the Documents folder.

General Controls no-brainer settings:

For beginners: Show Desktop when in background: Off. Show Launcher at system startup: On. Shut Down Warning: On. Folder Protection: On for both. Insertion Point Blinking: Fast. Menu Blinking: 3 times. Documents: Documents folder.

For more advanced users: Show Desktop when in background: On. Show Launcher at System Startup: Off. Shut Down Warning: Your call. Folder Protection: Off for both. Insertion Point Blinking: Fast. Menu Blinking: Off. Documents: Last folder used.

Internet

This control panel is covered in full and loving detail in Chapter 15, so I won't waste trees upon it here.

Keyboard

The Keyboard control panel modifies how your keyboard responds to your keystrokes. It's shown in Figure 12-16.

Figure 12-16:
The
Keyboard
control
panel
governs
how your
keyboard
responds.

The Keyboard Layouts section allows you to choose a different keyboard layout for languages other than United States English.

The Key Repeat Rate sets how fast a key will repeat when you hold it down. This feature comes into play when you hold down the dash key to make a line or the * key to make a divider.

The Delay Until Repeat option sets how long you have to hold down a key before it starts repeating.

Because changes to the Keyboard control panel take place immediately, you can open it and a word processor and experiment with its settings until you are comfortable.

Do not under any circumstances click the Options button unless you have good reason to use foreign keyboard layouts on occasion. The Command-Option-spacebar keyboard shortcut, when turned on, can cause unpredictable behavior if you later forget you've turned it on. Use this thingy with caution, especially if you use Photoshop (which uses Command-Option-spacebar as the shortcut for Zoom Out).

Keyboard no-brainer settings: Look at Figure 12-16. Duplicate its settings. If you live somewhere other than the United States and see a familiar-sounding keyboard layout in the scrolling part of the window, select it.

Launcher

Launcher is Apple's cheesy little file launcher. It lets you open items in its window with a single click, which saves you the trouble of rummaging through folders. The Launcher window's buttons reflect the contents of the Launcher Items folder in your System Folder.

To add an item to Launcher, drag it onto the Launcher window. This action automatically creates an alias for that item in the Launcher Items folder. To delete an item from Launcher, hold down Option and drag the item from the Launcher window to the Trash.

Whatever is in the Launcher Items folder appears as a button in the Launcher window. Single-clicking the button opens the item, which can be a file, a folder, a document, a control panel, or (better idea) an alias of a file, a folder, a document, or a control panel.

If you want Launcher to start up automatically, there's an option for that very thing in the General Controls control panel.

If you like Launcher, read up on how to make it better in Chapter 6.

Launcher is even less necessary now that the Finder has single-click buttons in any window. Why they don't retire this old hag is a mystery to me.

Memory

See Chapter 9, which covers nothing else.

Memory no-brainer settings: Click the Use Defaults button and be done with it.

Modem

The Modem control panel (shown in Figure 12-17) lets you choose which port your modem is connected to, as well as sound and dialing options (only available for internal modems, alas).

Figure 12-17:
The Modem control panel.

Monitors & Sound

Here's where you control your Mac's monitor and audio options.

Monitor

Click the Monitor button at the top of the window. You can now select the number of colors in the Color Depth scrolling list and Grays or Colors by clicking the appropriate radio button. If your monitor and video card support what is known as MultiSync, you can also change resolutions, as shown in Figure 12-18. Finally, some monitors let you adjust their brightness and/or gamma settings. If your monitor supports these features, you'll see brightness (as shown in Figure 12-18) and/or gamma (not shown) controls in this window. If you have these features, adjust them the way that looks best to your eyes.

Figure 12-18:
The Monitors & Sound control panels with the Monitor button at the top selected.

Sound

Click the Sound button at the top of the window. You can adjust all of your Mac's sound levels and stereo balance by dragging the appropriate slider. The System Volume Mute check box turns off your Mac's internal speaker. The Sound Output Quality pop-up menu lets you choose the quality of sounds (44.1 kHz is best; 11.025 kHz is worst). And finally, the Sound Monitoring Source pop-up menu lets you choose from External microphone, CD, Modem, or none; whatever you choose will be heard through your Mac speakers.

Note that some options shown in Figure 12-19 may not be available on all Mac models.

Figure 12-19:
The
Monitors &
Sound
control
panels with
the Sound
button
selected.

Alerts (beep sounds)

Click the Alerts button at the top of the window. Now you can choose your
Mac's System Alert sound, also known as its beep sound. (See Figure 12-20.)
The slider on the right controls System Alert (that is, beep) volume.

Figure 12-20:
The
Monitors &
Sound
control
panel with
the Alerts
button
selected.

If you have a microphone that works with your Mac, or have sounds you've
downloaded or traded with others, you can add additional beep sounds
using the SimpleSound desk accessory (for microphone recording) or by
dragging any sound file onto the System Folder icon (for stored sounds).

Don't believe me? Here's how to record your own sound (microphone
required, of course).

First, choose Apple menu⇨SimpleSound.

1. **Click the Add button.**

   A recording dialog box appears. (See Figure 12-21.)

Figure 12-21:
SimpleSound's
record-your-
own-beep-
sound
dialog box.

2. **Click the Record button.**

3. **Make your noise or sound.**

4. **Click the Stop button.**

5. **Name the sound.**

Bingo. That's it. Your new sound appears in the list of sounds. Select it now as your beep sound if you like. See. Told you it was a piece of cake (as long as you have the microphone).

Mouse

This control panel, shown in Figure 12-22, sets the mouse-tracking and double-click speeds.

Figure 12-22:
The Mouse
control
panel, where
speed is
king.

The Mouse Tracking setting governs the relationship between hand movement on the mouse and cursor movement on the screen. Fast mouse-tracking settings send the cursor squirting across the screen with a mere flick of the wrist; slow mouse-tracking settings make the cursor crawl across in seemingly slow motion, even when your hand is flying. Set it as fast as you can stand it. I like the fastest speed, as shown in Figure 12-22. Try it. You may like it.

The Double-Click Speed setting determines how close together two clicks must be for the Mac to interpret them as a double-click and not two separate clicks. The leftmost button is the slow setting. It lets you double-click at an almost leisurely pace. The rightmost is the fast setting (which I prefer). The middle button, of course, represents a double-click speed somewhere in the middle.

Changes in the Mouse control panel take place immediately, so you should definitely play around a little and see what settings feel best for you.

Mouse no-brainer settings: Mouse Tracking: Moderately fast to fast. Double-click speed: Middle setting.

Numbers

Use this control panel to change the decimal and thousands separators (the period and comma in $1,000,000.00) as well as the symbol used to denote currency ($ in the U.S., £ in England, and so on). Figure 12-23 shows the Numbers control panel.

You could go through your entire life without ever needing to open the Numbers control panel.

Figure 12-23:
Because you'll probably never see your own, here's a peek at my Numbers control panel.

QuickTime Settings

This one's a no-brainer. It's probably already configured properly, in which case, leave it alone. Just check to make sure it's set as follows:

First choose AutoPlay from the pop-up menu if it's not already selected; then uncheck both check boxes — Enable Audio CD AutoPlay and Enable CD-ROM AutoPlay. While these settings enable your Mac to automatically start playing all audio CDs and some CD-ROM titles, they also allow a nasty virus/worm called Autostart 9805 to infect your hard disk.

This topic brings up the bigger question of "Do I need an anti-virus program?" The answer is, "You do if you're at risk." How do you know if you're at risk? You're at risk if you:

✔ Download files from the Internet

✔ Receive e-mail with attachments

✔ Are on a network and share files with others

✔ Use floppy disks that have been inserted in anyone else's Mac

Those are the ways viruses spread, so if any or all of the above apply to you, you'd be well served running an anti-virus program, such as Dr. Solomon's Virex or Symantec's Norton Anti-Virus for Macintosh.

Now choose Connection Speed from the pop-up menu and select the speed of your Internet connection by clicking the appropriate radio button.

Ignore the Media Keys item. It says "Media keys authorize your access to secured media files." I still haven't figured out what it means. I guess if someone sends you a secured media file (or you download one) you can figure it out then. So far I've never seen one.

Now choose Music from the pop-up menu and make sure that QuickTime Music Synthesizer is selected.

Now choose QuickTime Exchange from the pop-up menu and click the Enable QuickTime Exchange check box so you can play files created on non-Mac computers.

Finally, if you want to purchase QuickTime Pro, choose Registration from the pop-up menu and click the Register Online button. If you choose to upgrade to QuickTime Pro, you'll be able to:

✔ Play back full-screen broadcast-quality video

✔ View high-quality streaming media in leading Internet browsers

✔ Access more than 85 percent of the multimedia content on the Web with one package

✔ Play more than 30 different audio and video file formats — on and off the Internet

✔ Edit and manipulate both existing and newly-created movies and audio

- ✔ Export movies using the best compression technology available
- ✔ Save audio and movie files for later use through a convenient pop-up menu
- ✔ View all the most popular Internet media formats with a single browser plug-in
- ✔ Resize movies to a variety of window sizes
- ✔ Copy and paste content from any supported format to create a new QuickTime movie
- ✔ Prepare and compress content for streaming delivery from any Mac OS or Windows-based Web server
- ✔ View images, including JPEG, BMP and PNG formats, from a wide variety of sources
- ✔ Enhance movies and still pictures with filters for sharpening, color tinting, embossing and more
- ✔ Save into the exciting new DV camcorder format for high-quality consumer video
- ✔ Create slide shows from any number of picture sources that play in any QuickTime application

All for just $29.99 with a 30-day money-back guarantee. There's no new software to install — just unlock the extended features of QuickTime 3, and you're ready to rock. I say it's worth every penny.

That'll do it. Close it and forget it.

Remote Access

Again, I won't waste trees on it. See Chapter 8 for the gory details.

Speech

(This control panel is available only if you install PlainTalk.)

Choose Voice from the Options pop-up menu (see Figure 12-24) to select the voice your Mac will use for speech-to-text applications. Now choose a voice from the 22 wild and wacky selections in the Voice pop-up menu. To check out your handiwork, click the speaker icon. Each voice says something different. My favorite is Fred, who says, "I sure like being inside this fancy computer." If you think that's fun, try this: Launch SimpleText, type a few words, and then choose Sound⇨Speak All (Command-J). Cute, eh?

Figure 12-24:
The Speech
control
panel —
choose from
22 wild and
wacky
voices and
make them
talk slower
or faster.

For a really good time, choose Talking Alerts from the Options pop-up menu and click both check boxes (as shown in Figure 12-25). Choose the Random from the list option from the Speak the phrase pop-up menu and then close the Speech control panel. The next time a program puts an alert box up on the screen ("Save changes to the document 'untitled' before closing?"), your favorite voice will speak it for you.

Even cuter. Here's my guess: You'll leave it turned on for maybe a week. Or less.

Figure 12-25:
This one will
really make
you puke;
set yours
like mine
and your
Mac will
speak alerts
to you.

Startup Disk

With this control panel, you choose which hard disk or hard disk volume (if you've partitioned your hard disk) should act as the startup disk when more than one drive with a System Folder is connected to the Mac. (See Figure 12-26.)

Figure 12-26:
This Mac
has three
hard disks
attached.
Spawn is
selected, so
it's the
startup disk.

TCP/IP

Sorry to disappoint again, but you'll have to read Chapter 15 if you want to
know about this alphabet soup.

Text

Another control panel you'll never need. Unless, of course, you have a
version of Mac OS 8.5 other than the United States version. If you use more
than one language on your Macintosh, you can choose between them in this
control panel, which is shown in Figure 12-27.

Figure 12-27:
You'll
probably
never need
to touch the
Text control
panel, but
here's what
it looks like.

Users & Groups

I'm sorry if I sound like a broken record, but I cover this one in great detail back in Chapter 8. If you need to know, that's where to go.

Web Sharing

I hate to sound like a broken record again, but you'll discover more than you can stand about this control panel in Chapter 15. Leave it turned off for now.

Chapter 13

How to Write an AppleScript in 21 Minutes

(The chapter title is, of course, a takeoff on Viki King's wonderful book about that other kind of script writing, *How to Write a Movie in 21 Days.*)

AppleScript is like a tape recorder for your Mac. It can record and play back things that you do, such as opening an icon or clicking a button.

Describing AppleScript to a Mac beginner is a bit like three blind men describing an elephant. One man might describe it as the Macintosh's built-in automation tool. Another might describe it as an interesting, but often overlooked, piece of enabling technology. The third might liken it to a cassette recorder, recording and playing back your actions at the keyboard. A fourth (if there were a fourth in the story) would assure you it looked like computer code written in a high-level language.

They would all be correct. AppleScript is the Mac's built-in automation tool (at least in System 7.5 and later, it's built in). It is a little-known (at least up to now) enabling technology. It is like a cassette recorder (for programs that support AppleScript recording). And scripts do look like computer programs (which could be because they are computer programs).

I call AppleScript a *time and effort enhancer*. AppleScript, if you just spend the time and effort it takes to learn it, will save you oodles of time and effort.

Therein lies the rub. This stuff isn't simple. There's no way in heaven I'm going to teach you how to use AppleScript in the next nine pages. Entire books have been written on the topic, for gosh sake!

And don't kid yourself. AppleScript is complicated and will take some effort to master. So rather than try to teach you how to use it, I try to show you what AppleScript can do for you, and I get you to the point where you can write a simple script of your own, all in about 21 minutes.

What the Heck Is an AppleScript, Anyway?

In the broadest sense, AppleScript is an enabling technology that lets you record and play back complex sequences of Macintosh events occurring in the Finder, in programs, or in any combination of the Finder and programs. In a narrower sense, AppleScript now makes it possible to automate multistep sequences, such as changing the bit depth of your monitor. What used to take at least three steps . . .

1. Open the Monitors & Sound control panel.

2. Click a number of colors.

3. Close the Monitors & Sound control panel.

. . . can now be performed instantly and effortlessly with one script. This feature may not sound like much, but it can sure save you time and effort. The more often you perform a task each day, the more you should consider automating it (if, of course, it can be automated — not all tasks can be automated, as you soon see).

The AppleScript components are installed automatically when you install Mac OS 8.5. (I discuss the components one by one after a brief rant.)

AppleScript has been around for a few years, but before System 7.5 it wasn't included in Apple System software releases. Instead, it came in separate Scripter and Developer packages at additional cost. So it never really caught on with the masses.

In the meantime, many forward-thinking developers have incorporated AppleScript support into their programs. Better still, that number is growing faster now that AppleScript is part of the System software.

Power users have been clamoring for this stuff for years. It's finally here, and it's only going to get better and more powerful as time goes on and more people get copies for free.

I encourage you, if you really want to master your Macintosh, to become familiar with at least a bit of basic scripting. This chapter is a start, but your investment of time spent finding out about AppleScript will be repaid tenfold in the time you save performing your daily tasks. And at the very least, some of the canned scripts that Apple provides — such as the one that turns file sharing on and off or the one that adds an items alias to your Apple menu — can save you time and effort every day.

The Script Editor requires at least 1,000K of free memory (Largest Unused Block in the About this Computer dialog box). If you don't have enough memory to use it, quit all open applications and try again. If that doesn't do it, open the Extensions Manager control panel, select the Mac OS 8.5 minimum option from the pop-up menu, and then restart your Mac. (Don't forget to turn this stuff back on later.)

What the Mac OS Installer Installs and Where It Installs It

Mac OS 8.5 includes a bevy of AppleScript-related items in various places on your hard disk. Some are essential to AppleScript's operation; the rest are merely convenient. Before you read about how to use them, here are your tools.

The AppleScriptLib and AppleScript extensions

(Located in the Extensions folder, which is in the System Folder.)

These extensions are installed in the Extensions folder (in the System Folder). They are the engine that make AppleScript work. If they're not in the Extensions folder at startup, AppleScript won't work. They require no care or maintenance.

The Scripting Additions folder

(Find this one in the System Folder.)

This folder contains add-on parts of the AppleScript system. AppleScript is modular, so you can add new commands to AppleScript by merely dropping a new item into the Scripting Additions folder. Leave it be.

The AppleScript Folder

(Located in the Apple Extras folder.)

This item consists of a SimpleText document called "About AppleScript," AppleScript Guide, the Script editor, the Automated Tasks folder, and the More Automated Tasks folder.

About AppleScript is a "read me" file. It's not as light and breezy as this chapter but is probably still worth reading. Check it out.

AppleScript Guide provides fodder for Mac OS Help. Without it, Mac OS Help won't be able to help you with AppleScript.

Script Editor is the program with which you edit scripts. Duh. You can play with it in a minute.

The Automated Tasks folder contains several useful scripts. Open and read the About Automated Tasks SimpleText document at your earliest convenience; it explains each of the tasks, so I won't waste the space.

An alias of the Automated Tasks folder is in your Apple Menu Items folder (Mac OS 8.5 put it there for you — isn't that thoughtful?), so you can select any of these useful scripts right from the Apple menu.

Last but not least is a folder called More Automated Tasks. They're more advanced than the plain old automated tasks; useful, but complicated to explain. Read the document "About More Automated Tasks" for more info.

Please note that Apple may have changed the names of some of the scripts before this book went to press. Also note that Apple will probably add and remove some scripts that the Installer installs as time goes by. So if you can't seem to find on your hard drive some of the scripts that I mention on the next few pages, there's nothing wrong with your System. Apple just changed the software.

But wait, there's more

If you want to use AppleScript with programs other than Mac OS 8.5 (much but not all of which is scriptable), they have to be AppleScript *enabled*, which means that they have to be adapted by their developers to work with AppleScript.

There are three levels of AppleScript support found in applications: scriptability, recordability, and attachability. Programs can support one, two, or all three levels.

Unfortunately, there is no easy way of telling whether a program is AppleScript enabled at all, much less if it's recordable or attachable. For what it's worth, the Finder supports all three levels.

Here are brief descriptions of the three levels of AppleScript support that you may find in third-party programs:

Scriptable programs

Scriptable means that the program can follow instructions sent by AppleScript scripts. Scriptable apps are the most common kind. If a program proclaims that it supports AppleScript, it's at this level at least.

Unfortunately, it's up to the developer to decide how much of the program is actually scriptable, so some programs are more scriptable than others. Microsoft Excel, FileMaker Pro, CorelDRAW 8, and Now Up-to-Date/Now Contact are a few scriptable programs I know of.

Recordable programs

Recordable programs go scriptable programs one better. *Recordable* means that you can record your actions in the program and automatically create an AppleScript script for future playback based on what you did within the program. Few programs are recordable yet.

Attachable programs

Attachable programs are even rarer than recordable ones. *Attachable* means that the program lets you attach a script to an item or element in a document, such as a cell in a spreadsheet, a button in a database, or a rectangle in a drawing. The Finder is attachable because you can attach a script to an icon.

What it all means

At this point, you should know at least this much:

- ✔ AppleScript is a kind of recording and playback mechanism for repetitive tasks on your Mac.
- ✔ Some programs, most notably the Mac OS 8.5 Finder, can be scripted to do some things under script control.
- ✔ A few programs can record and attach scripts.

Notice I didn't say *understand* up there, I said *know*. To develop true understanding would require far more pages than I have. But I had to mention this stuff so that when you try to use a script with a nonscriptable (or nonrecordable or nonattachable) program, you have at least a vague idea of why it's not working.

Writing a Simple Script

I agonized for a long time over this section. I wanted to teach you something useful, but it had to be easy enough to show in just a few pages.

I've realized that it can't be done. If a script is useful, it's going to require more explaining than I have space for. (And most of the easy, useful scripts are already done for you and thoughtfully placed in the Automated Tasks or More Automated Tasks folder.) So instead, I'm going to show how to write a script that's totally dumb but fun to watch.

If you want to see smart scripts, open any of the ones in the Automated Tasks or More Automated Tasks folder (in the AppleScript folder in the Apple Extras folder) and examine it closely.

1. **Launch the Script Editor application.**

   A new, untitled script appears on the screen.

2. **Type** My first stupid script **in the description field at the top of the document window.**

3. **Click the Record button.**

   After a brief pause, your screen should look more or less like Figure 13-1. Notice the tiny image of a cassette tape where the Apple menu's Apple logo used to be. It flashes to let you know that you're recording.

4. **Make the Finder active by clicking the desktop or any open windows or choosing Finder in the Application menu.**

5. **Close all open windows. (Either option-click any window's close box, press the Option key, and choose File⇨Close All or use the keyboard shortcut Command-Option-W.) If there are no open windows on your screen, ignore this step.**

6. **Create a new folder on the desktop (File⇨New Folder or Command-N).**

Figure 13-1:
Ready to
record a
script.

7. **Open the new, untitled folder and then click its title bar and drag it to a new location. The farther you drag it, the better.**

8. **Click the zoom box (the first of the two boxes on the far right side of the title bar) of the untitled folder window. Click it again.**

9. **Drag the folder to another new location.**

10. **Return to the Script Editor application and click the Stop button.**

That's it! You've written your first script. It should look something like Figure 13-2. Don't save it yet. (As you can see in the next section, you have choices yet to make about *how* to save your script.)

Figure 13-2:
Your first
script.

To see how your script works, click the Run button. Watch closely, as it happens fast. If you blinked and missed it, run the script again. It switches to the Finder, closes all open windows, creates a new folder, moves it, grows it, grows it again, and then moves it again.

I'm fudging a little when I say that you wrote a script. Actually, you recorded a script. If you had *written* it, you would have typed all the stuff between "tell application Finder" and "end tell" from memory, without actually performing the actions.

In fact, the most effective way to use AppleScript is a combination of recording and writing. First record your actions, then analyze the script, and then try to figure out ways to perform each action more efficiently by typing in different commands and trying them. To reach this level of scripting mastery, you'll need to know a lot more about the AppleScript language than this chapter can teach you.

Okay. You can return to the Finder and trash those untitled folders (one was created each time you ran the script).

So that's how to record a script.

You should know one more thing — unfortunately, many control panels are not scriptable.

If a Script Is Any Good, It Should Be Saved

There are a three different ways to save a script. If you choose Save or Save As from the File menu in the Script Editor, a pop-up menu in the Save dialog box gives you your choices. (See Figure 13-3.)

Figure 13-3:
So many
ways to
save a
script.

Save script as:

StupidScript.app

Kind: ✓ ◈ Application

◇ Compiled Script

▢ Text

- ✔ The Text option creates a text file of your script. This script can be opened in any text editor for editing or reopened by Script Editor.
- ✔ The Compiled Script option creates a Script Editor file. You can open, run, or modify the file with the Script Editor program.
- ✔ The Application option creates a self-running script that executes when you open its icon. (See Figure 13-4.)

The files in the Automated Tasks folder are scripts saved as applications.

If the Never Show Startup Screen check box is unchecked in the Save dialog box, your script displays a startup screen with a Run button before it executes, as shown in Figure 13-5.

If you check the Stay Open check box, the script application remains open until you quit it. Scripts saved with this option usually look for something to happen and then perform an action.

The Alert When Folder Changes script in the More Automated Tasks folder is one of these stay-open-and-watch applications.

Figure 13-4:
If you save
your script
as an
Application,
you have
even more
choices to
make.

Figure 13-5:
You can
eliminate
this startup
screen by
checking
the Never
Show
Startup
Screen
option in
the Save
dialog box,
as shown in
Figure 13-4.

Run Only means the saved file can't be edited. You would use the Save As Run Only command (in the File menu) if you had a spiffy script that you didn't want others to see or modify. Anyway, a Run Only script can never be modified. If you choose Save As Run Only instead of Save or Save As, the resulting file will be a Run Only application or compiled script (you can't save a Run Only text file). This script can never be modified or changed.

Chapter 14

What Can Stay and What Can Go

*T*his chapter is by far the most useful chapter in the book. In this chapter, I go through the entire System Folder, one item at a time. I show you how much RAM each item uses, how much disk space it occupies, and what (if any) side effects will occur if you delete or disable it.

There are no substitutes for RAM or hard disk space. But no matter how much you have, there will come a day when you need more of one or the other or both.

Yes, there are Band-Aids like Virtual Memory or RAM Doubler (for making your Mac think it has more RAM than it does) or StuffIt SpaceSaver or other compression software (for making your hard disk think it's bigger than it is). And yes, I think you can use programs like that safely most of the time.

Most of the time. RAM Doubler doesn't pose much threat, as it doesn't really deal with files or the file system. Compression software, on the other hand, adds another layer of complexity to your Mac. It's always expanding and compressing files in the background, reading and writing from the hard disk. So there's more chance for errors to occur. And all compression software extracts a noticeable performance penalty, slowing down your Mac anywhere from a little to a lot, depending on the compression software, your Mac model, and the speed of your hard disk.

My advice: Resort to those devices if you must, but *real* RAM and hard disk space are much better.

Reclamation Theory

RAM and hard disks are expensive. Therefore, I created this chapter — a first, I believe, in System software book history — dedicated to telling you how to get rid of the deadweight among the 110 or so megabytes of files (assuming a full install of Mac OS 8.5 and all its optional bells and whistles) in your System Folder by deleting or disabling.

Let's face it: Mac OS 8.5 puts a lot of files on your hard disk even if you don't choose one of the optional installations. If you do install all of the options, it installs a whopping 1,000+ files and folders, give or take a few. Not everybody needs every single one of these files; many of them can be deleted to free up (reclaim) hard disk space.

And another thing: Many control panels and extensions load into RAM at startup. So not only do they take up disk space, extensions and control panels can use up your valuable RAM too.

So if you want my advice about trashing stuff in your System Folder, here it is: Don't trash anything unless you're desperately short of hard disk space. And as far as RAM goes, it's a much better idea to just disable items you don't need by using Extensions Manager than to permanently delete them.

I'll go through the System Folder and see what each item costs you in terms of RAM and disk space and what, if any, repercussions you'll feel if you trash or disable the item.

This chapter lists every item that Install Mac OS 8.5 installs by default, which means it doesn't include such Custom installation options as QuickDraw GX, English Speech Recognition, Multilingual Internet Access, and so on. For further info on custom options, see Appendix B.

Life after Death: The Truth about Restoring Deleted Files

Before I can show you how to save RAM and disk space, I need to briefly cover a couple of important topics: backing up and reinstalling.

Other benefits of a lean, mean System Folder

Here are a bunch of other benefits to keeping your System Folder lean and mean:

- ✔ The Apple menu submenu for the Control Panels folder will be shorter.

- ✔ The Control Panels folder will contain fewer items and thus be easier to manage.

- ✔ The Chooser will be less cluttered after you get rid of printer drivers you'll never need.

- ✔ Your Mac may start up and run faster if you don't load unneeded extensions and control panels.

Back up first

If you don't have a backup and you don't have a Mac OS 8.5 CD-ROM, DO NOT DELETE ANY FILES! I repeat: If you don't have a backup and a Mac OS 8.5 CD, DON'T TRASH ANYTHING.

That said, if you're faithful about making backups (you should be, as you've heard me harp about it enough times by now; read Appendix B if you're still unclear), you can delete files with relative impunity. If you decide you miss them, restore them from your backup or reinstall Mac OS 8.5 from the CD.

Beware if you only have one backup set of disks or cartridges. Your backup software may keep a *mirror image* of your hard disk on the backup media. In other words, when you delete a file from your hard disk, the backup software may delete it from the backup disk(s). Read your backup software manual carefully.

Install Mac OS 8.5: Restorer of lost items

You can restore any System software file you delete if you have a Mac OS 8.5 CD-ROM. The degree of difficulty you encounter (and the amount of time it takes you) depends on what you need to restore.

To reinstall any extensions or control panels you delete, just run Install Mac OS 8.5 (see Appendix A) and reinstall anything and everything in one fell swoop.

Certain other Mac OS functions, such as English Text-to-Speech, Mac OS Runtime for Java, QuickDraw 3D, and others, can be installed individually. Click the Customize button in Install Mac OS 8.5 to see what's what.

Mac OS 8.5 *finally* allows you to choose individual components to reinstall. See Appendix A for complete instructions.

Anyway, that's all you need to know at this time. It's okay to trash any piece of Mac OS 8.5 as long as you have the Mac OS 8.5 CD-ROM so that you can reinstall it if you discover you need or want it.

Another thing to consider if you have a Zip, Jaz, SyQuest, or optical disk drive — perform a full install on a cartridge and set it aside for a rainy day. That way, if you delete something and later want it back, you can just drag it over rather than performing a complete reinstallation. Or once you're certain your System Folder is working just right, copy it to a cartridge just in case.

What, Exactly, Are Extensions and Control Panels?

Control panels and extensions appear first and second in the chapter because they make the most difference in reclaiming disk space and RAM. (I cover the rest of the System Folder later in the chapter.)

Extensions and control panels are a type of System software file with a special property: If they are not in the Control Panels or Extensions folder at startup, they do not load and/or will not function. (Or at least most won't. A few control panels can be used even if they aren't in the Control Panels folder at startup.)

Apple isn't the only one to make extensions and control panels. Many popular third-party programs, including famous names like After Dark, QuicKeys, RAM Doubler, and Speed Doubler, are extensions or control panels.

Most extensions and control panels grab a certain amount of RAM when they load at startup. If you choose Apple Menu⇨About This Computer right now, you can see how much RAM they're using by looking at the bar for your System software, which includes the RAM used by all loaded extensions and control panels.

Disabling 'em all with the Shift key

You can disable all control panels and extensions by holding down the Shift key during startup until you see the "Extensions Off" message appear beneath the "Welcome to Mac OS" greeting. That's what I've done in Figure 14-1. So my naked System software uses 14.7MB of RAM, leaving me 113.1MB available for running applications (the Largest Unused Block in Figure 14-1).

Figure 14-1:
No
extension
or control
panels
loaded =
14.7MB
used by my
System
Software.

Sharp-eyed readers will notice that there's two tenths of a megabyte of RAM missing in Figure 14-1 (128 – 113.1 = 14.9, not 14.7). That's the result of something called *memory fragmentation*. In simple terms, some programs don't release all the RAM they used when you quit them. There are two solutions: Restart your Mac or buy so much RAM the little bits you lose to memory fragmentation won't bother you.

Having lots of RAM is way cool. I never get "not enough memory to open the program" messages anymore — even with seven programs open at the same time.

Discriminating disabling with Extensions Manager

When I use the Extensions Manager control panel to turn on all the Mac OS 8.5 extensions and control panels (by choosing Mac OS 8.5 All from the Selected Set pop-up menu), the System software uses 24.8MB of RAM, leaving me less RAM for programs (the Largest Unused Block in Figure 14-2). Note that RAM used by System Software includes RAM grabbed at startup by extensions and control panels like QuickDraw 3D, QuickTime, and so on.

In the bad old days, disabling extensions and control panels was a messy affair that entailed moving them out of the Extensions or Control Panels folder manually and rebooting. It wasn't long before a wide variety of third-party extension/control panel managers appeared on the market. Prior to System 7.5, almost everyone I know used one.

Here's an example of why you might want to: You can reclaim a whopping half a megabyte of RAM just by disabling the ColorSync extension (which you probably don't need). That's what this chapter is about and why I feel it may be the most important part of this book.

Figure 14-2:
With all the
extensions
and control
panels
turned on,
the System
software
eats up
more RAM.

In the rest of the chapter, when I say how much RAM you save by disabling an extension or control panel, I mean that's how much RAM you save by turning it off (that is, unchecking it) in the Extensions Manager control panel. (Of course, you also save that amount of RAM if you delete the file totally.)

The disk space measurement for each file is the size shown in list view in the Finder. The Power Macintosh G3 I use has a 4GB hard disk. If you have a larger disk, the files may occupy slightly more space on your disk than the numbers shown in this chapter because of some things called file allocation blocks, which are complicated and not important.

In other words, your mileage may vary — and my disk-size figures are just estimates provided for your convenience.

I also formatted my hard disk using HFS+. This results in files taking up less space than if you format your disk using standard HFS. If your Mac came with Mac OS 8.5 pre-installed, chances are your hard disk is formatted using the more efficient HFS+ scheme; if your Mac is older, it probably uses standard HFS. To find out, select your hard disk icon and Get Info (File⇨Get Info or Command-I). If the Format type is Mac OS Extended, your hard disk is using HFS+; if it's Mac OS Standard, it's using standard HFS.

To convert a hard disk from Mac OS Standard (i.e. regular HFS) to the more efficient HFS+, you need to back up all your data (more than once if you're smart) and then reformat (i.e. erase) the disk using Special⇨Erase Disk and choosing HFS+ from the Format pop-up menu.

Or, in other, other words, many of the files that weigh 32K or less on my 4GB drive will weigh 64K or more on hard disks formatted using standard HFS instead of HFS+ due to that file allocation block thing you don't need to know about.

The same goes for my RAM measurements. Your mileage may vary slightly. I measured RAM usage with a wonderful shareware extension/control panel manager called Symbionts, of which I'm proud to be a registered owner. If you use other software — Conflict Catcher 8, for example — to measure RAM usage, your numbers may be slightly higher or lower.

One final thing: I performed all the testing for this chapter using a fresh, non-customized installation of Mac OS 8.5. If you have other files in your System Folder, they're either part of a custom installation that I cover in Appendix A or not part of the Mac OS.

In your System Folder, you'll see several folders with "(disabled)" after their names, such as Control Panels (disabled) and Extensions (disabled). Leave them alone. The Extensions Manager uses them to disable control panels and extensions by moving them into these folders. *Remember, if the control panel or extension isn't in the Control Panels or Extensions folder at startup, it doesn't load.*

Control Panels

I cover these control panels in Chapter 12. If you don't understand the cryptic comments or side effects, try reading that control panel's entry in Chapter 12.

Appearance
Disk space: 622K

RAM used: 0K

Side effects if disabled or deleted: Loss of control of window color, theme, highlight colors, system font, collapsing windows, and so on.

Comments: I'd keep it, especially until you've played with it enough to know how you'd like your Mac to look.

Apple Menu options
Disk space: 61K

RAM used: 265K

Side effects if disabled or deleted: Loss of Apple menu submenus and recent item tracking.

Comments: I'd keep it. I love submenus and recent item tracking. Unless I were terribly RAM-constrained (using a 16- or 32MB Mac, for example), I would never even consider disabling it, much less deleting it.

AppleTalk

Disk space: 207K

RAM used: 0K

Side effects if disabled or deleted: Possible loss of printing and network services (shared disks, e-mail, and so forth).

Comments: If you're on a network, you definitely need it. If you have a printer connected, you definitely need it. Because it uses no RAM, I'd say leave it alone unless you're horribly short of disk space, in which case you may trash it. (But trust me, you'll probably want it back soon for one reason or another.)

ColorSync

Disk space: 19K

RAM used: 0K

Side effects if disabled or deleted: Loss of capability to use ColorSync.

Comments: Get rid of it unless you use ColorSync on all your monitors, printers, and scanners. And note that its related extension, ColorSync extension, is a RAM hog, using almost half a meg of memory.

Control Strip

Disk space: 31K

RAM used: 0K

Side effects if disabled or deleted: Loss of use of Control Strip and all its modules.

Comments: If you like and use Control Strip, keep it; if you hate Control Strip and never want to see it again, trash it and its close relative, the Control Strip Extension.

To save another 250-plus kilobytes of disk space, also trash the Control Strip Modules folder in the System Folder while you're trashing the Control Strip control panel.

Date & Time

Disk space: 141K

RAM used: 0K

Side effects if disabled or deleted: Loss of capability to set Macintosh internal clock. Loss of menu bar clock.

Comments: Keep it.

DialAssist

Disk space: 32K

RAM used: 0K

Side effects if disabled or deleted: Loss of dialing assistance for Apple Remote Access.

Comments: Keep it if you use ARA; otherwise, feel free to dump it.

Energy Saver

Disk space: 190K

RAM used: 32K

Side effects if disabled or deleted: No automatic screen dimming and sleep (on Energy Star–compliant models only).

Comments: If it works with your Mac and monitor and you like it, keep it. If not, trash it. But I warn you: Trashing it is not ecologically correct.

Extensions Manager

Disk space: 170K

RAM used: 0K

Side effects if disabled or deleted: Loss of capability to enable and disable individual control panels and extensions.

Comments: You need it. Keep it. *See also* the EM Extension section.

File Exchange

Disk space: 600K

Ram used: 38K

Side effects if disabled or deleted: Loss of ability to use PC-formatted disks and file-translation capabilities for documents created by applications that don't reside on your hard disk.

Comments: It's a keeper.

File Sharing

Disk space: 630K

RAM used: 1K

Side effects if disabled or deleted: Loss of capability to turn file sharing (and Program Linking) on or off.

Comments: You only need it if you use file sharing. If you never use file sharing, make sure it's turned off before you delete it.

General Controls

Disk space: 43K

RAM used: 5K

Side effects if disabled or deleted: Too numerous to mention.

Comments: Keep it. If 43K of hard disk space or 5K of RAM makes a difference to you, you've got bigger problems, and disabling or trashing the General Controls control panel isn't going to help you.

You can get along without General Controls, but you won't be able to change any of its settings without first putting it back in the Control Panels folder and restarting your Mac.

Internet

Disk space: 304K

RAM used: 0K

Side effects if disabled or deleted: Too numerous to mention.

Comments: Keep it unless you never use the Internet, in which case feel free to trash it or turn it off.

Keyboard

Disk space: 41K

RAM used: 0K

Side effects if disabled or deleted: Loss of capability to specify key repeat speed and rate or choose foreign-language keyboard layouts.

Comments: Keep it.

Launcher
Disk space: 60K

RAM used: 0K

Side effects if disabled or deleted: Loss of Launcher window.

Comments: You can hear what I think about Launcher in Chapter 6, if you don't know already. I trashed mine.

Location Manager
Disk space: 370K

RAM used: 0K

Side effects if disabled or deleted: Loss of Location Manager; mostly only useful on a PowerBook.

Comments: Delete it unless you use a PowerBook and want to create custom locations.

Memory
Disk space: 40K

RAM used: 0K

Side effects if disabled or deleted: Too numerous (and awful) to mention. (See Chapter 9 for details.)

Comments: Do not delete!

Modem
Disk space: 137K

RAM used: 0K

Side effects if disabled or deleted: Possible loss or disruption of modem services.

Comments: If you use a modem, keep it.

Monitors & Sound

Disk space: 165K

RAM used: 0K

Side effects if disabled or deleted: Loss of capability to switch monitor color depths, alert sounds, and sound volume. Loss of additional capabilities if you have more than one monitor or a multisync monitor.

Comments: Keep it.

Mouse

Disk space: 28K

RAM used: 0K

Side effects if disabled or deleted: Loss of capability to change mouse tracking or double-click speed.

Comments: Keep it.

Numbers

Disk space: 16K

RAM used: 0K

Side effects if disabled or deleted: Loss of capability to change thousands of separators, decimal separators, and symbols for currency.

Comments: I've never used it.

QuickTime Settings

Disk space: 80K

RAM used: 0K

Side effects if disabled or deleted: Loss of AutoPlay features for CDs and CD-ROMs and some MIDI (Musical Instrument Digital Interface) configuration options.

Comments: Your call. If you need it, you probably know it. I'm keeping mine.

Remote Access

Disk space: 380K

RAM used: 0K

Side effects if disabled or deleted: Loss of ability to access your Mac remotely.

Comments: Like the old doctor joke, if you want to make remote connections to this Mac, don't trash it. Conversely, if you never dial in to this computer, trash that puppy.

Speech

Disk space: 104K

RAM used: 32K

Side effects if disabled or deleted: Loss of ability to use Talking Alerts and Text-to-Voice.

Comments: Your call. It does use a little RAM, and its 8MB Voices folder, which you can find in the Extensions folder, takes up a bit of disk space. I think the voices are cute and I am keeping them.

Startup Disk

Disk space: 25K

RAM used: 0K

Side effects if disabled or deleted: Loss of capability to choose a startup disk if more than one disk with a System Folder is connected at startup.

Comments: You may need it someday, especially if you're going to add an additional storage device — external hard disk; SyQuest, Zip, Jaz, or magneto-optical disk drive; or whatever. I say keep it.

TCP/IP

Disk space: 284K

RAM used: 0K

Side effects if disabled or deleted: Loss of ability to connect to Internet.

Comments: If you use the Internet, keep it; if you don't, you don't need it.

If you're on a network but don't use the Internet, check with your network administrator before trashing this (or any other) piece of System software.

Text

Disk space: 15K

RAM used: 0K

Side effects if disabled or deleted: Loss of capability to choose Text Behaviors.

Comments: If you only run the American version of Mac OS 8.5, you'll probably never need it.

Users & Groups

Disk space: 753K

RAM used: 1K

Side effects if disabled or deleted: Loss of capability to create users and groups for file sharing.

Comments: If you don't use file sharing, you don't need it.

Web Sharing

Disk space: 587K

RAM used: 0K

Side effects if disabled or deleted: Loss of capability to use your Mac as a personal Web server.

Comments: If your Mac isn't connected to the Internet full-time, you can't use Web Sharing, so you may as well delete it.

Control panels by RAM used

Table 14-1 is a quick-reference chart of the control panels in descending order of RAM usage.

Table 14-1	Control Panel RAM Usage
Control Panel	*RAM Used*
Apple Menu Options	265
File Exchange	38
Energy Saver	32
Speech	32
General Controls	5
File Sharing	1
Users & Groups	1

The rest of the items in your Control Panels folder use no RAM, even if they're in the Control Panels folder at startup.

Control panels by disk space used

To see a list of items in your Control Panels folder in descending order of size, choose View⇨As List and View⇨Sort List⇨by Size. The Control Panels folder window now displays its contents in descending size order.

Extensions

There are three main types of extensions among the approximately 113 items in your Extensions folder:

- ✔ System extensions
- ✔ Chooser extensions
- ✔ Apple Guide documents

Apple Guide documents use no RAM, nor do most Chooser extensions. System extensions, on the other hand, almost always grab a bit of RAM at startup. There are also a couple of other kinds of files in the Extensions folder; I talk about them after I finish with the big three.

To see these items by type, open the Extensions folder and then choose View⇨As List and then choose View⇨Sort List⇨by Kind. If the View by Kind option isn't available, choose View⇨View Options and check Kind under the Show Column heading.

System extensions

System extensions are the most important extensions. They do the most work (meaning they add useful features to the Mac OS), but they can also save you lots of precious RAM if you disable or delete them (if, of course, you don't need them).

EM Extension

Disk space: 6K

RAM used: 0K

Side effects if disabled or deleted: Loss of use of Extensions Manager control panel.

Comments: Keep it.

Why is EM Extension first in an alphabetical list? Because Apple ships it with a space before the E so that it is first in alphabetical lists. Extensions load alphabetically, and because this is the extension that gives Extensions Manager its powers, it must load before the other extensions in order to turn them on or off.

Hold down the spacebar just after you power up your Mac to use Extensions Manager *before* other extensions begin to load.

Apple CD/DVD Driver

Disk space: 101K

RAM used: 80K

Side effects if disabled or deleted: Loss of ability to use CD-ROM or DVD disks.

Comments: Since you almost certainly have a CD-ROM drive, you need it.

Apple Enet

Disk space: 371K

RAM used: 0K

Side effects if disabled or deleted: Loss of use of Ethernet.

Comments: If you use Ethernet, keep it; if not, disable it.

Apple Guide

Disk space: 664K

RAM used: 105K

Side effects if disabled or deleted: Loss of Apple Guide (interactive help).

Comments: Tough call. It uses a great deal of disk space (if you count all its Guide files) and a significant amount of RAM, but I think it's worth keeping. Delete or disable it only if you absolutely must.

Apple IX3D Graphics Accelerator

Disk space: 199K

RAM used: 312K

Side effects if disabled or deleted: Advanced features of IX3D video card disabled.

Comments: Disable it unless you have IX3D video card (many G3 models do; see your documentation for details).

Apple Photo Access

Disk space: 158K

RAM used: 0K

Side effects if disabled or deleted: Loss of capability to open PhotoCD files.

Comments: PhotoCD is the Kodak format for high-resolution image storage. PhotoCD files mostly come on CD-ROM disks. If you're likely to encounter PhotoCD files, keep it. If you don't have a CD-ROM drive, you definitely don't need it.

Apple QD3D HW Driver

Disk space: 15K

RAM used: 0K

Side effects if disabled or deleted: Loss of access to QuickDraw 3D–capable hardware.

Comments: If you use QuickDraw 3D–capable hardware, keep it. If not, delete it.

AppleScript

Disk space: 1MB

RAM used: 58K

Side effects if disabled or deleted: Loss of use of AppleScript scripts and Script Editor program.

Comments: You read Chapter 13, right? You know whether you want to keep AppleScript. (I would.)

Application Switcher

Disk space: 86K

RAM used: 0K

Side effects if disabled or deleted: Can't tear off application menu in upper-right corner of menu bar.

Comments: Keep it unless you never want to tear off the application menu.

ATI Driver Update, ATI Graphics Accelerator, ATI Video Accelerator

Disk space: 522K, 181K, and 36K, respectively

RAM used: 0K

Side effects if disabled or deleted: Loss of use of ATI-accelerated video, found in most newer Macs.

Comments: If you don't have ATI video, trash all three. If you have a newer Mac, like a G3, Powerbook G3, or iMac, leave 'em alone.

Audio CD Access

Disk space: 11K

RAM used: 0K

Side effects if disabled or deleted: Loss of capability to play audio CDs (that is, your David Garza and Elvis Costello CDs, or at least *my* David Garza and Elvis CDs).

Comments: If you don't have a CD-ROM drive, you don't need it. If you have a CD-ROM drive, you should probably keep it around, just in case.

Color Picker

Disk space: 488K

RAM used: 26K

Side effects if disabled or deleted: Loss of the new Apple Color Picker.

Comments: This whole shebang refers to which Color Picker you see in programs that use a color picker to choose among colors (most graphics programs).

The new Color Picker is, in my humble opinion, prettier than the old one and probably easier to use. Trashing this extension usually has little consequence, but if you use color graphics programs of any sort, you may want to keep it around.

ColorSync Extension

Disk space: 1MB

RAM used: 488K

Side effects if disabled or deleted: Loss of use of ColorSync (Apple's color matching system for monitors, printing devices, and scanners).

Comments: You probably don't need it unless you scan or print color images. And it uses a lot of RAM and disk space for something most people have no need for.

Contextual Menu Extension

Disk space: 74K

RAM used: 180K

Side effects if disabled or deleted: Loss of support for contextual menus in applications.

Comments: Keep it. Contextual menus are a cool new feature and are available in some applications. I'd keep it.

Desktop Printer Spooler

Disk space: 69K

RAM used: 0K

Side effects if disabled or deleted: Loss of desktop printer support.

Comments: Lets you drag and drop documents onto desktop printer icons and change printers without opening the Chooser. Keep it.

Ethernet (Built-In)
Disk space: 132K

RAM used: 0K

Side effects if disabled or deleted: Loss of use of Ethernet.

Comments: If you use Ethernet, keep it; if not, disable it.

FBC Indexing Scheduler
Disk space: 15K

RAM used: 0K

Side effects if disabled or deleted: Loss of ability to schedule indexing in the Find utility.

Comments: Keep it.

File Sharing extension
Disk space: 190K

RAM used: 4K

Side effects if disabled or deleted: Loss of file-sharing capability.

Comments: If you don't use file sharing, you can safely delete it.

Folder Actions
Disk space: 22K

RAM used: 0K

Side effects if disabled or deleted: Loss of capability to run AppleScripts attached to folders.

Comments: It's small and uses no RAM. I'd keep it even if you don't think you need it.

Foreign File Access

Disk space: 39K

RAM used: 135K

Side effects if disabled or deleted: Loss of capability to mount some CD-ROM disks.

Comments: If you have a CD-ROM drive, you need it; if you don't, you don't.

High Sierra File Access

Disk space: 19K

RAM used: 0K

Side effects if disabled or deleted: Loss of capability to mount some CD-ROM disks.

Comments: If you have a CD-ROM drive, you need it; if you don't, you don't.

Intel Raw Video, Indeo Video

Disk space: 253K and 13K, respectively

RAM used: 0K

Side effects if disabled or deleted: Loss of ability to view some types of video in your browser.

Comments: If you use the Internet, keep both.

Internet Config extension

Disk space: 95K

RAM used: 0K

Side effects if disabled or deleted: Internet configuration options won't be shared among applications.

Comments: Your browser and other Internet programs may not work properly without it. If you use the Internet, keep it.

Iomega Driver

Disk space: 66K

RAM used: 54K

Side effects if disabled or deleted: Loss of ability to mount Iomega Zip or Jaz disks automatically when inserted.

Comments: If you have an Iomega storage device — a Zip or Jaz drive — keep it. Otherwise you can safely trash it.

ISO 9660 File Access

Disk space: 20K

RAM used: 0K

Side effects if disabled or deleted: Loss of capability to mount some CD-ROM disks.

Comments: If you have a CD-ROM drive, you need it; if you don't, you don't. (I'm sorry if I sound like a broken record, but that's my advice.)

LocalTalkPCI

Disk space: 56K

RAM used: 0K

Side effects if disabled or deleted: Slower file transfers on LocalTalk.

Comments: If you use a LocalTalk network — AppleTalk or Ethernet — keep it.

MacinTalk 3 and MacinTalk Pro

Disk space: 351K and 790K, respectively

RAM used: 0K

Side effects if disabled or deleted: Loss of speech capabilities; see Speech control panel.

Comments: If you want your Mac to talk to you, keep them; if not, don't. Don't forget to also trash the Voices folder (see next section), Speech control panel (previous section), and Speech Manager extension if you decide to trash these two.

Printer Share

Disk space: 79K

RAM used: 12K

Side effects if disabled or deleted: Loss of capability to share certain devices, such as plotters, that could not be shared previously. Also, loss of the capability to password-protect color printers that use expensive printing materials.

Comments: If you're on a network, ask your network administrator before deleting or disabling.

QuickDraw 3D

Disk space: 1.4MB

RAM used: 0K

Side effects if disabled or deleted: Loss of use of QuickDraw 3D.

Comments: Keep it unless you're horribly pressed for disk space.

QuickTime, QuickTime MPEG Extension, QuickTime Musical Instruments, and QuickTime PowerPlug

Disk space: 2.6MB, 265K, 2MB, and 2.4MB, respectively

RAM used: Approximately 425K for all four pieces.

Side effects if disabled or deleted: Loss of capability to play QuickTime movies or use QuickTime applications.

Comments: I leave mine enabled all the time, but I probably have more stuff that requires QuickTime than you do. If you use QuickTime, even occasionally, leave these items alone.

QuickTime VR

Disk space: 585K

RAM used: 2K

Side effects if disabled or deleted: Loss of support for QuickTime VR.

Comments: QuickTime VR is a cool 3-D format used on some Web sites and games. Delete it if you don't go to multimedia sites and if you're sure that you don't have any games that need it.

Remote Only

Disk space: 4K

RAM used: 0K

Side effects if disabled or deleted: Can't access Mac from remote computer(s).

Comments: Keep it if you use Remote Access; dump it if you don't.

Shared Library Manager and Shared Library Manager PPC

Disk space: 165K and 207K, respectively

RAM used: 0K

Side effects if disabled or deleted: Many programs and utilities cease to function.

Comments: You need these. Don't delete them.

Sound Manager

Disk space: 370K

RAM used: 53K

Side effects if disabled or deleted: Sounds may not work properly.

Comments: Keep it.

Speech Manager

Disk space: 31K

RAM used: 11K

Side effects if disabled or deleted: No speech. See also MacinTalk extensions, Speech Control Panel, and Voices in this chapter.

Comments: Keep it if you want your Mac to speak.

SystemAV

Disk space: 320K

RAM used: 0K

Side effects if disabled or deleted: Monitors & Sound control panel quits working.

Comments: Don't delete it. Keep it.

Time Synchronizer

Disk space: 43K

RAM used: 0K

Side effects if disabled or deleted: Loss of ability to automatically update your computer's clock for daylight savings time and to synchronize your clock with a network time server.

Comments: I'd keep it. It's not essential and nothing bad happens without it, but I'm keeping mine anyway.

UDF Volume Access

Disk space: 252K

RAM used: 0K

Side effects if disabled or deleted: You won't be able to read UDF formatted volumes, which include DVD disks.

Comments: If you don't have a DVD drive, you can trash it.

Video Startup

Disk space: 69K

RAM used: 26K

Side effects if disabled or deleted: Loss of use of Apple Video Player application.

Comments: If you use Apple Video Player, keep it. If you use QuickTime, keep it. Otherwise, you can trash it if you like.

Web Sharing Extension

Disk space: 349K

RAM used: 0K

Side effects if disabled or deleted: Loss of ability to use your Mac as a Web server.

Comments: Dump it unless you use your Mac as a Web server, which is unlikely.

~AppleVision

Disk space: 598K

RAM used: 185K

Side effects if disabled or deleted: Only required if you have an AppleVision monitor. If so, you need it to use the Monitors & Sound control panel.

Comments: If you don't have an AppleVision monitor, by all means dump this sucker. (By the way, in case you were wondering, the tilde at the start of this extension's name forces it to the bottom of this alphabetical list.)

Chooser extensions

Chooser extensions are extensions that appear in the Chooser desk accessory when you open it. AppleShare is one of them; all the others are *printer drivers*, the software that your Mac requires to talk to a printer.

AppleShare

Disk space: 293K

RAM used: 195K

Side effects if disabled or deleted: Loss of use of file sharing.

Comments: If you use file sharing, you need it; if you don't, you don't.

Printer drivers

The Installer puts several printer drivers into your Extensions folder for you: Color SW 1500, Color SW 2500, Color SW Pro, ImageWriter, LaserWriter 8, StyleWriter 1200, and LaserWriter 300/LS.

Disk space: Between 46K and 845K each

RAM used: 0K

Side effects if disabled or deleted: None, as long as you leave the driver for *your* printer(s) — that is, the printer(s) that you use — in the Extensions folder.

Comments: You only need the driver or drivers that match the printer(s) you use. If you never use any color printer, for example, get rid of every Chooser extension with the word *color* in its name. If you never use an ImageWriter, get rid of all the ImageWriter Chooser extensions. And so on.

Apple Guide documents

There may be as many as ten Apple Guide documents in the Extensions folder.

Disk space: 4K to 500+K

RAM used: 0K

Side effects if disabled or deleted: Loss of use of Apple Guide interactive help.

Comments: If you don't use Apple Guide, you can safely delete all of the Guide files. But I'd leave them alone. You never know when you'll need help, and if you delete these files, help won't be available when you need it.

Other items in the Extensions folder

At least one of the following is not even an extension, and the rest you should probably leave alone.

Desktop PrintMonitor

Disk space: 77K

RAM used: 0K

Side effects if disabled or deleted: Loss of capability to print in background.

Comments: Keep it.

Desktop PrintMonitor is not an extension, although it lives in the Extensions folder. It is an application. Thus, it only uses RAM when background printing is taking place.

If you have problems with background printing, try increasing Desktop PrintMonitor's preferred memory size (in its Get Info window).

OpenTptAppleTalkLib, OpenTptInternetLib, OpenTptModem, OpenTpt Remote Access, OpenTpt Serial Arbitrator, and OpenTransportLib

Disk space: about 800K altogether

RAM used: about 200K

Side effects if disabled or deleted: Loss of ability to use Internet and networking features.

Comments: Leave these alone if you use a network or the Internet. Even if you don't, you may someday need these things. Disable them in Extensions Manager if you must, but leave them on your hard disk if you can.

Anything with the word "Lib" or "Library" in its name

The extensions in this category include any item that is of the Library *kind*. If you sort your Extensions folder *by kind* when you're in List view, you can see all of the various libraries.

Disk space: Varies

RAM used: under 100K total

Side effects if disabled or deleted: Lots of stuff will stop working.

Comments: Don't trash or disable any "Lib" or "Library" files. If you're horribly short of disk space, you're better off trashing a game you never play or some documents you may never need again.

Folders in the Extensions folder

There are several folders in the System Folder; you may or may not need them or their contents.

ActiveX Controls

This folder contains 112K of files your browser may someday need. Trash it at your own risk if you use the Internet.

Find

Stores searches and indexes. If you want Find to work properly, leave it alone.

Global Guide Files

This folder contains additional Apple Guide files for Monitors, Sound, and Color. Feel free to trash any that you don't need.

Location Manager Modules

This folder contains 260K of modules for the Location Manager, used with PowerBooks to customize network and Internet connections. Trash them if you don't have a PowerBook.

Modem Scripts

This folder contains over 400K of modem stuff, most of which you don't need. You can trash all the scripts except for the one whose name matches your modem if you need the disk space.

MRJ Libraries

This folder contains over 11MB of Java-related stuff. You'll need it if you use MRJ (Macintosh Runtime for Java) to view Java-enabled Internet sites. If you don't use the Internet, you can trash it.

Multiprocessing

You don't need this folder or its contents unless your Mac has multiple processors (few do, at least so far).

PPP Connect Scripts

This folder contains files used by your modem to connect to an ISP or other online service. If you use a modem, leave it alone. If you don't use a modem or connect to the Internet, you can trash it.

Printer Descriptions

This folder in your Extensions folder contains printer description files for 33 Apple printers. They require from 21K to 130K of disk space and use no RAM. You can delete all but the one (or ones) that match your printer (or printers).

Voices

This 8MB folder contains the voices used by Speech and MacinTalk. If you don't need the voices, you don't need the folder. And if you only use a couple of voices, delete the ones that you don't use.

Extensions by RAM used

Table 14-2 is a quick-reference chart of the extensions, sorted in descending order by RAM usage.

Table 14-2	Extension RAM Usage
Extension	*RAM Used*
ColorSync Extension	488K
QuickTime, QuickTime MPEG Extension, QuickTime Musical Instruments, and QuickTime PowerPlug	425K for all four pieces
Apple IX3D Graphics Accelerator	312K
AppleShare (Chooser Extension)	195K
~AppleVision	185K
Contextual Menu Extension	180K
Foreign File Access	135K
Apple Guide	105K
Apple CD/DVD Driver	80K
AppleScript	58K
Iomega Driver	54K
Sound Manager	53K
Color Picker	26K
Video Startup	26K
Printer Share	12K

All other extensions use 5K or less of RAM.

Extensions by disk space used

To see a list of items in your Extensions folder in descending order of size, first use the View⇨Views Options to turn on Calculate Folder Sizes; then choose View⇨As List and then View⇨Sort List⇨by Size. The Extensions folder window now displays its contents in descending size order.

The Rest of the Stuff in Your System Folder

The installer installed more than just control panels and extensions. Here's what the rest of it does:

The difference between applications and desk accessories

I promise in Chapter 4 to explain the difference between an application and a desk accessory (DA) here in Chapter 14. Being a man of my word, here goes:

Desk accessories are a throwback to System 4 and earlier, when there was no multitasking and no way to run more than one program at a time. Desk accessories were mini-programs that could be used even while other programs were open.

These days, now that opening multiple programs is the norm, desk accessories are the same as other programs — with three little differences:

- In list view, under the Kind category, desk accessories are listed as desk accessories (duh), not applications.

- You can't change a desk accessory's Minimum or Preferred Memory Requirements.

- Every desk accessory uses 20K of RAM (in About This Computer).

For all intents and purposes, a desk accessory is the same as an application program.

Appearance (folder)

Contains stuff associated with the Appearance control panel. If you want to use themes or sounds, leave it alone.

Apple Menu Items (folder)

The Apple Menu Items folder, which I cover extensively in Chapter 4, contains some folders, some desk accessories, and some applications.

The items in your Apple Menu Items folder only use RAM after you open them. So don't get rid of them to save RAM. If you're really short on disk space, use the old "View as list, sort by size" trick to find out how much each Apple Menu Item uses.

The only one that's an easy call is Jigsaw Puzzle, which is totally useless. (My wife Lisa chimes in: "Don't tell them that! I like the Mac jigsaw puzzle — the kids can't hide the pieces.") The other items are all useful in some way, and I'd recommend keeping them around.

Application Support (folder)

Some programs stash their "stuff" in this folder. I suggest you leave it alone or some programs may quit working.

Clipboard

Disk space: Varies

RAM used: 0K

Side effects if disabled or deleted: Loss of Clipboard contents at the moment of deletion.

Comments: This file is like a chameleon's tail — it regenerates if it's damaged or destroyed. So don't bother deleting it, it'll just grow back. Besides, why would you want to?

ColorSync Profiles (folder)

Disk space: 1.3MB, more or less

RAM used: 0K

Side effects if disabled or deleted: ColorSync won't work without it.

Comments: Don't delete it if you use ColorSync. Feel free to delete the entire folder if you don't use ColorSync.

Control Strip Modules (folder)

Disk space: 285K, more or less

RAM used: 0K

Side effects if disabled or deleted: Loss of use of module if it's not in this folder.

Comments: Don't delete it if you use Control Strip. Feel free to delete individual modules you don't use if you feel like it.

Favorites (folder)

Contains aliases of your favorite items created by choosing Add to Favorites from the contextual or File menus. Leave it be.

Finder

Disk space: 2.3MB

RAM used: Not applicable

Side effects if disabled or deleted: Loss of use of Mac.

Comments: Don't even think about it. Your Mac won't boot without a Finder.

Fonts (folder)

Contains your fonts; leave it be.

Help (folder)

Contains files your Help system requires. Leave it alone.

Internet Search Sites (folder)

Contains information the Find utility needs to search the Internet. You can delete it if you never use the Internet. Otherwise, leave it be.

Launcher Items (folder)

Contains the items that show up in Launcher; you need it if you use Launcher. So if you use Launcher, leave this folder alone. If you don't, feel free to trash it.

MacTCP DNR

Contains information used by TCP/IP. You need it if you use the Internet. If you're not planning to log on, you can delete it.

Preferences (folder)

The Preferences folder is where all programs, extensions, control panels, and desk accessories store their preferences files. These files store information that the program (or extension, control panel, or desk accessory) needs to remember between uses.

Most preferences files regenerate themselves when deleted, so trashing them is usually a waste of time.

When you get rid of a program, extension, control panel, or desk accessory, there's a good chance that it has left behind a preferences file in the Preferences folder. It's not a bad idea to go into your Preferences folder every so often and trash any files that appear to belong to software no longer on your hard disk.

For example, if you decide that you never want to use the Launcher control panel again, you can delete the Launcher Preferences file. Though Launcher Preferences only uses a few K of disk space, after a while, your Preferences folder may become quite crowded with preferences files that belong to software you don't even have on your hard disk any more.

Ack! I just looked at the Preferences folder on my main Mac and discovered more than 200 preferences files, at least half from programs that I no longer have or use.

I'll be right back — I'm going to practice what I preach and clean it up by trashing unneeded and unwanted prefs files.

I'm back. While I was doing my spring cleaning, I remembered another good tip having to do with preferences files: Trashing a program's preferences file can sometimes fix problems with the program itself.

If you have a program, extension, control panel, or desk accessory that's acting strange in any way — crashing, freezing, quitting unexpectedly — look in the Preferences folder and see if it's got a preferences file. If it does, try deleting it. Then restart your Mac.

This tip doesn't always work, but it's worth a try if a program that used to work starts acting funky.

By the way, some programs store all your customized settings (key combinations, macros, window positions, serial number, and so on) in their preferences files. If you delete these files, you may have to reset some of your customized settings in these programs or reenter your serial number. In most cases, that's no big deal, but in the case of, say, my Microsoft Word preferences, I'd have to spend about three hours recustomizing all my menus and keyboard shortcuts. Not fun. In fact, I keep a backup copy of my Word prefs on a floppy just in case the file gets corrupted or somebody comes along and changes things when I'm not around.

Print Monitor Documents (folder)

It'll just come back if you delete it and do any background printing. So just leave it.

Scrapbook File

Disk space: Varies

RAM used: 0K

Side effects if disabled or deleted: Loss of contents of Scrapbook.

Comments: If you don't use Scrapbook, you can delete it. But if you have anything you care about in the Scrapbook, you'll lose it when you trash this file.

Scripting Additions (folder)

Contains files used by AppleScript. If you don't intend to use AppleScript, it's safe to trash this folder.

Scripts (folder)

Contains files used by AppleScript. If you don't intend to use AppleScript, it's safe to trash this folder.

Shutdown Items (folder)

Put aliases of items you want to execute when you shut down your Mac in here. Leave it.

Startup Items (folder)

Put aliases of items you want to execute when you start up your Mac in here. Leave it.

System

Disk space: 9.7MB

RAM used: Not applicable

Side effects if disabled or deleted: Loss of use of Mac.

Comments: Don't even think of it. Your Mac won't boot if this file isn't in the System Folder.

System Resources

Disk space: 711K

RAM used: Not applicable

Side effects if disabled or deleted: Loss of use of Mac.

Comments: Don't even think of it. Your Mac won't boot if this file isn't in the System Folder along with the System and Finder files.

Text Encodings (folder)

Required for foreign language versions of Mac OS. If you only use one language, you can delete the other items in this folder if you like. I strongly suggest that you don't delete Unicode Encodings and Western Language Encodings, though. Your Mac may not work properly without them.

Chapter 15

Internet-Working

● ●

In This Chapter

▶ An overview of the Internet

▶ The Internet Setup Assistant

▶ Surfing with Internet Explorer

▶ E-mail with Outlook Express

▶ The Internet-related control panels

● ●

The Internet, sometimes referred to as the Information Superhighway, is a giant worldwide network of computers. With an Internet connection, you can view text and graphics on your computer, even if the text and graphics are sitting on a computer in Tokyo. The Internet enables you to send and retrieve messages and computer files to and from almost anywhere in the world — in milliseconds. Simply put, the Internet connects your Mac to a wealth of information residing on computers around the world. Lucky for you, Mac OS 8.5 has the best and most comprehensive Internet tools ever shipped with Mac OS.

I admit right now that this chapter covers only the barest minimum of stuff you need to know to connect to the Internet. There's so much more to say that you could write a book about it, and in fact, Charlie Seiter has. So if you're really interested in knowing more about Macs and the Internet, look for the 3rd Edition of *The Internet For Macs For Dummies* by Charles Seiter at fine bookstores everywhere.

Internet Overview (Brief)

The Internet, which is really nothing more than a giant conglomeration of connected computers, offers many kinds of services. This chapter covers the top two: the World Wide Web and electronic mail.

Other services offered on the Internet include live online chatting, bulletin board discussions called newsgroups, FTP (file transfer protocol) and video conferencing. After you've got your connection set up (something I cover in a moment), I urge you to check out these nifty features. Unfortunately, while this is way-interesting stuff, it's also beyond the purview, so that's all I'm going to say about them.

The most interesting part of the Internet, at least in my humble opinion, is the World Wide Web, the part of the Internet that lets you *surf* to *Web sites* and view them on your computer with software called a *browser*.

Mac OS 8.5 offers built-in Internet connectivity right out of the box. While most previous versions provided some of the plumbing, in the form of MacTCP, it was still up to you to assemble appropriate programs — browsers, PPP client (you don't need to know what that means yet, but you will in a moment), FTP client, e-mail program, and so on — on your own. Mac OS 8.5 comes with its own built-in PPP client (for making modem connections to the Internet) plus Microsoft Internet Explorer, the browser that allows you to browse the World Wide Web, download remote files via File Transfer Protocol, and more, and Microsoft Outlook Express, for e-mail and news reading.

Because Mac users like things to be easy, Mac OS 8.5 includes a cool piece of software called Internet Setup Assistant to help you get and configure an account with an Internet Service Provider. Once your Internet connection is up and running you can use the included Internet Explorer or use your own copy of Netscape Navigator or Netscape Communicator to cruise the Internet.

Or you can even use all three if you've got enough disk space. There's no reason you can't; just launch the one you feel like using when you're ready to surf.

But before I can talk about Internet Explorer or Outlook Express, I must first help you configure your Internet connection. When that is done, you can play with Internet Explorer and Outlook Express to your heart's content.

Getting Set Up for Surfing

If you're a typical home user, there are three things you need to surf the Internet:

- A modem (or other connection to the Internet such as ISDN, ADSL, cable, or satellite)
- An account with an ISP (Internet service provider) or America Online.
- Mac OS 8.5's default installation

If you use your Mac in an office setting or have a fast Internet connection via ISDN, ADSL, cable modem, or other scheme, you may use something other than a regular modem. Your network administrator (the person you run to when something goes wrong with your computer) or ISP is going to have to help you set up your Mac if you use one of these schemes instead of a modem, as setting up those other configurations is, once again, beyond the purview of this book.

It starts with the modem

A *modem* is a small, inexpensive device that turns data (that is, computer files) into sounds and then squirts them across phone lines. At the other end, another modem receives these sounds and turns them back into data (that is, your files).

There are two things to know if you're going out to buy a modem.

- ✔ Make sure it runs at 56 Kbps (or higher), or you'll be very unhappy with the speed at which you surf. Most modems today run at 56 Kbps.
- ✔ Make sure it includes a Mac cable. WinDoze computers require a different kind of modem cable, so be sure to ask.

Now plug a phone line into the modem and plug the modem cable into the modem port on the back of your Mac. It's the one with the little phone icon next to it. Finally, plug the modem into an AC power source.

Your Internet service provider and you

Now that you have a modem, you need to select a company to provide you with access to the Internet. It's kind of like choosing a long-distance company — prices and services offered vary, often from minute to minute.

Once you've done that you can launch and use Internet Explorer or Outlook Express to your heart's content.

If you have already used your Mac with an ISP under a previous version of Mac OS, you may not have to do anything at all. Chances are, everything is already configured. To find out, launch Internet Explorer (look in the Internet folder that was installed with Mac OS 8.5) or your favorite browser. If it connects to the Internet when you launch it, you're golden. If not, follow the instructions in the upcoming section, "Using Internet Setup Assistant if you already have an ISP."

Finding an ISP

Here's a chicken and egg situation for you. The good news is that I found three great Web sites to help you choose an ISP:

- http://www.barkers.org/online/
- http://webpedia.ispcheck.com/
- http://thelist.internet.com/

The bad news is that you'll need a Web connection to view them, and if you don't have an ISP yet, you don't have a Web connection. With any luck, you can use a friend's computer or one at a public library; just make sure that it is connected to the Internet.

If you are an America Online subscriber you don't need to do anything more than install the AOL software and log on to AOL. You can ignore the rest of this chapter except for the parts about surfing with Internet Explorer and the control panel section at the end. You don't need Outlook Express if you get your mail via AOL.

The going rate for unlimited access to the Internet is $19.95 per month. If your service provider asks for considerably more than that, find out why.

Anyway, first select a provider. Several national online services that you've probably heard of provide Internet access. They include CompuServe, America Online, and Prodigy. There are also pure Internet service companies like Earthlink, Netcom, AT&T, and perhaps even your cable company, so shop around for the deal that works best for you.

Mac OS 8.5's Internet Setup Assistant lets you start an account with Earthlink, a decent national ISP. The advantage of this method, if you're looking for a new ISP account, is that the Internet Setup Assistant configures your whole setup automatically. The drawback is that you can't choose an ISP; your only choice using this option is Earthlink. But, as I said, it's not bad as ISPs go.

Signing up with Earthlink using Internet Setup Assistant

After you've installed Mac OS 8.5, you can find the Internet Setup Assistant in the Internet folder on your hard disk. Or you can choose if from the Internet Access submenu in your Apple Menu. It will take you through the process of setting up an account with Earthlink. You can also use it to configure or modify an existing account. We'll talk about that a bit later. For now, let's concentrate on setting up your new account with Earthlink.

The Internet Setup Assistant consists of a series of screens. You answer questions about yourself and your modem and then sign up with Apple's preferred ISP, Earthlink.

Of course, you don't have to use Earthlink. But Apple and Earthlink are probably offering some kind of incentive for you to do just that. For example, when I wrote this they were offering a $25 discount (they waived the usual $25 setup fee), but that deal could change by the time you read this. In any event, I don't think Earthlink is a bad choice. Their prices are similar to other ISPs, and they do understand Macs, something that can't be said for all ISPs.

That said, just do it:

1. **Launch Internet Setup Assistant.**

   The first screen asks "Would you like to set up your computer to use the Internet?"

2. **Click the Yes button.**

   The second screen asks "Do you already have an Internet account?"

3. **Click the No button.**

   (If the answer is yes, skip ahead to the section called, "Using Internet Setup Assistant if you already have an ISP."

   After a few moments, the first actual Internet Setup Assistant screen appears, with more information about setting up your account.

4. **Read the Internet Setup Assistant screen and then click the right arrow at the bottom of the screen to move to the next one.**

   The Modem Settings screen appears, as shown in Figure 15-1.

5. **Choose your modem from the upper pop-up menu and the port it's connected to — usually the Modem Port — from the lower pop-up menu.**

6. **Click the radio button for tone or pulse dialing — usually Tone — and leave the Ignore Dial Tone checkbox unchecked.**

7. **Enter any dialing prefixes (like 9, to get an outside line or *70 to turn off Call-Waiting) that you'll need to make a toll-free phone call.**

8. **Click the right arrow at the bottom of the screen when you've finished making your selections in the Modem Settings screen. Oh, and make sure your modem is connected and turned on.**

   Screen 3 appears, telling you about ISPs.

9. **Read Screen 3 and then click the right arrow at the bottom of the screen.**

   Screen 4 appears.

Figure 15-1:
The Internet
Setup
Assistant
walks you
through
setting up
your
modem.

10. **Choose your country from the pop-up menu, type in your area code and phone number prefix, and then click the Register button.**

    Your modem emits a shriek or two as it dials Apple's ISP referral server. After a few moments, Screen 5 appears.

11. **Read Screen 5 and then click the right arrow yet again.**

    Screen 6 appears.

12. **Click the Go Ahead button.**

Microsoft Internet Explorer launches and you can start the process of getting signed up for an Internet account with Apple's preferred service provider, Earthlink, by clicking the Begin Registration button on the Web page Internet Explorer is displaying.

When you've entered all of the information Earthlink asks for, including your credit card number, you're in business. You have an Internet account — and best of all, the software you need to use it is all configured and ready to go. Congratulations. You can skip the next section and start surfing the Web.

If you decide you don't want to sign up with Earthlink, click the Cancel Registration button. Once you've chosen another ISP, you can follow the instructions in the next section, "Using Internet Setup Assistant if you already have an ISP." But Earthlink is probably as good (or as bad) a choice as any ISP.

Using Internet Setup Assistant if you already have an ISP

If you opted not to sign up with Earthlink, or if you already have an ISP, there's still some work to do before you can get out there and surf. (Funny, that's what my mom used to say to me.)

You need a bunch of information to configure your Internet connection; you should be able to get it all from your ISP:

✔ Your domain name server (DNS) addresses and/or domain name.

✔ Type of configuration. (I cover modem here, but you could be using Ethernet, Mac IP, or something else completely. If you are, see your network administrator or call your ISP for details.)

✔ Whether you need a PPP Connect Script or not.

✔ Whether you use a Proxy Server or not.

✔ Your IP address, subnet mask, and router address.

✔ Your ISP's dial-up phone number.

✔ Your user name and password.

When you have all these pieces assembled, you're ready to do some configuring.

Actually, with Internet Setup Assistant, "configuring" is an awfully strong way to put it. Sure, you'll enter all the information you'll need to connect to the Internet, but you don't have to get lost in a maze of jargon and control panels to do it. Just open up Internet Setup Assistant and follow the arrows. What could be simpler?

1. **Launch Internet Setup Assistant.**

   The first screen asks "Would you like to set up your computer to use the Internet?"

2. **Click the Yes button.**

   A second screen appears and asks "Do you already have an Internet account?"

3. **Click the Yes button.**

   (If the answer is no, go back to the previous section and follow the directions there.)

   Screen 1 appears and reminds you of the info you'll need before you can configure your account. If something's missing, call your ISP before you go any further. Assuming you've got everything you need, click the right arrow at the bottom of the window.

4. **Name your Internet account.**

   I called mine Bob's Account (see Figure 15-2).

5. **Click the Modem radio button and then click the right arrow at the bottom of the screen.**

   The Modem Settings screen — Screen 3 — appears.

Figure 15-2:
Give your
Internet
account a
logical
name.

6. **Choose your modem from the upper pop-up menu and the port it's connected to — usually the Modem Port — from the lower pop-up menu. (Refer back to Figure 15-1.)**

7. **Click the radio button for tone or pulse dialing — usually Tone — and leave the Ignore Dial Tone checkbox unchecked.**

8. **Click the right arrow at the bottom of the screen. Oh, and make sure your modem is connected and turned on.**

   Screen 4 appears. Now you'll do some real configuring.

9. **Enter your ISP's phone number, your user name, and your password, just like I did in Figure 15-3, and then click the right arrow at the bottom of the screen.**

   Screen 5 appears and asks if you need a PPP Connect Script. Only your ISP can tell you the answer to this question.

Figure 15-3:
Tell your
Mac where
to call and
who you are
with this
Internet
Assistant
screen.

10. **So ask your ISP and then click the proper radio button — yes or no — and move on by clicking the right arrow at the bottom of the screen.**

    Screen 6 appears. Everyone who connects to the Internet uses an *IP address,* a set of unique numbers that identifies your computer. Sometimes an ISP assigns you an IP address to use with your account. Most providers, though, assign you an IP address each time you connect. It really doesn't matter how you get an IP address, as long as you get one. The only time you have to worry about it is the first time you configure your account. That would be right now.

11. **In Screen 6, if your ISP gave you an IP address, choose Yes. If not, leave No checked. Click the right arrow.**

    Screen 7 appears. Even if your ISP didn't give you an IP address of your own, you probably did get what's called a DNS address. Basically, that's the IP address of your ISP. Often, there are several. Look at Figure 15-4 to see how a DNS address (sometimes called a server address) should look. You'll also see a blank for a domain name. That's the equivalent of the DNS address in words. For my provider, it's outer.net.

Figure 15-4:
This is where you enter your ISP's DNS address and domain name.

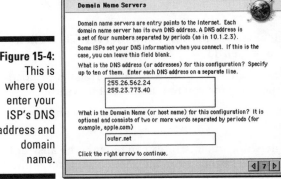

12. **Enter the DNS address and domain name and then click the right arrow to go to Screen 8.**

13. **Enter your e-mail address and password, and then click the right arrow to go to Screen 9.**

    Your e-mail address is the address you give to people who want to send you e-mail, and it's the address that appears at the top of messages you send.

14. **In Screen 9, enter the e-mail account and SMTP server address, as shown in Figure 15-5, and click the right arrow when you're done.**

    Sometimes, the account is the same as your e-mail address. Sometimes it's a little different. In this example, my e-mail address is `levitus@outer.net`, but my SMTP server is `smtp.outer.net`. The SMTP server is the machine that processes mail for your ISP.

Figure 15-5:
Enter your
e-mail
account
and SMTP
server
information
here.

15. **In Screen 10, enter the name of your ISP's news server. Then click the right arrow to go to Screen 11.**

    A news server is also called an NNTP (Network News Transfer Protocol) server, and it makes it possible for you to read Usenet newsgroups.

16. **In Screen 11, tell Internet Setup if you use proxy servers and then click the right arrow.**

    Only your ISP or your network administrator can tell you the answer to this question. Often, if you're setting up an Internet account for home use, you don't have proxy servers to worry about.

    The final Internet Setup Assistant screen gives you the chance to review your work, enable your new configuration, and get online right away.

17. **If you'd like to see what you've done, click Show Details.**

    If anything doesn't look right, click the left arrow to go back and fix it.

18. **When you're happy with your new configuration, click Go Ahead.**

    The Setup Assistant updates a few control panels while you wait.

That's it. You're good to go. Let's move on and meet your new Web browser, Microsoft Internet Explorer.

Surfing with Internet Explorer

Apple made a deal with Microsoft back in 1997, so the browser you get with your Mac is theirs, Internet Explorer. May Apple's ill-fated Cyberdog rest in peace. While some will argue that Netscape makes a better browser, Internet Explorer (IE for short) is a darn good one, and there's no reason not to use it unless you already use another browser and prefer it.

There are an amazing four ways to launch Internet Explorer:

✔ Double-click its icon in your Internet folder.

✔ Choose Apple Menu⇨Internet Access⇨Browse the Internet.

✔ Choose Apple Menu⇨Internet Access⇨Connect To... (then type in a Web address, also called a URL).

✔ Double-click the Browse the Internet icon on your desktop.

When you first launch it, you'll see that it has automatically connected you to the Internet and is displaying an Apple Web page designed especially for new Net surfers (see Figure 15-6).

If you click on the underlined words "Personalize this page" near the upper left corner of the window, you can customize this startup page to display only stuff you like. Try it, you'll like it.

Figure 15-6: Open Internet Explorer and you'll see a Web page that looks something like this.

Your copy of IE comes with some pointers — known in Web parlance as *bookmarks* — that will take you to other nifty Mac sites you'll want to check out.

Pull down the Favorites menu and take a look at the list your pals at Apple have put together. You'll find bookmarks to Apple sites (see Figure 15-7), hardware and software vendors, Mac publications, and more. Choosing any item from the Favorites menu takes you to that Web page almost immediately.

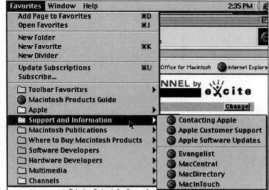

Figure 15-7: Your copy of Internet Explorer comes with a set of useful bookmarks.

Be sure and explore all of the included bookmarks when you have some time; they're all worth knowing more about.

There's a lot to IE that I don't have time to describe, but I'll hit the highlights from the top of the screen.

The buttons along the top of the window — Back, Forward, Refresh, Home, and so on — do pretty much what their names imply. Play with them a bit and you'll see what I mean.

Click the Search button to get to a *search engine* that can help you find Web pages on the Internet.

You don't have to launch IE to search the Internet at all. Just use the Finder's Find command — Sherlock — and click the Search Internet tab.

The Address field is where you type URLs you want to visit. Just type one in and press Return to surf to that site.

Web addresses (also known as URLs) almost always begin with `http://www.` But Internet Explorer does a cool trick: If you just type a name, you usually get to the appropriate Web site that way without typing `http`, `//`, or `www.` For example, if you type **Apple** into the Address field then press Return, you go to `http://www.apple.com`. Or if you type **Microsoft**, you're taken to `http://www.microsoft.com`. Try it; it's pretty cool.

Beneath the Address field are some more buttons that take you directly to pages that might interest you such as the Apple Web site, the Apple tech support Web site, the Apple Store, and so on. Click one of them to be transported instantly to that page.

Finally, to manage your bookmarks, choose Favorites⇨Open Favorites (Command-J) or click the Favorites button near the top of the window. To delete a bookmark, select it and then press Delete or Backspace.

Getting Your Mail with Outlook Express

You can use different applications to read Internet mail. Netscape Navigator and Netscape Communicator, for example, both have a built-in mail reader. But the easiest and best mail reader around (that means, the best one on your hard disk right now) is probably Outlook Express. And you can't beat the price; it's free.

Remember the handy Browse the Internet icon that got Internet Explorer up and running? Well, you'll find another icon on your Mac OS 8.5 desktop. This one looks like a hand holding a letter and is called Mail. Double-click the Mail icon to send and receive mail.

Outlook Express is fast and easy to use. It lets you send and receive messages and create an address book that includes the addresses of your friends and family. Outlook Express's main window looks like Figure 15-8.

Figure 15-8:
The Outlook
Express
main
window.

Here's how to create a message.

1. **Choose File⇨New⇨Mail Mesasge (Command-N) from the Mail menu.**

2. **Fill in the To field with someone's e-mail address.**

   (My address is `levitus@outer.net` if you don't know anyone else to send mail to.)

3. **Press Tab three times and type in a subject for this message.**

   Once you've finished addressing a mail message, you can add the recipient to your Outlook Express address book. From then on, you'll be able to type the first few letters of the recipient's name, and Outlook Express will fill out the address for you. Neat, huh?

4. **Click in the main "message" portion of the window, as shown in Figure 15-9, and type your message.**

Figure 15-9:
Using
Outlook
Express to
compose a
message.

5. **When the note says just what you want it to say, click Save to save it in the Drafts folder or Send to send it immediately.**

   If you save it into the Drafts folder (so you can write more later, perhaps), you can send it by opening the Drafts folder, double-clicking the message, then clicking Send.

Now, I know what you're thinking: How do I check my mail? Easy. Just click the Send and Receive mail button at the top of the window.

I'd love to tell you about reading newsgroups with Outlook Express, but I'm out of space. Blame my editor. He said we've already killed enough trees with this tome and that if I write one more page on this subject, he'll brain me. And I've still got four control panels I have to cover! So if you want to know more about IE or OE, I urge you to explore their help systems (available in each program's Help menu).

Four Internet-Related Control Panels

You may be wondering what happened to all the information you provided to Internet Setup Assistant. The answer is the Setup Assistant stashed it in the appropriate control panel.

If your Internet connection is working now, you have no need to even look at any of the control panels covered in the following sections. Still, in the interest of completeness (and because I said I would cover them here way back in Chapter 12), I will discuss each one briefly.

Internet control panel

The Internet control panel (shown in Figure 15-10) stores many of the settings your computer needs to connect to the Internet. It remembers stuff like your name, e-mail address, company name, user name for mail, mail server name, password (optional), and so on. If you ever need to change one of these items, the Internet control panel is the place to do it.

If you're familiar with the freeware program Internet Config, the Internet control panel does pretty much the same stuff. Choose Edit⇨User Mode and then click the Advanced buttong to reveal features such as firewalls, helper apps, fonts, and so on.

If you have multiple users, you can create a *set* of settings for each one. Just choose File⇨New Set (Command-N), name it something relevant, and fill out the information on all four tabs (Personal, E-Mail, Web, and News) for the other user or users. If the new set is similar to an existing set, you may find

Figure 15-10:
The Internet control panel stores most of the information your Mac needs to use the Internet.

it easier to use the Duplicate Set command, which is File⇨Duplicate Set (Command-D). This command creates a set with all the settings of the original set; you can then modify only the things you want to change instead of starting from scratch.

In the upper-right corner of the Internet control panel, you'll see a question mark in a circle. Click it and you'll get a ton of excellent help and information about this control panel.

TCP-IP control panel

The TCP-IP control panel stores settings your computer needs to make a connection to your ISP, including your IP address, subnet mask, router address, domain name, and name server address. If you ever need to change any of these settings, this is the place to come.

To create a set of TCP-IP settings, choose File⇨Configurations (Command-K), choose the set most like the set you wish to create, and then click the Duplicate button. Make the appropriate changes and close the TCP-IP control panel. You'll be asked if you want to save your changes. Click OK.

If you need additional information on this control panel, open Mac OS Help and search for *tcp-ip*. You'll find out more than you need to know.

Modem control panel

The Modem control panel stores settings about (what else?) your modem. It's here that you choose the brand and model of modem that you're using, whether sound should be on or off, tone or pulse dialing, and whether to ignore the dial tone.

To create a set of modem settings, choose File⇨Configurations (Command-K), choose the set most like the set you wish to create, and then click the Duplicate button. Make the appropriate changes and close the TCP-IP control panel. You'll be asked if you want to save your changes. Click OK.

In the lower-left corner of the Modem control panel is a question mark in a circle. Click it and you'll get a ton of excellent help and information about this control panel.

Location Manager control panel

If you have a PowerBook or use your computer in more than one place, this is going to be your favorite control panel (see Figure 15-11). It allows you to store and immediately switch your settings for AppleTalk, TCP/IP, Printer,

Extension Set, File Sharing State, Internet Set, Remote Access Settings, Sound Level, and Time Zone. It also allows you to specify items — such as your browser or other program — that you want to open automatically when you switch to a Location.

To configure a location, choose File⇨New Location (Command-N) and give the location a descriptive name. Next, click each item — AppleTalk, TCP/IP, Printer, Extension Set, File Sharing State, Internet Set, Remote Access Settings, Sound Level, and Time Zone — and click the Get Info button. Follow the instructions for each item to configure it. In some cases, you may have to open and configure a control panel manually; in other cases, clicking the Edit button will open the control panel you need. Just do what it says when you click Get Info and you can't go wrong.

When you close the Location Manager control panel, you are given the opportunity to save your settings.

Figure 15-11: The Location Manager control panel lets you change many settings at once.

Once you've configured one or more locations, you can switch locations from the control strip as shown in Figure 15-12.

In the upper-right corner of the Location Manager control panel is a question mark in a circle. Click it and you'll get a ton of excellent help and information about this control panel.

Figure 15-12: The Location Manager lets you switch locations from the control strip.

Part IV
The Infamous
Part of Tens

The 5th Wave   By Rich Tennant

In this part . . .

*W*e're in the home stretch now. Just three more chapters and you're outta here.

These last three are a little different — they're kind of like long top ten lists. I'd like you to believe that it's because I'm a big fan of Dave Letterman, but the truth is, IDG Books has always put a "Part of Tens" in books with *...For Dummies* in their titles, and this book must continue the tradition. Because IDG pays me, I'm doing these chapters their way. (Actually, it's kind of fun.)

First, I'll briefly describe ten (actually, 12) pieces of Mac OS 8.5 that you might someday need (and that haven't been discussed much previously). I'll tell you what they do and why you might need them. A couple of them might actually be useful to you someday.

I'll then move on to a subject near and dear to my heart: Ten awesome things for your Mac that are worth spending money on.

Finally, you'll take a tour of Dr. Mac's top ten troubleshooting tips, for those times when good System software goes bad.

Chapter 16

At Least Ten Pieces of Mac OS 8.5 That You Might Someday Need

• •

In This Chapter

▶ Internet Access

▶ Apple Remote Access

▶ Personal Web Sharing

▶ QuickDraw 3D

▶ Text-to-Speech

▶ Mac OS Runtime for Java

▶ ColorSync

▶ QuickDraw GX

▶ English Speech Recognition

▶ MultiLingual Internet Access

▶ CloseView

▶ Easy Access

• •

When you run the Mac OS 8.5 installer, there are a bunch of things that you can choose to install or not install.

If you just perform a "standard" installation, the Install Mac OS 8.5 program automatically installs Internet Access, Apple Remote Access, Personal Web Sharing, QuickDraw 3D, Text-to-Speech, Mac OS Runtime for Java, and ColorSync, plus the core components of Mac OS 8.5. (Of course, you can choose a *custom* installation and elect not to install one or more of these components. But I'm getting ahead of myself; custom installations are covered in Appendix A.)

In addition to these pieces that are installed automatically, you can choose a custom installation and also install QuickDraw GX, English Speech Recognition, MultiLingual Internet Access, CloseView, and Easy Access.

In this chapter, I tell you what each of these pieces of Mac OS does and whether or not it makes sense for you to install it. (For details on *how* to perform custom installations, see Appendix A.)

Unfortunately, due to space limitations, I can't really explain how to *use* each of these potentially useful goodies. Instead, I'll briefly describe each one and then provide some insights on whether you need it or not.

Internet Access

The Internet Access installation consists of a set of tools for accessing the Internet. Included in this set are several extensions, control panels, and utilities required to access the Internet, plus Microsoft Internet Explorer, Microsoft Outlook Express, and Netscape Navigator. An installation of all of the pieces in the Internet Access software package uses about 47 megabytes of hard disk space.

Internet Access is installed automatically unless you choose a custom install (see Appendix A).

Bob sez

If you use the Internet, of course you need this stuff. But if you don't use your Mac to connect to the Internet and don't expect to, you can save almost 50 megs of disk space by choosing not to install it.

Apple Remote Access

The Apple Remote Access installation consists of the tools you need to connect to a remote Mac OS computer via modem (direct) or via the Internet using PPP and a modem. It includes the Apple Remote Access software, Apple Remote Access Modem Scripts, and X.25 Modem scripts. An installation of all of the pieces in the Apple Remote Access package uses about 2 megabytes of hard disk space.

Apple Remote Access is installed automatically unless you choose a custom install (see Appendix A).

Bob sez

If you intend to use your Mac to connect to other Macs via modem or the Internet, by all means install it. If you don't, then don't.

Personal Web Sharing

The Personal Web Sharing installation consists of software that allows others to share documents on your computer via the World Wide Web. It includes the Personal Web Sharing control panel and control strip module, plus documentation. An installation of all the pieces in the Personal Web Sharing package uses about a megabyte of hard disk space.

Personal Web Sharing is installed automatically unless you choose a custom install (see Appendix A).

Bob sez

If you want to make files on your Mac available to others via the World Wide Web, by all means install it. If you don't, then don't.

One thing you should know is that Personal Web Sharing only works while your Mac is connected to the Internet. As long as your computer is connected to a TCP/IP network (intranet or Internet) and your server is running (turned on in the Web Sharing control panel), the server's content is available to users of the network. In other words, if you use a modem, this stuff won't be a lot of use to you unless you keep your modem connected to the Internet 24 hours a day.

QuickDraw 3D

The QuickDraw 3D installation consists of software required to view and manipulate 3D images with your Mac. It includes the actual QuickDraw 3D software, drivers for Apple's QuickDraw 3D Accelerator Cards, a special version of SimpleText, and the Scrapbook that work with 3D images and some sample 3D files. An installation of all the pieces in the QuickDraw 3D package uses just under 7 megabytes of disk space.

QuickDraw 3D is installed automatically unless you choose a custom install (see Appendix A).

Bob sez

Unless you use 3D programs or games, or view 3D stuff on the Internet, you can probably do without it. Still, it doesn't use much space and you never know when you're going to encounter a document, program, image on the Internet, or game that requires this software. I'd leave it installed if I were you.

Text-to-Speech

The Text-to-Speech installation consists of software — extensions and voice files — you need to have your computer read text and alert messages aloud. A complete installation includes the actual Text-to-Speech software, a set of high-quality voices, MacinTalk3 and MacinTalk Pro, plus Speech Manager. An installation of all the pieces of Text-to-Speech uses about 21 megabytes of disk space.

Text-to-Speech is installed automatically unless you choose a custom install (see Appendix A).

Bob sez

Text-to-Speech is kind of cool, but I never use it. The talking alerts are fun but again, I don't use them. And this stuff does use a little bit of RAM. If you're tight on disk space or memory, you can probably do without it.

If you do install it and then discover that you never use it, don't forget to turn it off using Extensions Manager — or uninstall it.

Mac OS Runtime for Java

Mac OS Runtime for Java (MRJ) is Apple's version of Java. Java is a programming language (or a platform, depending upon who you ask) that is most frequently used in Web pages you view on the Internet. Stand-alone Java programs, mostly called *applets,* are beginning to become available as well.

MRJ lets you run programs written in Java on your Mac with the included Applet Runner program, with most popular Web browsers, or with any other Java-enabled Mac OS application.

A complete installation of Mac OS Runtime for Java includes the MRJ software, the Apple Applet Runner and demonstration applets, and two extensions necessary for reading foreign language text and using MRJ with older Macs.

Mac OS Runtime for Java is installed automatically unless you choose a custom install (see Appendix A).

Bob sez

If you use the Internet (and who doesn't these days), use stand-alone Java applets, or use a Java-enabled Mac OS program, this is the implementation of Java you want. It's better and faster than any before it.

ColorSync

The ColorSync installation consists of software that helps ensure color accuracy when scanning, printing, and working with color images. A complete installation includes the ColorSync software, ColorSync profiles for a variety of monitors, scanners, and printers, and Photoshop plug-ins that let you use ColorSync from within Adobe Photoshop. An installation of all of the pieces of ColorSync uses about 6 megabytes of disk space.

ColorSync is installed automatically unless you choose a custom install (see Appendix A).

Bob sez

If you're not a graphic artist working with color files and calibrating monitors and printers to achieve accurate color matching, you don't really need it.

QuickDraw GX

QuickDraw GX was Apple's advanced printing architecture, but it has been discontinued. The QuickDraw GX installation includes the QuickDraw GX software, some QuickDraw GX fonts, and Adobe Type Manager for QuickDraw GX. An installation of all the pieces of QuickDraw GX uses just over 6 megabytes of disk space.

QuickDraw GX is not installed unless you explicitly choose to install it using a custom install (see Appendix A).

Bob sez

Unless you're one of the unlucky few who depend upon a program that requires QuickDraw GX, you don't need it.

English Speech Recognition

English Speech Recognition allows your Mac to recognize and respond to human speech, so you can say stuff like "Get my mail" to your Mac and have it actually get your mail. A complete installation consists of the English Speech Recognition software and uses about 3 megabytes of disk space.

English Speech Recognition is not installed unless you explicitly choose to install it using a custom install (see Appendix A).

Bob sez

It's clever and kind of fun, but it uses a bit of RAM and a few megs (5) of hard disk space, and it requires a microphone. And I've never gotten it to work well enough to continue using beyond a few days. Still, it's kind of neat (and it is a freebie), so you might want to install it and check it out just for kicks.

Multilingual Internet Access

Multilingual Internet Access allows multilingual programs and Internet applications to display and edit text in languages other than English. A complete install provides software to view and edit Arabic, Devanagari, Gujarati, Gurmukhi, and Hebrew text, plus software to view Japanese, Korean, Simplified Chinese, and Traditional Chinese text. You can choose to install any or all of these options. A complete installation uses about 20 megabytes of disk space.

Multilingual Internet Access is not installed unless you explicitly choose to install it using a custom install (see Appendix A).

Bob sez

If you only use your Mac for English language stuff, you don't need it. If you need one of the foreign languages just mentioned, install the one you need.

Two More Things You Should Know About

A few items are usually not installed when you choose the Easy Install option in the Mac OS 8.5 Installer program. I talk about them in Appendix A, but two of these custom-install items are so well worth knowing about that I'm going to go over my quota of ten items in this chapter and include them here.

Easy Access

Easy Access (shown in Figure 16-1) is a control panel designed primarily for people with impaired mobility. That doesn't mean it might not come in handy for anyone.

Figure 16-1:
The Easy
Access
control
panel may
come in
handy for
any user.

Easy Access lets you do three things:

🖊 Use the numeric keypad on your keyboard (instead of the mouse) to control the cursor on the screen.

🖊 Type keyboard shortcuts without having to press both keys at the same time.

🖊 Type very slowly.

Mouse Keys

When you turn on Mouse Keys, the numeric keypad, instead of the mouse, controls the cursor. The 5 key is the mouse button; the 0 key is the click and hold button. The rest of the numbers control the cursor direction (see Figure 16-2).

The keyboard shortcut Command-Shift-Clear toggles Mouse Keys on and off. If you have the audio feedback option checked, you'll hear a whoop when Mouse Keys is turned on and another when it's turned off.

Figure 16-2:
The
numeric
keypad
controls the
cursor. The
5 key is a
click; the 0
key is a
click and
hold.

The Mouse Keys radio buttons control the delay before movement occurs (after you press the key) and the speed at which the cursor travels across the screen.

Slow Keys

Slow Keys delays the Mac's recognition of keystrokes. In other words, if the acceptance delay is set to Long, you would have to hold down a key for almost two seconds for it to be recognized. This feature is designed to filter out inadvertent and accidental key presses.

Sticky Keys

Sticky Keys lets you type keyboard shortcuts one key at a time. In other words, to open an icon, you'd ordinarily press the Command and O keys simultaneously. Sticky Keys makes it possible to press the Command key first and then the O key after it.

The keyboard shortcut for turning Sticky Keys on and off is to press the Shift key five times in rapid succession. To lock the modifier key down, press it twice in rapid succession.

As illustrated in Figure 16-3, when you press the modifier key, you'll see a little icon in the upper-right corner of your menu bar that gives you visual feedback on the state of Sticky Keys.

My take: Easy Access can come in handy. For example, in programs that don't have a nudge command for moving objects one pixel at a time using the arrow keys, Mouse Keys makes a decent substitute. It might be worth keeping around for this feature alone. You can always turn it off using Extensions Manager.

Figure 16-3:
Sticky Keys
turned on
(left);
modifier key
pressed
and waiting
for
keystroke
(center);
and
modifier key
locked
(right).

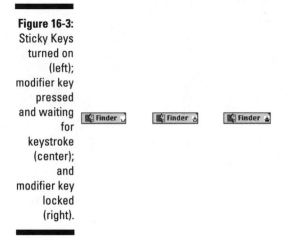

CloseView

CloseView blows up your screen. No, it doesn't make it explode; it enlarges the image, and it can all be done with keyboard shortcuts.

The CloseView control panel appears in Figure 16-4. The black frame around it is the area that will be displayed when I turn magnification on (in Figure 16-5).

CloseView uses a lot of memory — from a few hundred K to more than a thousand K. If you can afford the RAM, it's a useful little doohickey to have around. It can give you a zoom feature in programs that don't allow zooming. On the other hand, hundreds of K is a lot of RAM to waste if you don't use CloseView often.

My take: Install it but turn it off using Extensions Manager. If you need it, enable it in Extensions Manager and restart.

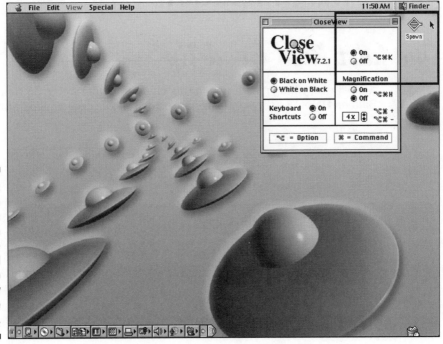

Figure 16-4:
If I turn on magnification now, the area in the frame will be blown up to fill my screen (see Figure 16-5).

Figure 16-5:
Ta-da! This
image fills
my entire
monitor.

One Last Real Good Tip

Almost everything mentioned in this chapter includes Mac OS Help and/or Balloon Help. Use them to learn more about how these goodies work.

Chapter 17

Ten Ways to Make Your Mac Better by Throwing Money at It

· ·

In This Chapter

▶ Stuff I think you ought to buy

· ·

*T*his is one of my favorite chapters. As you've probably figured out by now, I love souping up my Mac. I live to find ways of working smarter, saving time, and saving hand motion. And I revel in tweaking my Mac and Mac OS 8.5. So it gives me great pleasure to share this chapter, my personal top ten (actually, eleven, but don't tell my editor) things you can buy for your Mac to tweak it and make it faster, easier to use, and (I hope) more fun.

The items listed in this chapter are things I have, use every day, love dearly, and would buy again.

✔ **RAM:** It's worth every penny. If you have anything less than 64MB in your Mac, you'll like it a lot better if you upgrade to 64MB or more. If you like to do a few things at once, 64 or more megs of RAM will make you a happier camper. (For what it's worth, RAM has never been cheaper than it is today.)

✔ **Backup software:** There are only two kinds of Macintosh users: Those who have lost data and those who are going to. If your work means anything to you, get something that helps automate the task of backing up your files. Retrospect or Retrospect Express, both from Dantz Development, are the names to trust. Remember these words: "If you don't back it up, you will someday lose it." And please, please read Appendix B.

✔ **Big monitor:** You'll spend less time scrolling and rearranging windows. You'll spend more of your time getting actual work done, which is a good thing, right? If you still have a tiny monitor, get a bigger one. I use a multisync Sony 20sfII and love it to death. I also love my Apple flat-panel Studio Display a lot.

✔ **Modem:** Your capacity to communicate will increase tenfold. Join an online service, surf the Internet, e-mail your friends, and much, much more. Get a modem that can do 33.6 or 56 Kbps. 14.4 Kbps doesn't cut it anymore; nor does 28.8. If you're a real Internet hound, check out ISDN, ADSL, or cable modems for even faster Net access.

✔ **Games:** I just love MYTH from Bungie Software. It may just be the best game ever invented. I still like all the episodes of You Don't Know Jack. I loved Titanic — the game *and* the movie! The Marathon trilogy and Quake are cool too. My point: Gaming on the Mac has never been better.

✔ **CD-ROMs:** There are some great games, references, and educational titles out there. You'll love 'em, and so will your kids.

✔ **Some big honking speakers with a subwoofer:** Turn your boring Mac into a multimedia entertainment and education center. If you don't have great external speakers, you absolutely need them if you want the full CD-ROM or game experience on your Mac. Crank it up!

✔ **Action Files:** This utility puts Mac OS 8.5's Open and Save dialog boxes on steroids. Basically, it adds a menu bar that lets you get info, duplicate, create an alias, label, move to trash, and rename files and folders. Plus it has menus and keyboard shortcuts for easy fast access to frequently-used files and folders. You can download a demo from www.actionutilities.com/. Use it for a week, and you'll wonder how you lived without it.

✔ **QuicKeys or OneClick:** These utilities create macros called *shortcuts* that can perform a task or a series of tasks (a *sequence*) with a single command — a keystroke or mouseclick. It's like AppleScript, only better. Download a QuicKeys demo from www.cesoft.com. There wasn't a demo available for OneClick when I wrote this, but you might check www.westcodesoft.com and see if perhaps there is one now.

✔ **NetObjects Fusion:** If you're going to build a Web site and you're graphically-challenged like me, this is the program you want. Don't believe me? I don't know HTML from Jack, but I built my entire Web site — at www.boblevitus.com — in NetObjects Fusion in a matter of hours. If you want to make a Web site yourself and aren't a graphic artist, it's a must-have.

✔ **A New CPU:** If you've got any money left, consider upgrading to a newer, faster Mac. They've never been faster, cheaper, or better-equipped.

So there you have it: Eleven awesome ways to spend a big chunk of change. So ladies and gentlemen, start your checkbooks. Go forth, throw money at your Mac, and most of all, have fun.

Chapter 18

At Least Ten Things to Try When Good System Software Goes Bad

I said Chapter 14 was "easily the most useful chapter in the book." It is. Unless you wake up one morning to find your Macintosh sick or dying. Then (and only then) is this chapter more useful because it's the one that is going to save your bacon.

As a bleeding-edge Mac enthusiast with almost eleven years of Mac under my belt, I've had more than my share of Mac troubles. Over those years, I've developed an arsenal of tips and tricks that I believe can resolve more than 90 percent of Macintosh problems without a trip to the repair shop.

Disclaimer: Of course, if your hardware is dead, there's nothing you or I can do about it. But if your hardware is okay, there's a 90-percent chance that something (or a combination of things) in this chapter will get you up and running.

I know that there are *more* than ten things in this chapter. My editor says it doesn't matter, that the "Part of Tens" in *...For Dummies* books is sort of just for show, and I don't really have to have ten of anything as long as I use the word *ten* in the chapter name. Cool, eh?

Think of this chapter as yet another occasion where I give you more than your money's worth.

Dem Ol' Sad Mac Chimes of Doom Blues

One thing we all dread is seeing the Sad Mac icon (see Figure 18-1) and hearing that arpeggio in G minor, better known as the Chimes of Doom.

The Sad Mac usually indicates that something very bad has happened to your Mac, often that some hardware component has bitten the dust. But Sad Macs are rather uncommon — many users go years without seeing one. If you've got one, don't despair. Yet. There is something you can try before you diagnose your Mac as terminal — something that just might bring it back to life. Try this:

1. **Shut down your Mac.**

2a. **If your Mac came with a Disk Tools floppy disk, insert it.**

    or

2b. **If your Mac has an internal CD-ROM drive and came with a bootable CD-ROM System Software disk, insert that or the Mac OS 8.5 CD instead.**

3. **Restart your Mac.**

4. **If you are using a CD, you have to hold down the C key on your keyboard during startup.**

    Some Macs require AppleTalk to be on for CD-ROM boot to work. Go figure.

If you see the Mac OS startup screen when you boot off your Disk Tools or CD-ROM, there's hope for your Mac. The fact that you could boot from another disk indicates that there's a problem with your hard disk or your System Folder. Whatever it is, it will more than likely respond to one of the techniques discussed throughout the rest of this chapter, so read on.

If the forthcoming techniques don't fix the problem, or you still see the Sad Mac icon when you start up with Disk Tools or CD, your Mac is toasted beyond my help and needs to go in for repairs (usually to an Apple dealer).

Before you drag it down to the shop, you might try 1-800-SOS-APPL. They may well suggest something else you can try.

Flashing Question Mark Problems

Go through these steps in sequence. If one doesn't work, move on to the next.

Now would be a good time to reread the "Question Mark and the Mysterians" section of Chapter 1, which explains the flashing question mark and why Disk Tools or a bootable CD-ROM are the ultimate startup disks. Both are things you need to know before you continue.

The bootable Mac OS CD-ROM is *soooo* important, it's a good idea to have more than one copy around. That way, if one gets misplaced, damaged, eaten by the dog, scuffed, scratched, or otherwise rendered useless, you won't be totally out of luck. An older version of Mac OS or the CD that came with your computer are examples of "extra" bootable CDs you might have hanging around. The Mac OS 8.5 CD is bootable as well.

I keep the Mac OS 8.5 CD in my middle desk drawer and several other bootable CDs on the bookshelf.

If you have a removable media drive like a Zip or a Jaz or a SyQuest, it's a good idea to create a bootable cartridge (by installing Mac OS 8.5; see Appendix A) and stash it someplace safe, just in case.

If you don't have a bootable CD-ROM, preferably a Mac OS 8.5 Install CD-ROM, you can't do the rest of the stuff in this chapter. So if you don't have one handy, go find it now.

Start with something easy: Rebuild the desktop

Before attempting more drastic measures, try rebuilding the desktop.

Actually, rebuilding the desktop should go under the heading of preventive maintenance. Apple recommends rebuilding the desktop once a month, and so do I.

1-800-SOS-APPL

This is a very good number to know. It's Apple's technical support line, and it's good for all Apple-branded products. If nothing in this chapter brings you relief, call Apple before you lug the box down to the repair shop. Maybe they know something I don't.

In the bad old days, Apple's stance on technical support was "Ask your Apple dealer." That position, as you might guess, wasn't very satisfying — at least not to users. So a few years ago, Apple saw the light and instituted direct, toll-free technical support via the aforementioned 1-800-SOS-APPL, a big win for Macintosh users.

I have, since the line opened up several years ago, called a few times a year, often with an obscure problem. I have to say that they are very well informed at Apple tech support — they are batting close to 1,000, believe it or not. These guys and gals do know their stuff.

There is a drawback to this service: You may have to wait a bit. Some days it takes 30 minutes to get a live person on the phone. And some products are now covered only by "pay-to-use" support. Still, it's worth giving this number a try before you proceed any further.

Call using a speaker phone. Enjoy the soothing music and continue with your work until you hear a live person.

On the other hand, I've often had my call answered on the first ring. I think it's easier to get through first thing in the morning; they're open from 6 to 6, Pacific time.

Another good time to rebuild the desktop is if you notice icons disappearing, changing or being replaced by generic icons (see Figure 18-2). This problem is usually a result of a desktop that needs rebuilding.

Figure 18-2:
If your formerly colorful icons turn generic, like these, try rebuilding the desktop.

The desktop you're rebuilding is an invisible database that keeps track of every file on your hard disk, manages what icon goes with which file, and manages which program launches when you open a document.

More strictly speaking, the desktop is a pair of invisible files called Desktop DB and Desktop DF. They're stored at root level, but you can only see them with special software designed to work with invisible files. Leave them alone.

Another good time to rebuild the desktop is if you start getting "An application can't be found for this document" errors when you know that you have the application or have assigned a substitute using File Exchange.

Anyway, to rebuild the desktop, hold down the Command and Option keys during startup until you see the dialog box in Figure 18-3.

Figure 18-3:
Yes, you do
want to
rebuild the
desktop.
Click OK.

Are you sure you want to rebuild the desktop file on the disk "Spawn"?

Cancel | OK

After you click OK, you'll see a progress window as the desktop is rebuilt. In a moment or two, it disappears and you're off and running.

If you have more than one hard disk or hard disk partition, a dialog box like the one shown in Figure 18-3 will appear for each disk that mounts on the desktop at startup. Click OK for every disk.

If you booted from a CD, you won't be asked if you want to rebuild its desktop 'cause it's not a recordable device. Its desktop, like the rest of the data on it, can't be changed.

Just remember to rebuild your desktop monthly to keep your Mac in tip-top shape. And rebuild it again if you see the flashing question mark.

You're going to attempt to boot from your hard disk now, so remove the Disk Tools disk or bootable CD from the drive and restart.

If you still see the flashing question mark, it's time to . . .

Send for the ambulance: Run Disk First Aid

The next step in the program is to run the Disk First Aid application.

The desktop isn't the only place where hard disks store information about themselves. There are BTrees, extent files, catalog files, and other creatively named invisible files involved in managing the data on your disks. Disk First Aid is a program that checks all those files and repairs ones that are damaged.

You'll find the Disk First Aid program in the Utilities folder that was installed with OS 8.5.

The version of Disk First Aid in Mac OS 8.5 is the first ever to be able to verify and repair the startup disk. Before this you had to boot from another disk or CD to repair your startup disk. Yuck.

Here's how to make Disk First Aid do its thing:

1. **Launch the Disk First Aid application (see Figure 18-4).**

   It's probably in a folder called Utilities.

Figure 18-4:
It's Disk
First Aid to
the rescue.

Disk First Aid

2. **Click the icon for your hard disk at the top of the Disk First Aid window (see Figure 18-5).**

Figure 18-5:
Click your
hard disk's
icon and
then click
Repair; Disk
First Aid
does
the rest.

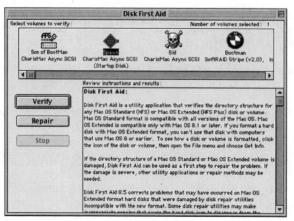

3. Click the Repair button.

Your Mac will whir and hum for a few minutes, and the results window will tell you what's going on (see Figure 18-6).

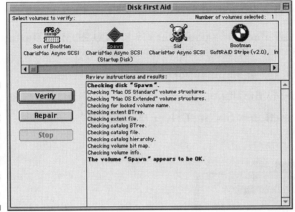

Figure 18-6:
Disk First
Aid runs
some
tests and
offers its
diagnosis.

Ultimately, Disk First Aid will tell you (you hope) that the disk appears to be okay. If so, then go back to work.

If Disk First Aid finds damage that it's unable to fix, a commercial disk-recovery tool such as Norton Utilities for the Macintosh or TechTool Pro may be able to repair the damage.

If the software *can't* repair the damage, you'll have to initialize your disk. But that's okay, right? You have that backup software and you use it.

If everything checks out with Disk First Aid, try to boot from your hard disk again. If you still get the flashing question mark, try . . .

Installing new hard disk drivers

This section applies to Apple-brand hard disks only. If you have a third-party hard disk, the procedure is different. That means if you have a Mac clone or you bought your hard disk from anyone but Apple, read your manual and do what it says. You may not want to (or even be able to) use Apple's Drive Setup application. Sorry.

What you're going to attempt next is to install (update) your hard disk drivers.

Drivers are little invisible bits of code that tell your hard disk how to communicate with a Mac. They occasionally become damaged and need replacing. Done properly, the technique is completely harmless and can make the flashing question mark disappear. Mac OS 8.5 installs new drivers automatically (on Apple-brand hard disks) when you first install it.

Here's how you actually install a new hard disk driver:

1. **Restart your Mac using your Mac OS 8.5 CD-ROM as startup disk (remember to hold down the C key at startup).**

2. **Launch the Drive Setup application.**

   It should be in the Utilities folder.

3. **Choose Functions⇨Update Driver (Figure 18-7).**

Figure 18-7: To update (install new) hard disk drivers using Drive Setup, choose Functions⇨ Update.

You should see a message telling you that the new driver won't be available until you restart your computer.

Do not click Initialize or choose Functions⇨Initialization Options! If you initialize your hard disk, it will be erased completely and irrevocably.

You get a warning or two first, but if you're not paying attention, a few false clicks (or presses of the Return or Enter key) and your hard disk is blank.

So update, don't initialize, okay?

If that solution doesn't get you up and running, and you're still seeing that danged flashing question mark when you try to boot from your hard disk, don't despair. There are still a few things you can try, such as . . .

The latest dance craze: Zapping the PRAM

Sometimes your parameter RAM (PRAM) becomes scrambled and needs to be reset.

The PRAM is a small piece of memory that's not erased or forgotten when you shut down. It keeps track of things like printer selection in the Chooser, sound level, and monitor settings.

Try zapping your PRAM if your Monitors & Sound control panel or your Chooser seem to forget their settings when you shut down or restart.

Restart your Mac and hold down Command-Option-P-R (that's four keys — good luck; it's okay to use your nose) until your Mac restarts itself again. It's kind of like a hiccup. You see the smiling Mac or flashing question mark for a second, and then that icon disappears and your Mac restarts.

Zapping the PRAM returns some control panels to their default settings (but, interestingly, not the date or time), so you may have to do some tweaking after zapping the PRAM.

SCSI voodoo

It is said that connecting more than one SCSI device — an external hard disk, SyQuest, Zip, Jaz, optical disk, scanner, and so on — requires the luck of the gods.

The first bugaboo is SCSI termination. According to Apple, the first and last device on a SCSI chain must have a terminator. No devices in between should have termination. Internal hard drives are always terminated. And the total length of a SCSI chain can be no more than 22 feet.

But sometimes you can't get your SCSI chain to work by following the rules. Sometimes it requires terminating a drive in the middle of the chain as well as the first and last drives. Other times, a chain won't work if the last device *is* terminated. The physical order of devices matters. And, of course, there are those SCSI ID numbers.

So if you're seeing a flashing question mark still, and you have any external devices attached, shut down your Mac and unplug them. After they're all disconnected, try restarting your Mac and booting from the Mac OS 8.5 CD.

Never plug or unplug SCSI devices with the power on. Turn both your Mac and the device off before you attempt to connect or disconnect any cables.

If your Mac starts up when no SCSI devices are connected, you've got a problem on the SCSI chain: a termination problem, a bad cable, or a SCSI ID conflict.

I'll be back: The terminator

A terminator is a plug that fits into the empty cable connector of the last device on your chain. Many newer external hard disks have termination built in. Consult your hard disk manual if you're not sure.

Some terminators are *pass-through* connectors, which can have a cable connected to them. Others block off that connector completely; these are known as block terminators.

If you see the flashing question mark and your last device isn't terminated, terminate it. If it is terminated, unterminate it. If you have more than one device and your terminator is a pass-through terminator, connect it to a device in the middle of the chain (instead of the end) and try to start your Mac.

If you have two terminators and two or more devices, try two terminators, one in the middle and one at the end. This trick isn't recommended, but sometimes that's what it takes to make it work.

If all this terminator juggling isn't working for you, try changing the physical order of the devices. If right now your Mac is connected to the hard disk, which is connected to the Zip drive, then try connecting the Zip drive to the Mac and the hard disk to the Zip drive.

I add and subtract SCSI devices more often in a year than most people do in two lifetimes. I'm always firing up some new storage device that someone wants me to check out. And I've had good luck since switching to a drive with Digital Active Termination.

Digital Active Termination senses how much termination your SCSI chain requires and then supplies it automatically. It's almost a miracle, and it's included on almost all storage devices from APS Technologies. Just put any device with Digital Active Termination at the end of your chain, and you are virtually guaranteed perfect termination, regardless of the number of devices in the chain or the physical order of the devices.

Cables: Cheap is bad

When troubleshooting SCSI problems, you should check your SCSI cables. If you can borrow others, try that option. Cheap cables, usually ones that are thin and flexible, are more prone to failure than heavy, shielded cables. Again, APS has excellent thick cables at fair prices.

Gotta have some ID: Unique SCSI ID numbers required

If you have multiple SCSI devices, don't forget that each must have a unique SCSI ID between 0 and 7. Your internal hard disk has ID 0, so external devices can have numbers from 1 to 6. Internal CD-ROM drives are frequently assigned the ID number 3.

You usually select the ID number using a wheel or button on the back of the device. Just make sure that each drive in the chain has a unique number and you're all set.

Try again to restart from your usual startup disk.

If nothing so far has cured the flashing question mark, you have to suspect damage to the System software on your hard disk.

So now you're going to try to replace your old System software with fresh, new System software.

Reinstalling the System software

The reason that this procedure comes last in this section is that it takes the longest. The procedure is detailed at great length in Appendix A, affectionately known as "Anyone Can Install Mac OS 8.5."

Read it and follow the instructions.

If nothing has worked so far

If none of my suggestions have worked, if you've rebuilt the desktop, run Disk First Aid, installed new hard disk drivers, zapped your PRAM, disconnected all SCSI devices, and reinstalled your System software, and you're still seeing the flashing question mark, then you've got big trouble.

You may have any one of the following problems:

- ✔ Your hard disk is dead and so is your floppy drive.
- ✔ Your hard disk is dead but your floppy drive is okay.
- ✔ You have some other type of hardware failure.
- ✔ All of your startup disks — your Disk Tools and Install Disk 1 floppies and/or your System software CDs — are defective (unlikely).

The bottom line: If you're still seeing the flashing question mark after trying all the stuff in the previous pages, you almost certainly need to have your Mac serviced by a qualified technician.

If You Crash at Startup

More of a hassle to solve than flashing question mark problems, but rarely fatal, startup crashes are another bad thing that can happen to your Mac.

A *crash* is defined as a System Error dialog box, frozen cursor, frozen screen, or any other disabling event.

At startup is defined as any time between flicking the power key or switch (or restarting) and having full use of the Finder desktop.

A startup crash may happen to you someday. If it does, here's what to do.

Restart without extensions and control panels

The first thing you need to do is establish whether an extension or control panel is causing the crash by starting up with all of them disabled.

If your Mac is already on, choose Special⇨Restart, holding down the Shift key until you see "Extensions Off" in the Welcome to Mac OS window. After you see "Extensions Off," you may release the Shift key.

If your Mac is off, power it up and hold down the Shift key until you see "Extensions Off" in the Welcome to Mac OS window. Again, you can release the Shift key after "Extensions Off" appears.

If your Mac starts up successfully when you hold down the Shift key but crashes or freezes when you don't, you can deduce that one (or more) of your extensions or control panels is responsible for the crash. Read the section "Resolving extension and control panel conflicts" below.

If your Mac still crashes when you hold down the Shift key, you can deduce that something is wrong with your System or Finder. Read the section "How to perform a clean System reinstallation" later in this chapter.

Resolving extension and control panel conflicts

If you're reading this section, you have an extension or control panel that is causing your Mac to crash at startup. The trick now is to isolate which one (or, occasionally, more than one) is causing your troubles. Chances are, it's a third-party extension or control panel, but you can't rule out Apple extensions and control panels either. They too can conflict with other extensions or control panels or become corrupted and not function properly.

Because you know that your Mac will start up with the Shift key down, you use Extensions Manager to track down the rogue extension or control panel file.

I'm so happy Apple included Extensions Manager as part of System 7.5 and improved it a lot for Mac OS 8.5, I could turn backflips. You'll see why when I show you how to resolve your difficulties with Extensions Manager. Just imagine what a hassle it would be without EM. Of course it's even better with Casady & Greene's aptly-named Conflict Catcher 8.

The first step is to establish whether any of the Apple Mac OS 8.5 extensions or control panels is causing problems.

1. **Launch the Extensions Manager control panel.**
2. **Choose Mac OS 8.5 All from the pop-up menu (see Figure 18-8) and then click the Restart button.**

Figure 18-8: Choose Mac OS 8.5 all to load only the standard-issue Mac OS extensions and control panels. Then click the Restart button.

Situation 1: You can now boot successfully, which means that the culprit must be one of your third-party extensions or control panels.

Situation 2: You still crash at startup, which means that the culprit must be one of the Mac OS extensions or control panels.

In Situation 1, repeat these steps until you crash again:

1. **Power up or restart your Mac and then press and hold the spacebar until the Extensions Manager window appears.**
2. **Add one extension or control panel to the enabled list by clicking it so that a check mark appears.**
3. **Click the Continue button to begin the startup process.**

If you start up successfully, you know that the extension or control panel you just added is not the culprit. Repeat these three steps, enabling one new item each time you restart, until you crash. When you do, the last extension or control panel you enabled is the culprit.

See the section called "Dealing with recalcitrant extensions and control panels" for possible solutions.

In Situation 2, repeat these steps until you stop crashing:

1. **Power up or restart your Mac and then press and hold the spacebar until the Extensions Manager window appears.**

2. **Disable one of the currently enabled extensions or control panels by clicking it so that its check mark disappears.**

3. **Click the Continue button to begin the startup process.**

Repeat these three steps, disabling one item each time you restart, until you stop crashing. When you do, the last extension or control panel you disabled was the culprit.

See the next section, "Dealing with recalcitrant extensions and control panels," for some things you can try.

Sometimes you can tell which extension or control panel is causing your crash by looking carefully at the little icons that appear on the bottom of your screen during startup. Each icon you see represents a control panel or extension loading into memory. If you can determine which icon was the last to appear before the crash, you can try disabling it before going through the iterative and frustrating process of determining the culprit as described above. You might get lucky and save yourself hours of boring detective work.

If you have a good memory, enable or disable a few at a time in Step 2. Just keep track of what you're doing and you can reduce the number of restarts it takes to find your offender.

Dealing with recalcitrant extensions and control panels

In the previous section, you determined which particular extension or control panel was giving you fits. In this section, I have a couple of suggestions — replace and reorder — that may let you use the offending item anyway.

How to replace a recalcitrant file

1. **Delete the guilty control panel or extension from your hard disk by dragging it to the Trash.**

2. **Open the Preferences folder in your System Folder and delete any preferences file with the same name as the guilty file.**

3. **Replace the guilty file with a fresh copy from a master disk.**

If it's an Apple extension or control panel, use the Mac OS installers as described in Appendix A. If it's a third-party product, follow the installation instructions in its manual.

Restart and see if the problem reoccurs.

If it does, you may *still* be able to use the recalcitrant extension or control panel by diddling with the loading order of extensions and control panels at startup.

How to reorder a recalcitrant file

To understand how to reorder, you must first understand why you need to reorder.

In some cases, extensions and control panels crash only if they load before or after another extension. Ergo, by diddling with the loading order, you can force one file to load before another.

How do you diddle the loading order, you ask? When extensions and control panels load at startup, they load in alphabetical order by folder. To wit:

1. The Extensions folder's contents, in alphabetical order.

2. The Control Panels folder's contents, in alphabetical order.

3. Control panels or extensions loose in your System Folder (that is, not in the Extensions or Control Panels folders), in alphabetical order.

So, if you have a recalcitrant extension or control panel, try forcing it to load either first or last. This trick works more often than not.

To force an offending control panel or extension (Snapz Pro in this example) to load first, precede its name by several spaces and move it into the Extensions folder if it's a control panel. It will then load before any other extensions or control panels (Figure 18-9).

By putting the Snapz Pro control panel in the Extensions folder (so that it loads before items in the Control Panels folder or System Folder) and preceding its name with several spaces, I ensured that Snapz Pro would be the first control panel to load.

Figure 18-9:
The first
item to load
will be the
control
panel I
renamed
"Snapz
Pro."

Name	Date Modified	Size	Kind
Snapz Pro	Today	282 K	control panel
EM Extension	7/24/98	6 K	system extension
About Apple Guide	8/7/98	4 K	Apple Guide document
▷ ActiveX Controls	Yesterday	—	folder
Apple CD/DVD Driver	Today	101 K	system extension
Apple Color SW Pro CMM	4/26/95	39 K	system extension
Apple Enet	8/25/98	371 K	system extension
Apple Guide	8/5/98	664 K	system extension
Apple IX3D Graphics Accelerator	6/13/98	199 K	system extension

Extensions — 116 items, 83.4 MB available

Going the other way, to force an extension or control panel to load last, precede its name with several °°° (Option-8) and move it out of the Extensions folder and into the System Folder itself (see Figure 18-10).

By preceding the item's name with tildes and moving it out of the Extensions folder and into the System Folder itself, as shown, I've ensured that Snapz Pro will be the last extension or control panel to load.

More sophisticated startup managers, such as Casady & Greene's Conflict Catcher 8, let you change the loading order of extensions and control panels by dragging them around, avoiding the inconvenience of renaming or moving them manually. I wish Extensions Manager had this capability. If you find yourself resolving many conflicts with extensions or control panels, Conflict Catcher 8 is a good investment.

It performs the conflict resolution three-step boogie automatically. You just restart, tell the software whether the problem is gone, and then restart again. The software does all the enabling and disabling and keeps track automatically. At the end, it tells you which file is the culprit. If you have many of these conflicts, CC8 is a worthwhile upgrade to the bare-bones Extensions Manager.

If you're still reading and your problem hasn't been resolved, there's one last thing you can try; namely, a clean System software installation.

Figure 18-10:
The last
item to load
will be the
control
panel I
renamed
"°°°°°Snapz
Pro."

Name	Date Modified	Size	Kind
▷ Scripts	Yesterday	—	folder
▷ Shutdown Items	Today	—	folder
▷ Shutdown Items (Disabled)	Today	—	folder
▷ Startup Items	Today	—	folder
▷ Startup Items (Disabled)	Today	—	folder
System	Today	9.7 MB	suitcase
▷ System Extensions (Disabled)	Today	—	folder
System Resources	9/4/98	711 K	file
▷ Text Encodings	Yesterday	—	folder
°°°°Snapz Pro	Today	282 K	control panel

System Folder — 34 items, 82.5 MB available

How to perform a clean System reinstallation

This is a drastic final step. If nothing so far has fixed your startup problems, a clean System reinstallation, also known as *clean install,* very well may. I saved this solution for last because it's the biggest hassle, and you don't want to go through the trouble if something easier can fix you up. So if you're doing a clean install, it's more or less your last hope.

Don't worry. This solution will most likely get you back on your feet. This one will fix all but the most horrifying and malignant of problems. So let's get to it.

Prior to System 7.5, clean installs were performed manually and were much harder to explain.

Thankfully, there is now a barely hidden shortcut in the Install Mac OS program that lets you perform a clean install automatically, with no muss or fuss. Here's how:

1. **Start up or restart your Mac with the Mac OS 8.5 CD in your CD-ROM drive.**

   Remember, you have to hold the C key to boot from the CD.

2. **Launch the Install Mac OS 8.5 program.**

3. **Click Continue in the first screen you see.**

   The Select Destination screen appears.

4. **Choose the appropriate hard disk if you have more than one and then click the Options button as shown in Figure 18-11.**

5. **Click the checkbox for Perform Clean Installation and click OK. (See Figure 18-12.)**

Figure 18-11: It's never been easier to perform a clean install. Just click the Options button.

Figure 18-12:
After you click the Options button, the clean installation option appears.

When the Install Mac OS program is through, you have a brand spanking new System Folder on your hard disk. Your old System Folder has been renamed Previous System Folder. Nothing has been removed from it.

The folder called Previous System Folder contains all your old third-party extensions, control panels, and fonts. Because it's possible, even likely, that one of these items contributed to your problem, I recommend that you reinstall them one item at a time. In other words, move one extension or control panel from Previous System Folder onto the new System Folder's icon. Then restart and work for a while to see if any problems occur before reinstalling another.

Clean versus regular installation

To understand why you need to do a clean install, or even what a clean install is, you have to understand a little about how the Install Mac OS program works and what *resources* are.

Resources are the building blocks from which all programs, control panels, extensions, and so on, are built. The Install Mac OS program is, technically, a resource installer. It installs the resources that become programs, control panels, extensions, and so on.

And the Install Mac OS program is very smart about which resources it installs. It looks at your hard disk; then, if it sees a System Folder containing a System and a Finder, it installs only the resources it thinks you need. So, for example, if the Install Mac OS program sees a System and Finder, it looks to see if they contain the proper resources. If they do, it doesn't install anything, even if the resources are damaged.

Therein lies the rub. The Install Mac OS program can sometimes outsmart itself. If the reason your Mac is crashing is that a resource inside the System, Finder, a control panel, or an extension has become damaged or corrupted, the Install Mac OS program may not replace the defective resource if you perform a Regular Install.

A clean install, on the other hand, ensures that every single file and every single resource is replaced with a brand spanking new one. In fact, a clean install gives you a brand new System Folder.

It's a good idea to trash the System and Finder in the Previous System Folder as soon as possible after performing the clean install.

It's simply a bad idea to have two System Folders on one hard disk, and as long as Previous System Folder has a System and a Finder in it, your Mac could confuse Previous System Folder with the real System Folder, and that confusion could cause you major heartache.

So delete the old System and Finder files, the ones in the Previous System Folder, now. Just in case. Thanks.

Don't forget that the System Folder is smart. If you drag a control panel or extension onto its icon (but *not* into its open window), it puts the file in the proper folder for you.

Part V

Appendixes

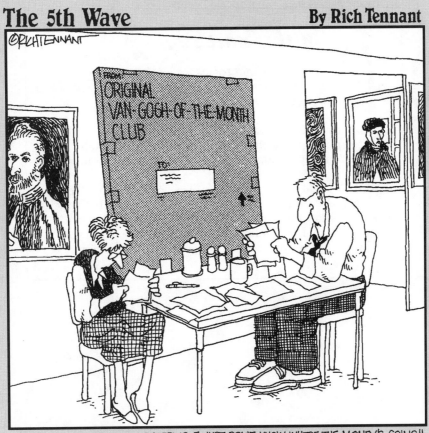

The 5th Wave   By Rich Tennant

ORIGINAL VAN-GOGH-OF-THE-MONTH CLUB

"SINCE WE BEGAN ON-LINE SHOPPING, I JUST DON'T KNOW WHERE THE MONEY'S GOING."

In this part . . .

I saved some important topics for last because, as an intelligent Mac user, you already know much of what I cover in these appendixes.

First, I cover installing Mac OS 8.5. The whole process has gotten quite easy with this version of the System software. You may wonder why I bothered to write about it.

Second, I deal with the whole process of backing up. You know that your files are important, and I'm sure that you already know how to copy files from your hard disk to a floppy or some other form of media. But just in case you don't, you'd better read this appendix.

Appendix A
Anyone Can Install Mac OS 8.5

● ●

*T*he Mac OS 8.5 CD-ROM can install more than just System software. So in the first section, I discuss the plain vanilla installation that'll happen if you just keep clicking OK and Continue and Agree.

An easy install includes the basic system software, Internet Access, Apple Remote Access, Personal Web Sharing, QuickDraw 3D, Text-to-Speech, Mac OS Runtime for Java, and ColorSync. If for some reason you don't want to install those components (read about them in Chapter 16), click the Customize button and then uncheck them as shown in Figure A-1.

After that, I explain how to install each item that requires a separate installation.

Finally, there are several other optional pieces of System software — such as Easy Access and CloseView (see Chapter 16) — that require a separate custom installation process in the main Mac OS installer program. I cover them in the final section.

If the reason you're installing (actually reinstalling) Mac OS 8.5 is that your Mac is acting up, you may need to perform a *clean install*. See the section in Chapter 18.

The procedure for installing Mac OS 8.5 is the same regardless of whether you're upgrading from an earlier version of System software or installing Mac OS 8.5 on an empty hard disk.

Ready? Take a deep breath.

Figure A-1:
To avoid
installing
Internet
Access,
Apple
Remote
Access,
Personal
Web
Sharing,
QuickDraw
3D, Text-to-
Speech,
Mac OS
Runtime for
Java, and/or
ColorSync,
uncheck
them in the
Custom
Installation
and
Removal
window.

Installing Mac OS 8.5

Shut down your Macintosh if it's turned on. Insert the Mac OS 8.5 CD-ROM and turn on your Mac. If you're starting up from a CD, hold down the C key on your keyboard.

Your Mac will start up. Launch the Install Mac OS 8.5 program. You'll see a comforting welcome screen like the one in Figure A-2.

(Are you beginning to detect a pattern? Macs are warmer and fuzzier than other personal computers?)

Click the Continue button. The Select Destination window appears. Choose a disk to install Mac OS 8.5 onto from the pop-up Destination Disk menu. Of course, if you only have one hard disk it will be automatically selected for you by the nice installer program.

Figure A-2:
The
opening
screen of
the Install
Mac OS 8.5
program.

Click the Select button. Now read some important information about this software.

Print it and read it. Really. It's important, and I'm not going to repeat it all here.

When you're done, click the Continue button. The License Agreement window appears. Read it if you like. Then click the Continue button. You may have to click an Agree button now (I did with some versions of the installer and didn't with others).

Eventually the Install Software screen appears (see Figure A-3).

This is where you choose what software you want to install. For a normal (easy) install, just click Start. Internet Access, Apple Remote Access, Personal Web Sharing, QuickDraw 3D, Text-to-Speech, Mac OS Runtime for Java, and ColorSync will be installed along with the basic system software. Or if you want to add or delete components now, click the Customize button. (Refer back to Chapter 16 to find out what they are and what they do.)

Figure A-3:
The Install
Software
window,
ready to
rock.

Click the Start button. The installer checks your destination disk with Disk First Aid to make sure it's in tip-top shape. It then updates your hard disk drivers automatically if you have an Apple hard disk.

If you have more than one hard disk, or a hard disk that's wasn't made by Apple, you may see a warning that the installer is not going to try to update these disks. That's okay; it's what you want.

Hard disk drivers are little bits of computer code installed by the software that formatted your hard disk. They manage how the disk talks to the Mac. Old disk drivers may be incompatible with new system software, so it's always a good idea to check with the manufacturer before installing a new version of Mac OS if you have a non-Apple hard disk. Apple hard disks, of course, have their drivers updated automatically as part of the installation process.

If you have a non-Apple hard disk, you should contact its manufacturer before installing Mac OS 8.5. This could be important. You need to know whether you need to update your hard disk drivers. Though you might be able to install Mac OS 8.5 without updating your hard disk drivers, it's a bad idea. Your Mac may not boot after the installation if your current hard disk drivers are incompatible with Mac OS 8.5.

After clicking that Start button, just kick back and relax for a few minutes.

After whirring and clicking for a while, your Mac politely informs you that the installation was successful. Quit, restart your Mac, and away you go.

That's it. Your hard disk now has Mac OS 8.5 installed. Piece of cake. The waiting is the hardest part. Onward!

Custom Installs

To install or remove Internet Access, Apple Remote Access, Personal Web Sharing, QuickDraw 3D, Text-to-Speech, Mac OS Runtime for Java, ColorSync, QuickDraw GX, English Speech Recognition, or Multilingual Internet Access, click the Customize button on the Install Software screen, then check or uncheck their names before clicking the Start button.

Don't forget that Internet Access, Apple Remote Access, Personal Web Sharing, QuickDraw 3D, Text-to-Speech, Mac OS Runtime for Java, and ColorSync were probably installed when you first installed Mac OS 8.5. Unless you manually deselected them when you first installed Mac OS 8.5, they're already installed. The instructions that follow show you how to install them if you haven't already.

Follow the instructions in the first section of this chapter right up to the part where you click the Start button. Then, instead of clicking the Start button, click the Customize button. The Custom Installation and Removal window appears. Click next to the names of the options you want to install, and choose Custom Installation from the Installation mode pop-up menu.

You can quickly check an item's installation status (as shown in Figure A-4); it changes depending on whether or not its box is checked.

Figure A-4:
Custom
installation;
Mac OS 8.5,
Internet
Access,
Apple
Remote
Access,
Personal
Web
Sharing,
and Mac
OS Runtime
for Java will
be installed
when I click
the Start
button.

In this example, the Mac OS 8.5, Internet Access, Apple Remote Access, Personal Web Sharing, and Mac OS Runtime for Java installers will run in sequence when I click Start.

The Install Mac OS 8 program is nothing more than a little launcher program that launches the installer for each piece of the System software. Don't believe me? Look in the folder called Software Installers. Each custom installation option has its own personal installer program. If you want to save time, you can launch these installers separately and avoid dealing with the Install Mac OS 8.5 program completely.

Optional Mac OS Items

Some Mac OS components — including useful ones such as Easy Access and CloseView — require separate installation using the Custom Install feature.

To install these optional components, follow the directions in the first section of this appendix right up until the part where you click the Start button.

Instead of clicking the Start button, click the Customize button. Now deselect everything but Mac OS 8.5.

Now choose Customized Installation from the Installation mode pop-up menu. A new window appears where you can select individual Mac OS 8.5 features to install (see Figure A-5). You'll find Easy Access and CloseView in the Universal Access folder.

When you've selected the items you want to install, click OK and then click the Start button or press Return.

After some whirring and clicking, you're told that the installation was successful. Click the Quit button.

Figure A-5:
The Select
Mac OS 8.5
features
to install
window,
ready
to rock.

Select Mac OS 8.5 features to install.

Selection: Custom

Feature	Size	
▷ ☐ Mobility	3,937K 🖹	
▷ ☐ Multimedia	15,536K 🖹	
▷ ☐ Networking & Connectivity	9,557K 🖹	
▷ ☐ Printing	14,379K 🖹	
▽ ☑ Universal Access	45K 🖹	
☑ CloseView	33K 🖹	
☑ Easy Access	12K 🖹	
▽ ☐ Utility	5,655K 🖹	
☐ AppleScript	2,073K 🖹	
☐ Application Switcher	84K 🖹	

Selected size: 45K

Cancel   OK

Appendix B
Back Up Now or Regret It Later

• •

*A*lthough Macs are generally reliable beasts, someday your hard disk will die. I promise. They all do. And if you haven't backed up your hard disk, there's a good chance that you'll never see your files again. And if you do see them again, it'll only be after paying Scott at the DriveSavers data recovery service a king's ransom, with no guarantee of success. DriveSavers is the premier recoverer of lost data on hard disks. They do good work and can often recover stuff nobody else could. (Ask the *Simpsons'* producers about the "almost-lost" episodes.) They charge accordingly.

I'm going to give you DriveSavers' phone number. It's 415-883-4232. Now pray you never need it. Back up often, and you won't. If, somehow, none of this sinks in, tell Scott I said Hi.

In other words, you absolutely, positively, without question MUST BACK UP. Just as you've adopted the Shut Down command and made it a habit, you must learn to back up your hard disk and back it up often.

How often is often? That depends on you. How much work can you afford to lose? If the answer is that losing everything you did yesterday would put you out of business, you need to back up daily, or possibly twice a day. If you'd only lose a couple of unimportant letters, you can back up less frequently.

Backing Up Is (Not) Hard to Do

There are lots of ways to back up your hard disk. Some are better than others.

The manual, "brute force" method

Drag your files a few at a time to floppy disks.

Yuk. If it sounds pretty awful, trust me, it is. It takes forever; you can't really tell if you've copied every file; and there's no way to copy only the files that have been modified since your last backup. Almost nobody sticks with this method for long.

Commercial backup software

There's nothing else in this book that I insist that you buy, but you must buy backup software if you don't already have some.

For some unfathomable reason, Apple has almost never seen fit to provide backup software with new Macs or include it with System software releases. I know some Performas had a crummy backup program, but Apple has left millions of Mac owners clueless.

Mac owners get nothing more than a brief passage regarding backing up in the *Macintosh User's Guide.* It ought to be in big red letters, in the first chapter, and include a warning from the Surgeon General or something. And it wouldn't kill them to provide a backup utility either. Sheesh, even DOS has a backup command, albeit a lousy one.

C'mon, Apple, give Mac owners a fair shake. At least include the lame Apple Backup program some Performa owners got.

Fortunately, plenty of very good backup programs are available for well under $100, including the excellent Retrospect and Retrospect Express from Dantz Development. If you want the best, most flexible, most powerful, top-of-the-line backup software, spend a little more and pop for Retrospect.

Backup software automates the task of backing up. The backup software remembers what is on each backup disk and only backs up files that have been modified since the last backup. Your first backup with commercial software should take no more than 90 minutes and use a few dozen 1.4MB floppy disks. (Better: Zip, Jaz, SyQuest, Bernoulli, or magneto-optical disks.) Subsequent backups, called *incremental backups* in backup-software parlance, should only take a few minutes.

Be sure to label the disks that you use for your backups because, during incremental backups, the backup software is going to ask you to "Please insert backup disk 7." If you haven't labeled your disks clearly, you have a problem.

Why You Need Two Sets of Backup Disks

You're a good soldier. You back up regularly. You think you're immune.

Now picture this: One day you take a floppy disk to QuicKopyLazerPrintz to print your resume on their laser printer. You make a few changes while at QuicKopyLazerPrintz and take the floppy home and stick it into your Mac.

Unbeknownst to you, the floppy became infected with a computer virus at QuicKopyLazerPrintz. (I discuss viruses in the "Virus trivia" sidebar later in this appendix.) When you insert the disk into your Mac, the infection spreads to your hard disk like wildfire.

Then you back up. Your backup software, believing that all the infected files have been recently modified (well, they have been — they were infected with a virus!), proceeds to back them up. You notice that the backup takes a little longer than usual, but otherwise, things seem to be okay.

Virus trivia

A computer virus, in case you missed it in *Time* or *Newsweek*, is a nasty little piece of computer code that replicates and spreads from disk to disk. Most viruses cause your Mac to misbehave; some viruses can destroy files or erase disks with no warning.

If you use disks that have been inserted in other computers, you need some form of virus-detection software. If you download and use files from Web and FTP sites on the Internet, you need some form of virus detection as well.

Don't worry too much if you download files from commercial online services such as America Online or CompuServe. They are very conscientious about viral infections. Do worry about that Web site called Pirate's Den that an unsavory friend told you about.

On the commercial front, Virex and Norton Anti-Virus (formerly Symantec Anti-Virus) each have their fans. I'm using Virex right now, but I've used NAV for years have never gotten a virus while using either program.

The big advantage of buying a commercial antivirus program is that the publisher will contact you each time a virus is discovered and provide you with a software update to protect you against the new strain. Or, for a fee, the publisher can send you a new version of the software every time a new virus is found.

There are many shareware and freeware antivirus solutions. None that I know of are as trustworthy as Virex or Norton.

If you only use commercial software and don't download files from Web sites with strange names, you have a very low risk of infection. On the other hand, if you swap disks with friends regularly, shuttle disks back and forth to other Macs, use your disks at service bureaus or copy shops, or download files from various and sundry places on the Internet, you are at risk.

If you're at risk, do yourself a favor and buy a commercial antivirus program.

A few days later, your Mac starts acting strangely. You borrow a copy of that excellent virus-detection software, Virex or Norton Anti-Virus (formerly Symantec Anti-Virus), and discover that your hard disk is infected. "Aha," you exclaim. "I've been a good little Mac user, backing up regularly. I'll just restore everything from my backup disks."

Not so fast, bucko. The files on your backup disks are also infected.

This scenario demonstrates why you need multiple backups. If you have several sets of backup disks, chances are pretty good that one of the sets is clean.

I keep three backup sets. I use one set on even-numbered days, one on odd-numbered days, and I update the third set once a week and store it in my bank's vault. This scheme ensures that no matter what happens, even if my office burns, floods, is destroyed by a tornado or hurricane, or is robbed, I won't lose more than a few days' worth of work. I can live with that.

Index

IDG BOOKS WORLDWIDE BOOK REGISTRATION

Register This Book and Win!

We want to hear from you!

Visit **http://my2cents.dummies.com** to register this book and tell us how you liked it!

✔ Get entered in our monthly prize giveaway.

✔ Give us feedback about this book — tell us what you like best, what you like least, or maybe what you'd like to ask the author and us to change!

✔ Let us know any other ...*For Dummies*® topics that interest you.

Your feedback helps us determine what books to publish, tells us what coverage to add as we revise our books, and lets us know whether we're meeting your needs as a ...*For Dummies* reader. You're our most valuable resource, and what you have to say is important to us!

Not on the Web yet? It's easy to get started with *Dummies 101*®*: The Internet For Windows*® *98* or *The Internet For Dummies*®, 5th Edition, at local retailers everywhere.

Or let us know what you think by sending us a letter at the following address:

...*For Dummies* Book Registration
Dummies Press
7260 Shadeland Station, Suite 100
Indianapolis, IN 46256-3945
Fax 317-596-5498

™
FOR DUMMIES

BESTSELLING
BOOK SERIES
FROM IDG